The Unveiling

An Exhaustive Study
of
The Book Of Revelation

Keith Harris

All Scripture references quoted from the King James translation of the Holy Bible.

The Unveiling
Copyright 1999 by Keith Harris
P.O. Box 1353 Madisonville, Ky 42431
Published by The Olive Press, a division of Midnight Call Inc.
Columbia, South Carolina 29228

Copy Typist: Keith Harris
Proofreader: Angie Peters, Susanna Cancassi, Claire Bliesner
Lithography: Simon Froese
Cover Design: J Spurling

Library of Congress Cataloging-in-Publication Data

Harris, Keith
The Unveiling
ISBN 0-937422-48-7

Printed in the United States of America

The Unveiling
Table of Contents

This book is dedicated to all

who love God and His wonderful

Word; to those who

desire to know Him more.

Introduction

Do you want a real blessing from God? Well, it's there for you; just reach out for it. A very real and wonderful blessing is promised to those who read, to those who listen, and to those who keep the sayings of the book of Revelation. All you have to do to begin receiving these blessings is to open your mind and let the Spirit of God walk you through. Don't be afraid of Revelation; trust God that He will bless you through this most extraordinary book.

Revelation was written in such a manner as to tie all of Scripture together. Thus, one automatically receives a better insight into the Word of God by studying it. That is a great blessing within itself. Furthermore, as the Word begins to unfold, there arises a pattern of understanding, an "unveiling," a revelation. God's plan for man and the course of the end times shall emerge for you in a most awe-inspiring way. Study Revelation with great expectation; you'll not be disapointed.

Interpreting Revelation

Interpreting Scripture has always had its difficulties. So we need to know how. Have you ever whispered a phrase into the ear of the person sitting next to you and have it repeated from person to person in a large group? The end result, more often than not, comes out quite different than what you said to begin with. Have you ever taken a phrase, such as, "You can drive a car," and emphasize a different word each time you repeat it? The meaning changes each time according to emphasis.

So imagine, if you will, interpreting a book of symbols, metaphors, doctrines, and so on, with the added ingredient of personal concept. Due to personal concepts, doctrinal errors of times past have affected the message of Revelation, and indeed, the whole of Scripture. As a result, one may find just about any form of interpretation with which he desires to agree. That, of itself, is not good. Many interpretations have sprouted from great nearsightedness of scholars past, while other interpretations have been spawned from outright fallacies. Few scholars have grasped the foresight needed to stay within the bounds and intent of the Revelation message. This boundary and intent may only be correctly deduced by staying within the confines of Scripture, using it, as a whole, as a foundation. Scripture interprets Scripture. This includes everything from history to poetry and from metaphor to reality.

Through the centuries of Church history, events both digressive and progressive have provided variations of thought and speculation. It should come as no surprise that a hodgepodge of interpretations exist today concerning the book of Revelation. After sifting through the more obvious and erroneous belief systems, there are four major modes of interpretation which prevail:

1. The Preterist or Historical Interpretation.

This view holds that all of the book of Revelation was fulfilled during the time of Nero and/or Domitian or shortly thereafter. This interpretation concerns that era only and has little or no message for modern society. This view was developed by Jesuit Priests and is held by many of the Roman Church and some Protestants.

The Preterists' view has great weakness in that it deprives succeeding generations of the prophetic message of Revelation and gives light to the first century believers only. It makes God a respecter of persons in that the full blessing of Revelation was for the early Church only (1:3; 22:19). This view makes the prophecy of Revelation nothing more than history except for the Second Coming of Christ.

2. The Continuous Historical Interpretation.

This view relates the book of Revelation as a panorama of Church history from the Apostolic Era until the Second Coming of Christ. Most who accept this view maintain that Christ's return will be after the Millennial Age, also called "Post-Millennialism."

The Continuous Historical View asserts that chapters two and three of the Revelation hold historic significance, but are incorrect in respect to the total view.

Many of this belief suggest that Christ will return after the Millennial Age. However, compiled Scripture teaches that He will return before the Millennial Age. Although elements of the Continuous Historical View may be rightly applied, Scripture will fall prey to contradiction when accepting the Continuous Historical View in its totality.

3. The Idealist or Spiritualist Interpretation.

This view, also called the "Ammillennialist" view, maintains that the Apocalypse is not to be taken as a representation of actual events whether past or future.

Accordingly, the book of Revelation is only a symbol or metaphor depicting the great conflict between good and evil. This view, originated by Origen in and by the school of philosophy at Alexandria, is basically a marriage between pagan and Christian theology, a bad mix. It appeals to most liberals and some conservative Bible students today.

The Idealist or Spiritualist interpretation is absurd when taken wholly. We know that spiritual application may be applied to Scripture, however, to spiritualize the entire book of Revelation is to interpret at whim. The structure of Revelation thus falls flat. In addition, this view denies the book as prophetic. In all probability, Origen would be what is today termed a Jehovah's Witness.

4. The Futuristic Interpretation.

This view is most often called "Premillennialism," the belief that Christ will return to usher in the Millennial Age. This view was held by Anabaptists of the Reformation period. Numerous church fathers from the beginning of Christianity were advocates. This view falls into perfect harmony with the message of the entire Bible and fewer problematic enigmas exist.

This interpretation would obviously seem to be the most practical and informative. Note, however, that elements of the aforementioned interpretations fit harmoniously with the tenure of Scripture. This is often either overlooked or dismissed. Using one mode of thought to interpret Scripture is always fatal to a sincere quest for truth.

Proper Interpretation For Revelation

Although not an easy task, correct and proper interpretation may be found, that is to say, the one that God
intended. One of the most important things to keep in
mind when studying the book of Revelation is that it was
written so that God's Word would be preserved, through
time, until all it contains is fulfilled. Thus, we find sym-
bology and figurative speech and literal interpretation, as
well as spiritual application. We also find sequential puz-
zles, metaphors, and other such variations. This is where
one's ability to "rightly divide the word of truth" is put to
the test.

If we as God's people are to "rightly divide" the Word,
we must find a method, pattern, guideline, or rule-of-
thumb in order to keep our interpretation in check. One
thing is sure, proper interpretation cannot be found by taking one particular mode of interpretation and applying it
throughout a study.

The Key to Interpretation

All methods of Scriptural interpretation should work
in harmony and run parallel one to another, whether they
be literal, symbolic, prophetic.

In order to "rightly divide the Word" we must remember that Scripture does not and cannot contradict itself.
Common sense should tell us that. Scripture is not a
"whosoever shall interpret at will" work, but a structured,
magnificent work authored by Creator God. He is not only
faithful and true, but He is organized and proper in His
method of instruction. All Scripture is given by inspiration

of God, and thus, may be relied upon with all assurance
(II Tim. 3:16).

Concerning the whole, this study is to be deemed as
futurist in viewpoint, historic in the progression of Church
history, spiritual in vision, and prophetic in nature.
However, interpretation is not limited to these modes.

Note that the book of Revelation has twenty-two
chapters. This work, "The Unveiling," has twenty-two
chapters, each one corresponding with the given chapter
in Revelation. There are subtitles concerning each distinction of each chapter. With the aid of this work, I trust you
will enjoy the marvelous book of Revelation as God
reveals it to you through the Holy Spirit (Jn.16:13). May
God richly bless you as you study His Word.

Ω

The Apocalypse Begins
Chapter 1

John penned the book of Revelation during a time of great hardship and persecution, even for officials.

The Emperor, Nero, had a mind to give a make-over to the image of Rome. His intentions were to change its violent character into a more humane one. Romans, however, hated Nero's love for the Greek way of life. This resulted in the murder of Nero's mother, Agrippinia, and his legal wife, Octavia. Many of his advisors were either killed or exiled.

Things went from bad to worse. Nero, in a state of madness, had been accused of burning Rome and needed a scapegoat. He thus launched an attack against Christians living in Rome. Christians, although good citizens, were despised for not recognizing Roman emperors as gods. In the brutal attack against them, followers of Christ (including the apostles Peter and Paul) were martyred by the thousands.

This personal and local onslaught of violence brought great suffering and misery to God's Church, now only some sixty-plus years into the Christian era. Nero himself was exiled from Rome and took his own life.

With the end of Nero's reign, Domitian, also opposed to Christianity, yet less cruel, exiled Christians in the stead of martyrdom. He attempted to banish Christianity from the Empire without the enormity of bloodshed. While Nero's method of persecution had been one of martyrdom, Domitian's was one of exile. It is here, during Domitian's reign (AD 90's), that we find John, the beloved disciple, exiled to the Isle of Patmos. The Church world, now, was one with characteristics extending from that of falling from their first love, all the way to tolerating and falling prey to false doctrine. The Church as a whole had changed somewhat from the one Paul had pictured in the AD 60's and 70's.

With the death of all of the apostles, except John, the collective Church was on its own. At this time the stage was set for the Church to receive a new revelation and unveiling of Scripture; thus, the book of Revelation. John, the beloved disciple of Jesus, was called upon to be the scribe for the last book of the New Testament, the Apocalypse. Without this amazing book, Scripture would be incomplete.

What is the Apocalypse?

The word *"Apocalypse,"* or *"Apocalupsis,"* is the Greek word for Revelation and means "to unveil." Thus, we learn that Revelation is a book to be opened, not one to be shut up or put out of sight and mind. It is to be opened and studied. This is emphasized in the blessing promised to those who read, hear, and keep the words of this prophecy. The book opens and closes with this promise of blessing to its readers and hearers (1:3; 22:7).

In addition, the book of Revelation is the opening up of what Daniel was told to close up (Dan.12:4). It will continue to unveil and open until all is fulfilled and will remain as record forever (Matt. 24:35).

The Revelation of Jesus Christ

> The Revelation of Jesus Christ, which God gave unto him, to shew unto his servants things which must shortly come to pass; and he sent and signified it by his angel unto his servant John: Who bare record of the word of God, and of the testimony of Jesus Christ, and of all things that he saw. Blessed is he that readeth, and they that hear the words of this prophecy, and keep those things which are written therein: for the time is at hand. Rev. 1:1-3

Although the heading, in many Bibles, states that the Revelation is of John, it is not really of John but to John. It is the Revelation of Jesus Christ, as stated from the onset in verse one. God gave it by way of an angel to give assurance of the Second Coming of Christ and to reveal judgment that is coming upon the world.

The assurance is realized in the word "shortly" (v.2), which comes from two Greek words, "en," meaning "fixed," and "tachos," which means "brief." Hence, a "fixed briefness." Thus, the Second Coming and the events coinciding with it, are, "fixed, set, and certain to come to pass."

Grace Be Unto You

> John to the seven churches which are in Asia: Grace be unto you, and peace, from him which is, and which was, and which is to come; and from the seven Spirits which are before his throne; And from Jesus Christ, who is the faithful witness, and the first begotten of the dead, and the prince of the kings of the earth. Unto him

that loved us, and washed us from our sins in his own blood, And
hath made us kings and priests unto God and his Father; to him be
glory and dominion for ever and ever. Amen. Rev. 1:4-6

John was instructed to write the Revelation to seven of
the fourteen churches in Asia. These churches were chosen due to the traits which each held, both individually
and corporately. They would serve not only as addressees,
but as foundations from which the entire book could be
constructed, compared and understood. Many believe that
the book of Revelation cannot be understood and should
be shunned. That thought contradicts its very existence. It
was written to be studied and to convey blessings, warnings and hope. John not only introduces the seven churches here (v.4-6), but also the Eternal, unchangeable God,
who sends his grace. Thus, chapter one is an introductory
chapter.

We also find introduction to the seven Spirits which
are before God's throne. These Spirits are sent forth into
all the Earth. They are the seven horns and seven eyes of
the slain Lamb, Jesus Christ (5:6). Seven is the number of
completeness, hence, the total omnipotence and
omnipresence of the Lord in the personage of the Holy
Spirit. More detail will be given regarding the seven
Spirits in chapter three.

The salutation of verse five is not merely from John,
the beloved, or from the Godhead collectively (that is,
Father, Son and Holy Spirit), but from Jesus in particular.
The apostle Paul tells us that all the fulness of the
Godhead ("*theotes*," Gk. "divinity") dwells in Jesus (Col.
2:9). This second introduction of Jesus denotes, once
again, on whom the Revelation is focused.

Following suit, this mention of Jesus brings more detail of His character. He is called the "faithful witness." The psalmist David wrote of Jesus' witness (Psa. 89:36-37); Isaiah spoke of His witness to the people (Isa. 55:4); Jesus spoke it of himself (Jn. 3:11); John spoke of the same (Jn. 3:32). (See also, Jn. 8:14-16; 18:37; I Tim. 6:13; I Jn. 5:7-10.)

Jesus is also introduced here as the "first begotten of the dead." Could it not be said that the Zarephath widow's son whom Elijah raised from the dead was the first begotten of the dead (I Kings 17:20-24)? or the Shunammite woman's son whom Elisha raised (II Kings 4:32-37)? What about the man who was cast on Elijah's bones (II Kings 13:21)? How about Jairus' daughter (Mark 5:41-43)? Lazarus (John 11:43-44)? or Eutychus (Acts 20:9-12)? All but one of these instances took place before the resurrection of Jesus Christ. What then?

Acts 26:23 states that Christ should be the first to rise from the dead; Colossians 1:18 states that He is the first-born from the dead; I Corinthians 15:20-23 states that Christ is become the firstfruits of them that slept. Is this a contradiction? How then could it be said that Jesus is the first begotten of the dead?

Answer

The "first begotten of the dead" is more than an order of resurrection; it is a wonderful reference to the deity of Jesus. It is not a contradiction. Jesus is the parent, the head, the instigator of the resurrection. We find in Colossians 1:16 that Jesus created all things; He is God (Isa. 43:11, comp. Lu.2:11; Matt. 1:23; John 1:1-14; Col.

1:13-16; Heb. 1:8). He laid the foundation of the Earth (Heb. 1:10).

The resurrections listed above were neither by, nor of, Elijah, Elisha, or anyone else. They were through the power of God. Elijah and Elisha, as others, were God's representatives. Jesus is the image of the invisible God, the second personage of the three-fold embodiment of God. To be the "firstborn" or the "firstfruit" is a poetic way of saying that Jesus is heir to all things and resurrector of all who are resurrected.

To be the first to arise from the dead refers to being the first resurrected by His own power. Speaking of His death and resurrection, Jesus stated that He was to rise again by His own power (Jn. 10:17-18). Speaking of His body, He said, "Destroy this temple, and in three days I will raise it up" (John 2:19). Notice then, in Rev. 1:5, that it does not say the first-begotten from the dead, but of the dead. All resurrections come through Jesus Christ. He said, "I am the resurrection and the life" (Jn. 11:25).

Continuing verse five, we find that Jesus is the Prince, or ruler, of the kings of the Earth (Dan. 2:21,24) who has washed us from our sins in His own blood (Titus 3:5). He has made us kings and priests (I Peter 2:5). We were not born of ourselves into kingship or into a priesthood (Eph. 2:8,9,10), but have been adopted into a kingly and priestly family (Eph. 1:5). Those born again (born of the Spirit), are born of and by the Holy Spirit into God's family (John 3:6-8).

Behold He Cometh

Behold, he cometh with clouds; and every eye shall see him, and they also which pierced him: and all kindreds of the earth shall wail because of him. Even so, Amen. Rev. 1:7

Here we find a reference to the Second Coming of Christ. We must keep in mind that the Second Coming will be in two distinct stages: the Rapture ("catching away") of born again believers (I Thess. 4:16-18) and the Revelation of Jesus at the end of the Tribulation Period (Rev. 19:11).

There is much dispute over this "Rapture" or "catching away." The question concerns the order in which this event falls, whether before, during, or after the Tribulation, among other views. Some declare the Rapture to be a hoax altogether. The order of the event, that is to say, the placement of it, is beautifully portrayed in the book of Leviticus, the law book.

The apostle Paul informs us that the law contains shadows or types of things to come (Heb. 10:1). Thus, in Leviticus, the law book, 14:33-46, we find a beautiful illustration, a type, or shadow of God's order of events. It is a law concerning leprosy in a house. This, at first, seems to be an odd comparison.

The Lord gave this command to Moses and Aaron for the Israelites upon taking and dwelling in the land of Canaan. When the owner of a house would find leprosy (greenish or reddish mold) in his house, he would report it to the priest. The priest would inspect the house. If indeed leprosy existed, he would empty the house and shut it up for seven days. He would come again after the seven days to see if the leprosy was still in the house. If so, he would take away the stones which held the leprosy and replace them with good stones. After a time the priest would inspect the house again and if the leprosy had returned it was a fretting leprosy. The house was then to be broken down and taken out of the city to an unclean place.

This illustration gives us a shadow of God's order of events. Surely the world we live in now is a leprous house. Sin is rampant. (See chart, pg. 483)

We, many of us anyway, are calling to our priest, indeed our High Priest, Jesus Christ, beckoning His attention to our plague. At any moment He could come and empty the house, through the Rapture or "catching away." He will shut up the house (the world) for seven years, typified in the seven days. After seven years (the Tribulation Period), He will return (Second Coming). He will then judge the nations, casting many into Hell (removing stones), and exalt nations which will go into the Millennial Age (replacing stones). Satan will be bound (the cause of sin - leprosy) for 1000 years (Rev. 20:2). However, after 1,000 years, Satan will be loosed. This leprous house (world) will be inspected again. It is a fretting leprosy (Satan seduces nations). The house (world) will be torn down (burned with fire).

This "shadow" reveals the "catching away" as Pre-Tribulation or prior to the Tribulation Period. We will see the reality of the pre-trib Rapture throughout our study of Revelation.

Every Eye Shall See Him

Verse 7 states that "every eye shall see him, and they also which pierced him." Does this mean all who have lived and are alive at the appearance of Christ or only those who are alive at his coming? We do know that those who have lived and died for Christ and those who have been taken out prior to the Second Coming, at the "catching away" (I Thess. 4:16-18), will be with him (Zech. 14:5; Col. 3:4; I Thess. 3:13; Jude 14). Old and New Testament saints alike will certainly see him.

What about those who remain in Hell and those who are later cast there, during or immediately after the Tribulation?

The answer lies in the narrative of the rich man and Lazarus (Lu.16:19-31). Lazarus had no comprehension of the rich man in Hell, but the rich man had an awareness of Lazarus being in the bosom of Abraham, a reference to the great care of God as Father. The rich man could visualize paradise, but he could not partake of it. As "every eye" shall see Him, it stands to reason that those in Hades shall be made to visualize the event, along with those unsaved persons, surviving during the Tribulation Period. Their visualization of the Second Coming would vindicate today's message of Christ's return.

Those who pierced Him, some 2,000 years ago, the Roman soldiers, will undoubtedly be numbered among either the resurrected at the Rapture (those having repented) or with those found in Hell; thus, they will see Him. In all likelihood, "they that pierced Him" refers to the Roman government of Jesus' day. This reference coincides with a government existing at the time of Christ's return, the revived Roman Empire.

Alpha And Omega

I am Alpha and Omega, the beginning and the ending, saith the Lord, which is, and which was, and which is to come, the Almighty. Rev. 1:8

This verse reveals that all things are wrapped up in the determination and prescription of Jesus Christ, for His person has no beginning or end. Alpha and Omega are the first and last letters of the Greek alphabet. This reveals the totality of Jesus Christ as the Word of God which became flesh (John 1:1). The first half of this verse relates to the creation (all that is, for all things were created by the Word of God) and the last half to the person of Christ. He is Jesus, who *is* (Jehovah, meaning, self-existent or eternal), which *was* (the person of Christ in human form) and which *is to come* (To bring an end to the age and prepare all for eternity).

The Almighty

Jesus is the Almighty (v.8). This is very plain and easily understood although many have not grasped this profound truth. Jesus is God. Many think of Jesus as less than God. This is oftentimes due to the title given Jesus as the Son of God. Note that in the gospels Jesus is also the son of David, the son of Abraham, and the son of man. Why? Because as the son of David, Jesus has a right to the throne of David (Lu.1:32). As the son of Abraham, Jesus is entitled to the land of Israel, which includes the royal grant to Abraham. He is the son of man revealing His title to the Earth and the world. He is the Son of God, indicating that He is the heir of all things. Jesus is the second personage of the three-fold nature of Almighty God. He is God.

Note that Jesus thought it not robbery to be equal with God (Phil. 2:6). Why? Because He is Almighty God. In Isaiah 43:11, Jehovah God says, "I, even I, am the Lord;

and beside me there is no saviour." Yet the angel of the Lord proclaims, "For unto you is born this day in the city of David a Saviour, which is Christ the Lord" (Luke 2:11). Why? Because the Saviour, the Lord, Jesus, is God! Matthew says, "and they shall call his name "Emmanuel," which means, "God with us." Wow!

John tells us in the first few verses of his gospel that Jesus is God. "In the beginning was the Word, and the Word was with God, and the Word was God." The Greek for "Word," here, is "Logos," meaning "something said, utterance." John goes on to say that the "Word became flesh and dwelt among us." That's Jesus, God in the flesh! Note what the apostle Paul says concerning the deity of Jesus:

> Looking for that blessed hope, and the glorious appearing of the great God and our Saviour Jesus Christ; Who gave himself for us, that he might redeem us from all iniquity, and purify unto himself a peculiar people, zealous of good works. Titus 2:13-14

Paul says that Jesus is the great God and Saviour who gave "himself." Please don't let those who claim to be Jehovah's Witnesses tell you that Jesus is a lesser god. Jesus is God, the Almighty. Praise God, that's a revelation! Take it and run with it; you'll be blessed abundantly when that truth really grabs you.

The Isle of Patmos

> I John, who also am your brother, and companion in tribulation, and in the kingdom and patience of Jesus Christ, was in the isle that is called Patmos, for the word of God, and for the testimony of Jesus Christ. I was in the Spirit on the Lord's day, and heard behind me a great voice, as of a trumpet,... Rev. 1:9-10

Here, John writes a note to the seven churches. He knows of their troubles at home and lets them know that he feels their distress, for he himself had been exiled to Patmos, and this, for carrying the witness or testimony of Jesus.

From *Nelson's Illustrated Dictionary* we find this of the Isle of Patmos:

> a small rocky island to which the apostle John was banished and where he wrote the book of Revelation (Rev. 1:9). The island, about 16 kilometers (ten miles) long and ten kilometers (six miles) wide, lies off the southwest coast of Asia Minor (modern Turkey). Because of its desolate and barren nature, Patmos was used by the Romans as a place to banish criminals who were forced to work at hard labor in the mines and quarries of the island. Because Christians were regarded as criminals by the Roman emperor Domitian (ruled AD 81-96), the apostle John probably suffered from harsh treatment during his exile on Patmos. An early Christian tradition said John was in exile for 18 months.

Even in exile, however, John recognized the Lord's day. It is evident that John was in an attitude of worship and in the Spirit on this particular day. John is said to be "in the spirit" four times (1:10; 4:2; 17:3; 21:10). These mark the four major visions of Revelation. Here, in verse ten, Christ comes to John. In the next three visions John is told to "come." Thus, John, after the first vision, is taken from an earthly perspective to a heavenly perspective.

Write In A Book

Saying, I am Alpha and Omega, the first and the last: and, What thou seest, write in a book, and send it unto the seven churches which are in Asia; unto Ephesus, and unto Smyrna, and unto Pergamos, and unto Thyatira, and unto Sardis, and unto Philadelphia, and unto Laodicea. And I turned to see the voice that spake with me. And being turned, I saw seven golden candlesticks; And in the midst of the seven candlesticks one like unto the Son of man, clothed with a garment down to the foot, and girt about the paps with a golden girdle. His head and his hairs were white like wool, as white as snow; and his eyes were as a flame of fire; And his feet like unto fine brass, as if they burned in a furnace; and his voice as the sound of many waters. And he had in his right hand seven stars: and out of his mouth went a sharp two-edged sword: and his countenance was as the sun shineth in his strength. Rev. 1:11-16

In the Spirit, John heard a great voice as a trumpet. The voice of the Lord quickens John to his first recorded vision of the book. It was sent from the Alpha and Omega, Christ himself, the Word. John is thus commissioned to write the things he sees in a book, hence the book of the Revelation.

John turns, expecting to see the one speaking to him, but instead he sees seven golden candlesticks. These candlesticks represent the seven churches (v. 20). Christ is seen standing in the midst of these candlesticks. This reveals that Christ is present in all that takes place with these churches, and indeed, in all they represent.

We are then introduced to attributes describing Christ. John was so staggered by the awesome and frightening appearance of Christ that he falls to the ground as being dead (v.17).

The Description of Christ

John sees Christ in a long robe, wearing a breastplate having a golden belt. He has the wardrobe of a High Priest. We no longer have to go to a priest down the street somewhere to confess our sins, because Christ Jesus became our High Priest (Heb. 3:1; 4:14). Neither are we to call any man "father," in a religious sense, for one is our Father (Matt. 23:9).

Christ is seen as having a head and hairs like wool, white as snow. This reveals the attribute of the most pure and righteous judge, the ancient of days, yet without aging. His head and hair reveal the crown of glory. His eyes are seen as a flame of fire revealing the omnipresence of Christ.

His feet are like fine brass as if they had burned in a furnace. His feet are strong, tempered brass. This represents His ability to subdue His enemies. His feet have been tried, already, in the fiery furnace (Dan. 3:19-25).

The voice of the Lord is found to be both melodious and terrible (v.15). It has the soothing effect of flowing waters and the awesomeness of many waters. He holds in His right hand seven stars, which are the angels or messengers of the seven churches (v. 20).

> And when I saw him, I fell at his feet as dead. And he laid his right hand upon me, saying unto me, Fear not; I am the first and the last: I am he that liveth, and was dead; and, behold, I am alive for evermore, Amen; and have the keys of hell and of death. Rev. 1:17-18.

John was awestruck and having fallen down as being dead, is comforted by Christ, who, in His loving compassion, reaches with his right hand (signifying favor) to assure John, saying, "Fear not." Christ then identifies himself, "I am the first and the last: I am he that liveth (revealing the eternity of Christ), was dead (revealing the reality of the cross), and alive for evermore (revealing the reality of the resurrection)." We thus realize the deity, love, and power of Christ.

Keys of Death & Hell

A key, as we know, is for locking and unlocking. Christ has more than just a key, but keys (plural). He has the key of death, for He is the resurrection and life as mentioned earlier. He also holds the key to Hell, not only because He is Creator, but because He has been there. What? Christ has been in Hell!? That's right, He's been there. We are told this in Acts:

> Whom God hath raised up, having loosed the pains of death: because it was not possible that he should be holden of it. For David speaketh concerning him, I foresaw the Lord always before my face, for he is on my right hand, that I should not be moved: Therefore did my heart rejoice, and my tongue was glad; moreover also my flesh shall rest in hope: Because thou wilt not leave my soul in hell, neither wilt thou suffer thine Holy One to see corruption. Acts 2:24-27

Luke, here, quotes David (Psa. 16:8-11) and expressly states that he is speaking of Christ (Acts 2:25). Paul also speaks of Jesus' descent into Hell in Ephesians:

> Wherefore he saith, When he ascended up on high, he led captivity captive, and gave gifts unto men. (Now that he ascended, what is it but that he also descended first into the lower parts of the earth? He that descended is the same also that ascended up far above all heavens, that he might fill all things.) Eph. 4:8-10

Peter also mentioned Christ's descent into Hell:

> For Christ also hath once suffered for sins, the just for the unjust,
> that he might bring us to God, being put to death in the flesh, but
> quickened by the Spirit: By which also he went and preached unto
> the spirits in prison; Which sometime were disobedient, when
> once the longsuffering of God waited in the days of Noah, while
> the ark was a preparing, wherein few, that is, eight souls were
> saved by water. 1 Peter 3:18-20

Christ, between the crucifixion and the resurrection, by the Spirit, descended into Hades (Gk. for Hell) which is located within the Earth's core. He went to the "spirits in prison." Many contend the recipients of this message were those alive in Noah's day and that Christ, by the Spirit, traveled to Noah's day and preached to them. This reference, however, concerns the time immediately after Christ's death on the cross. It is then that the sin which Jesus became, on behalf of mankind, was delivered to its place (II Cor. 5:21). Then could our Saviour arise with a glorified body. It is there, also, that Noah's faith and example was vindicated. Christ did not go there to give those spirits a second chance, but to proclaim His triumph and vindicate the way of faith, the victorious faith, which Noah had held before them.

Two Compartments

Not only did Christ descend into Hades, but into the lower parts (plural). Before the resurrection of Christ, Hades had two parts. The one part being of torment and the other a paradise. These two parts had a great gulf separating them (Luke 16:26).

> And he said unto Jesus, Lord, remember me when thou comest
> into thy kingdom. And Jesus said unto him, Verily I say unto thee,
> To day shalt thou be with me in paradise. Lu. 23:42-43

Christ did not arise until three days later, yet He tells the thief on the cross that "to day shalt thou be with me in paradise." In addition, we have witness of paradise, the place of peace for Old Testament believers, as being within the Earth. The Philistines had come to war against Israel. King Saul inquired of the Lord about the matter, but the Lord didn't answer. In an impatient act, Saul went to the opposition for inquiry, a witch of Endor. He wanted her to bring up Samuel from the dead. Samuel's spirit did arise, but this was evidently a work of the Lord, for it scared the witch terribly. She apparently wasn't accustomed to seeing such a thing. She cried, "I saw gods ascending out of the earth." The point is, Samuel was quieted within the Earth. He said to Saul, "Why hast thou disquieted me, to bring me up" (I Sam. 28:11-15).

It was to the paradise side that Christ had taken the thief on the cross who had accepted Him. When Christ arose from the dead, he led captivity captive. That is, those in paradise were taken out and transported to the "Sea of Glass" directly beneath the throne of God (4:6). Samuel was in that crowd also. This was the time when Christ moved paradise from within the Earth to Heaven, beneath the throne of God, to the Sea of Glass (4:6). He led those captive in paradise, within the Earth, to captivity in paradise, or Heaven, under the throne of God, thus, leading "captivity captive."

The part within the Earth called paradise, now emptied, would be overtaken by the torturous side, for Hell continues to enlarge itself as it had begun to do in Isaiah's day (Isa. 5:14).

Why Did They Have To Wait?

Why were the Old Testament saints, upon death, taken into paradise within the Earth and not immediately taken into the presence of God under the Sea of Glass? Why did they have to wait? Answer: These saints could not enter into the presence of God because the ultimate sacrifice had not been made and could not be made until Christ. We find this in Hebrews 10:4, "For it is not possible that the blood of bulls and of goats should take away sins." These Old Testament saints could not go into the presence of the one Holy God until the perfect sacrifice for sin was made. That perfect sacrifice was Christ.

Christ has the key which no one else has. He is Creator of the place of eternal bliss for all who accept Him. That place is also called paradise. Christ also has the key of the place prepared for the devil and his angels, Hell. He, and He alone, can traverse into and out of such a place. He has walked in the fire with the three Hebrew children, He has feet like unto fine brass as if they had burned in a furnace. He has been there, but His very being did not see corruption. (The three stages of Hell discussed in chapter nine.)

Three-fold Purpose Of Revelation

Write the things which thou hast seen, and the things which are, and the things which shall be hereafter; The mystery of the seven stars which thou sawest in my right hand, and the seven golden candlesticks. The seven stars are the angels of the seven churches: and the seven candlesticks which thou sawest are the seven churches. Rev. 1:19-20

Here we find the three-fold purpose of which John is to write:

1. The purpose at hand: telling of Christ in the midst of the churches.

2. The historical purpose: relaying the message of Christ for every generation of believers.

3. The godly purpose of "Revealing Jesus Christ." This is realized in verse nineteen: "Write the things which thou hast seen, and the things which are, and the things which shall be hereafter."

The chapter ends revealing the mystery of the stars and the candlesticks. They are the seven angels, or messengers, and the seven churches. Thus, the unveiling of the Revelation begins.

Ω

The Seven Churches In Asia

Part 1
Chapter 2

"But why do I get one thing out of Scripture lessons one time and something else out of the same Scripture another time?" ..... "But, I thought it meant.....?"

Have you ever heard statements like these? As we grow spiritually, more and more "meat" is given to us (Heb. 5:12-14). This does not mean that the principles of Scripture we first learn (the milk) are no longer valid, but only that a deeper and fuller revelation is given to us in addition to the first principles.

This is where the truth of Scripture will run parallel whether spiritual, literal, or symbolic interpretations are used. Whether "milk" or "meat," truth may be found without contradiction. Such is the case with this chapter and the one following. Several interpretative methods will be incorporated for a fuller effect of the overall picture.

Chapter 2 concerns four of the seven churches. These churches, as well as those of chapter three, are prime examples of why we should use various interpretative methods. They were not only placed near the beginning of the book as addressees, but also as representatives.

The Seven Churches Of Asia

The first question to be answered is: Was the message of Revelation written for only seven of the churches of

Asia?

> ...What thou seest, write in a book, and send it unto the seven
> churches which are in Asia; unto Ephesus, and unto Smyrna, and
> unto Pergamos, and unto Thyatira, and unto Sardis, and unto
> Philadelphia, and unto Laodicea. Rev 1:11

Scripture relates that there were several churches in
Asia at the time of John's writing. There was, in addition
to the seven mentioned above, Troas (Acts 20:5; II Cor.
2:12), Miletus (Acts 20:17), Colossae (Col. 1:2), and
Hierapolis (Col. 4:12). There were also other churches in
Asia at this time. John was surely aware of them. The
question, then, is why was the Revelation message
addressed to only these seven churches and not to all
churches?

As discussed earlier, there is a blessing given to
whosoever reads, hears, and keeps the words of the
prophecy. And we know that the very nature of the title,
"Revelation," means to unveil, open up, and not to close
up or stop off with a message to only seven churches in
Asia. Revelation, then, is for all believers. It is the opening of what the prophet Daniel was told to shut and seal
up until the time of the end (Daniel 12:4). Hence, the
seven churches were specifically chosen for a greater purpose than just being addressees or historical references.

The seven churches were chosen for their particular
traits which apply to all of Christendom. Thus, these
seven churches were not only literal, but also representative. Found in their characteristics are not only practical
teaching and doctrinal beliefs, but also an outline for
Christian and anti-Christian history. These churches set
the tone and foundation for the entire book of Revelation

concerning the true Church and the false church. The false church is the one over which the coming false prophet and the one-world religion will preside. As representatives, however, they carry historical, symbolic, spiritual and prophetic meaning as well. The key to proper application, as mentioned in the introduction, is that these aspects of interpretation work in parallel and cannot conflict. It is here that we must again "rightly divide the word of truth."

Taking all this into consideration, we will study, in this chapter, four of the seven churches by applying as many of the aforementioned modes of interpretation as possible. We will thus begin to see the formation of a pattern that will serve as a foundation on which the remainder of the book can rest. Note that the churches concern the religious world, not the political, that is, the coming one-world government. The political aspect begins in chapter six.

Defining the Pattern

The definitions concerning the seven churches (chapters 2-3), will be applied as follows:

1. Literal Interpretation: Actual, real.

2. Spiritual Interpretation: Relating the spiritual atmosphere and condition in which the literal Church existed.

3. Historical Interpretation: More than just literal existence, but historical interpretation which applies to the development of church history. This extends from John's day until the Second Coming of Christ. This will include moral progressive stages and digressive

stages of the church world. (See chart, pg. 490)

4. Symbolic Interpretation: A symbol is something that represents something else. These churches hold religious doctrinal application for today. In a figurative sense, a type, or metaphor for modern application.

5. Prophetic Interpretation: This interpretation may include all of the above definitions, with the addition of parallels for interpreting future Biblical realities.

6. In the Background: In addition to the various interpretative methods, there will be references to those things going on behind the scenes which are relevant to the overall picture and interpretation of Revelation. These sections will aid in understanding the culmination of Christian history as well.

Each church will be studied as literal, spiritual, symbolic, historic, and so on under the given church name in order that one may see and feel the progression of church history. A straight-through study is recommended. However, for a quick, comparative study or quick-reference study, each section of any particular church is cross-referenced. For example: Ephesus Spiritual to Symrna Spiritual, or Ephesus Historical to Smyrna Historical and so on. These are linked by page number to the next succeeding topic.

To Those Who Have Ears

"He that hath an ear, let him hear what the Spirit saith unto the churches."

This statement is given following each letter to each church. It is a call to recognize the speaker, the hearer, and the message. The hearers are to hear with a spiritual ear, that is, let the Spirit speak in a most personal and revealing way. No wonder so many interpretations have arisen concerning the book of Revelation. One must be spiritually-minded and open-minded to the truth (I Cor. 2:14). Today many Biblical matters are portrayed through book, television and computer mediums; however, many Biblical matters are squandered away by unscriptural and unspiritual minds. This is a terrible tragedy for the hearer as well as the speaker.

We must remember that those things written in the Scriptures are spoken by the Spirit of God, thus are "God breathed" words (II Tim. 3:16). These words cannot be properly collated and understood unless given to man by the Holy Spirit as He, the Spirit, hears from Heaven.

> Howbeit when he, the Spirit of truth, is come, he will guide you into all truth: for he shall not speak of himself; but whatsoever he shall hear, that shall he speak: and he will shew you things to come. John 16:13

To Ephesus

THE SALUTATION - Unto the angel of the church of Ephesus write; These things saith he that holdeth the seven stars in his right hand, who walketh in the midst of the seven golden candlesticks; COMMENDATION - I know thy works, and thy labour, and thy patience, and how thou canst not bear them which are evil: and thou hast tried them which say they are apostles, and are not, and hast found them liars: And hast borne, and hast patience, and for my name's sake hast laboured, and hast not fainted. COMPLAINT - Nevertheless I have somewhat against thee, because thou hast left thy first love. WARNING - Remember therefore from whence thou art fallen, and repent, and do the first works; or else I will come unto thee quickly, and will remove thy candlestick out of his place, except thou repent. PRAISE - But this thou hast, that thou hatest the deeds of the Nicolaitanes, which I also hate. PROMISE - He that hath an ear, let him hear what the Spirit saith unto the churches; To him that overcometh will I give to eat of the tree of life, which is in the midst of the paradise of God. Rev 2:1-7

Ephesus Literal

This city, at its height, was the most important of some 230 that dotted the coastline of Asia minor. It was a great commercial mecca and a strategic force until its harbors fell into ruin. The efforts to save the harbors were only half-hearted. Trade eventually fell and shifted to other cities. The church at Ephesus was planted by Paul (Acts 19). (Ref. pg. 45)

Ephesus Spiritual

The Ephesian believers lived in a city which held religious conflict. The population was given over to the worship of Diana, as seen in Acts 19:23-35. False teachers and false prophets came against them from every side. The Ephesian Christians, however, were steadfast in defending their faith in Christ.

They were commended for being a church made up of hard workers. These people held great patience as they labored, yet would not tolerate those persons or groups that were evil. They detested the false teaching of the Nicolaitanes and "put to the test" those who claimed to be apostles, finding them to be liars (2:2).

Christian Zeal

We can readily see the zeal of the Ephesian Christians

in their standing for truth. They had good works, labor, and patience, yet, there was a complaint against them. They had become complacent in personal worship. Although they were busy defending the faith and disputing heresies, they had lost their first love, that is, they had drifted from the all-important one-on-one relationship with Christ. They were thus a spiritually backslidden church. Paul had warned them of this (Acts 20:29,30). If only they would look and see, the believers in Ephesus could relate to becoming relaxed and half-hearted by the example and lax effort displayed by the city to rebuild and repair the harbors.

Who Are The Nicolaitanes?

The Ephesian Church turned away the belief system and doctrine of the Nicolaitanes. The Lord commended the Ephesus Church for their stand and stated, that he too, hated the system of the Nicolaitanes ("hate," *miseo,* Gk, "to detest," "to love less").

Although many scholars mention very little of this sect, its doctrine has been an outstanding force throughout most of church history, particularly in the period of the Dark Ages, and, consequently, in modern times. It is a cohort with the Balaam instigators, who brought idolatry into the early church congregations. (See under, "Pergamos Spiritual" pg. 52)

The word Nicolaitanes, from the Greek, *Nikolaites,* h comes from *Niko,* "to conquer," or "overthrow," and *laos,* "the people, or laity."

The Nicolaitanes wished to set up an order of holy men to control the laity. This evidently began with a proselyte named Nicolas (Acts 6:5). Being a "proselyte" meant that he was a Gentile from another region who converted to Judaism before becoming a Christian. The church fathers accused Nicolas of denying the true Christian faith and founding the heretical sect known as the Nicolaitanes. His name means "conqueror of the people."

Whether Nicolas had anything to do with it or not, there were those who wished to set up an "apostolic succession," especially after the death of the apostles. Such succession would include clergy, bishops, archbishops, cardinals, popes, and so on, to over-lord the people. This is foreign to the New Testament teaching of calling the leaders pastors, deacons, evangelists, teachers, and so forth. (Ref. pg. 45)

Ephesus Historical

Ephesus, as well as the other six churches, represent not only spiritual and moral instruction, but it displays an outline for church history. Remember that the overall study of this book is that of a futurist viewpoint. However, the progress of church history cannot be overlooked. The historical aspect will stand to reveal either spiritual progression and digression as the wheel of history turns.

The term "church," in connection with church history, applies to collective Christianity. In its true meaning, the "church" is not a building or a particular sect; the true Church (assembly) is made up of believers of many denominations, many nations, and many races. They are those who have accepted Jesus Christ as Lord and Savior and who live for Him. They are those "born again of the

Spirit."

A fair historical outline of the Ephesian church age would be from around the time of the destruction of Jerusalem in AD 70, until around AD 170, a time of drastic change for the church world. Having to survive on its own due to the passing of most of the apostles, the Church collectively would suffer growing pains.

After the complete destruction of Jerusalem in AD 70, a Roman city was built on the site. Jerusalem was off-limits and regarded as forbidden ground for the Jews. These Jews were the ones who often plagued the Church with contentions.

The Church had become one of contending for the faith above that of developing a personal relationship with Christ. These Christians were committed to Christ, but had fallen prey to doctrinal contention. The lack of personal relationship would bring the church world into a more drastic stage of Christian history. It would be a stirring toward commitment through persecution as seen in the second church of Revelation.

Notes of concern:

1. The dates given are approximate. They are not meant to be a stopping-off of a given church or thoughts which align with them. They are given only because they fit that particular portion of Church history. Example: AD 70 to AD 170 is best fitted to Ephesus.

2. Remember that all modes of interpretation will remain in tact and continue to unfold as history progresses. EXAMPLE: The "Prophetic Aspect" was

prophetic for the people of John's day, however, it is both prophetic and historical for us. Thus, we can realize the written prophecy while looking back upon its foundation and fulfillment. We can also realize symbolic and spiritual qualities for today. The "Historical Interpretation" as displayed in this book is given only to reveal the outline of church history and to show its relevance to the entire book of Revelation. (Ref. pg. 47)

Ephesus Symbolic

The modern church world has fallen prey to the spirit of Ephesus. Contending for the faith has become a must, just as in the early Church (Jude 1:3) and is commendable. However, without a personal commitment to Christ, contending for the faith leads to vanity. Alongside the ingredient of contending for the faith should be personal commitment, thus, adding power to our contending.

The warning for the Ephesian Church in verse five was to repent and do their first works, or else, "I will come unto thee quickly, and will remove (*kino,* Gk."to stir") thy candlestick out of his place, except thou repent." The name "Ephesus" means "to relax." This relaxed characteristic would breed less Christian principle and a more "religious" attitude.

This church stands as a symbol to every Christian who becomes relaxed in spiritual commitment and more "religious" than Christian. A removing or "stirring" (Gk) will be the result (See the author's book *"The Bridal Feast"*).

False prophets in Ezekiel's day told Israel to relax, that God would not suffer Jerusalem to be destroyed (Ez.

13). They did not listen and would not repent. The "stirring" into Babylonian captivity was the terrible result. Let us take note of the warning to Ephesus and remain alert to the importance of a one-on-one relationship with Christ.

Overcomers

It is said of the overcomers of Ephesus that they are to become partakers of the Tree of Life, which is in the midst of the paradise of God. This is the same tree that was found in the Garden of Eden. After Adam lost dominion to the serpent, he and Eve were banished from the Garden (Gen. 3:23-24). Because of his sin, he could not partake of the Tree of Life, lest he "eat, and live for ever" (Gen. 3:22). The Tree of Life will again be in the paradise of God, which will be in the new city on the new Earth (Rev. 22:2; 22:14). (Ref. pg. 49)

In the Background

The seven churches of Asia, indeed, all the churches mentioned in New Testament Scripture, were within the boundaries of the Roman Empire. Persecution, brought upon Christianity, more often than not had to do with religious conflict not only with the Jews, but also between Christian and pagan principles. This, along with the Christians' refusal to recognize Roman emperors as gods, was intolerable for religious Rome.

What Is Paganism?

Paganism is a polytheistic system of religion, a doctrine based on belief in gods, and/or goddesses. Paganism has existed alongside Christianity and has played a major role in the development of the anti-christ systems of religion today. Understanding the roots of paganism will help us to better understand Revelation.

The belief in many gods first sprang forth at the infamous tower of Babel. This was several years after the flood of Noah. During that time, cities began to be built. Those who built the cities were revered as gods, an aspect of adoration which survived well into the period of the Roman Empire.

The most famous cities of the time were Babylon, Erech, Accad, and Calneh. These cities were built by the most outstanding Biblical character who lived between the flood and Abraham. His name was Nimrod. He was revered as the "god" of these cities. His first dominion, however, began at Babel (Gen. 10:10).

Nimrod was also a mighty hunter before the Lord. This title not only revealed his military ability, but also his protectiveness at a time when wild animals were a continual menace. The word "mighty" (*gibbowr*, Hebrew) means "warrior, tyrant." A tyrant is one who exercises power in a harsh, cruel manner.

Nimrod is also known in history as a hunter of men. The latter part of the phrase, "before the Lord," mentioned above, revolves around the word "before" which comes from the Hebrew word *paniym* meaning - "the face" (as the part that turns). We see, then, that Nimrod was a tyrant who turned his face from the Lord. This is why the Hebrew people referred to him later as "the rebel" or "rebellious one."

Nimrod, the revered god, is credited as being the instigator of the infamous tower of Babel. History and appellation, however, names his father, Cush, as the original instigator. The name Cush is a Chaldaic form of the name

"Chaos," which means "confusion." Nimrod's first dominion was at Babel, revealing a shift of power to him.

During the building of the tower of Babel, God confused the languages of the people and the building was stopped. The Bible states that the whole world was of one language and speech prior to this event (Genesis 11). At the "confusion of languages," people could no longer speak the name of their god. Thus, Nimrod, their chief god, was now known by multiple names due to multiple languages.

As Nimrod had so many things attributed to him, it was only reasonable for people, now in segregation, to adopt the portion of belief best interpreted by each group. Thus, we find diverse religious attributes and beliefs, yet peoples remaining reverent to their god. We find various names for Nimrod in Scripture: Chemosh, Molock, Merodach, Remphan, Tammuz (reincarnated) and Baal, to mention only a few of the some 38 Biblical titles and representative aspects given to this revered god.

Goddesses

Goddesses also came from the confusion at this infamous tower. Nimrod's father Cush was married to Semiramis (name found in classical history). After the death of Cush, Semiramis gained control and notoriety through Nimrod. She married him. Nimrod is also known in history as the "husband of the mother." At the confusion of languages, she also came to be known by multiple names.

She is known as Ashtaroth in the Old Testament and Diana in the New. After Nimrod was killed by his great uncle, Semiramis became with child and claimed this child to be the reincarnated Nimrod, who had ascended to the sun (beginning of sun worship). She was often depicted as a mother holding her child. The child, reincarnate Nimrod, was known as Tammuz, the Egyptian Horus (Nimrod reincarnate).

Nimrod and Semiramis are one and the same in ancient Egypt under the names of Osiris and Isis, to name a few appellations. In India, Semiramis is known as Iswara and Isi, in Asia as Deoius and Cybele, and in Rome as Jupiter and Fortuna ("Venus," and so on). In Greece, Semiramis is Ceres, the Great Mother, with the babe at her breast, or Plutus and Irene. In Thibet, in China, and Japan, she is Shing Moo, the Holy Mother bearing a child in her arms.

Many modern religions are descended from the religious system of Nimrod and his mother, Semiramis. As we shall see, paganism has had, and does have, great bearing on the message of Revelation, especially in recognizing "Babylon the Great."

To Smyrna

THE SALUTATION - And unto the angel of the church in Smyrna write; These things saith the first and the last, which was dead, and is alive; TRIAL OF PERSECUTION - I know thy works, and tribulation, and poverty, (but thou art rich) and I know the blasphemy of them which say they are Jews, and are not, but are the synagogue of Satan. EXHORTATION - Fear none of those things which thou shalt suffer: behold, the devil shall cast some of you into prison, that ye may be tried; and ye shall have tribulation ten days: be thou faithful unto death, and I will give thee a crown of life. PROMISE - He that hath an ear, let him hear what the Spirit saith unto the churches; He that overcometh shall not be hurt of the second death. Rev 2:8-11

Smyrna Literal

Symrna was a beautiful city. Its people were proud of their commercial wealth, refined culture and beautiful surroundings. Smyrna's main commercial trade was myrrh, a product used for perfume (Psa.45:8), for embalming (Jn.19:39), for oil (Ex.30:23) and for purification of women (Est.2:12). It was also used for dulling pain (Mrk.15:23). The failing harbors of Ephesus had caused the shifting of much trade to Smyrna. It grew more and more prosperous because of Ephesus's relaxed state. (Ref. pg. 52)

Smyrna Spiritual

The pride of this city, however, gave rise to widespread vanity. The atmosphere was one of "keeping up with the Joneses," and, indeed, of trying to surpass them. Such competition bred indifference, degradation, and eventually an outward display of cruelty to those deemed inferior. This gave leverage to a sect of Christian haters called the Jews.

What Constitutes a Jew?

A great number of Jews lived in Smyrna, but they were not Christian Jews. They were those steeped in Old Testament law who had rejected Christ as the Messiah. They despised the Christians of Smyrna.

Christ calls these Jews (who hated the Church) blasphemers, and then says, "they say they are Jews, and are not, but are of the synagogue of Satan" (v.9). They were not only well-versed in Old Testament law, but also in the prophecies concerning the Messiah (Jesus) although they had rejected him (Jn.1:11). These persons remained hardened against change and thus rejected the new Covenant as given by Christ. To remain unchanged toward the Messiah, Jesus, would cause these Jews to be un-Jew, blasphemers.

The term "Jew" was not ascribed to God's chosen people (Israel - Deut. 7:6) until sometime around BC 490 to 480, when it was used to describe Mordecai, a Benjamite. "Jew," however, had been given to describe a descendant of Judah. Why was this title given to Mordecai?

The explanation springs from the time of the Babylonian captivity, somewhere around BC 600. Members of the tribe of Judah formed, by far, the larger portion of the remnant of the covenant people. Thus, "Jew" became the appellation of the whole nation of Israel (II Macc. 9:17; Jn. 4:9; Acts 18:2,24). The original designation of the Israelite people was "Hebrews," as the descendants of Eber and Abraham.

However, the New Covenant was to make a new Jew (Rom. 2:17-29; Gal. 3:7). Thus, a Jew is not a person of an earthly race or creed (Rom. 9:6-9). A true Jew is any person who believes and accepts Jesus Christ as the only Lord and Saviour (Rom. 4:11). He is someone who has the same faith as that of Abraham (Gal. 3:7). In retrospect, those who rejected Christ Jesus as the Messiah became un-Jew and blasphemers.

Hold To Christ

The salutation to Smyrna comes from the "first and

the last, which was dead, and is alive" (v.8). This was a message from Christ, revealing that although the atmosphere for the Smyrna Christians was distressing, He is ultimately in control. No matter how severe the mockery, cursing, and abuse, they were to hold their testimony for Christ. Christ was assuring them that He knew their works and their troubles.

The Jews at Smyrna were doing all they could to influence city officials to stamp out Christianity. Thus, the church at Smyrna became impoverished. Many lost their jobs or had their goods confiscated for "breaking the law." Christ was reminding them that although they were in poverty, they were rich, spiritually rich (Matt.6:19 21). The church at Smyrna represents the persecution that would befall the Church in years to come. (Ref. pg. 52)

Smyrna Historical

Not only was poverty bringing hardships, but the Church was beginning to be severely persecuted. The name "Smyrna" means "bitterness" (from myrrh). This, indeed, fit the situation for Smyrna Christians. The Smyrna period resulted from the relaxed state of the Ephesus period.

The Ephesus period, AD 70 to AD 170, a time of religion over a personal relationship with Christ, would lead the church world into great persecution, that is, a removing, or better, a great stirring, of the candlestick. The church world was warned of this through the Ephesus example (2:5). This "removing," or "stirring," would occur during the Symrna church age.

Losing its first love, the church world would now fall

into persecution. Such persecution would cause one of two things: either a sincere stand for Christ, or, an outward refusal of Him. The allegiance to Christ, however, prevailed in hearts; men and women literally gave their lives for their Lord under the severest of persecutions and even unto death. Many, however, fled, thus spreading the gospel with greater fervency to surrounding areas.

Note: There have been persecutions before and after the beginning of the New Testament Church, and they will continue, in one form or another, to be present until Christ returns. Such persecutions are separate in their own right from that of the Smyrna church age persecution. Smyrna represents that portion of church history extending from around AD 170 to AD 312. During this period, the Church suffered the severest persecutions by the Roman government. The last ten years of the Emperor Diocletian's reign brought fierce persecutions upon Christianity, hence, the Church. This is reflected in verse ten, "and ye shall have tribulation ten days: be thou faithful unto death" (myrrh is associated with death).

Those who had taken a stand against the devil (v.10), those of literal Smyrna, and all who have tasted death since those times, for the cause of Christ, are promised a crown of life. This is the martyr's crown. They will escape the second death (v.11).

What Is The Second Death?

To understand this, we must briefly mention two major judgments that are yet to come: The Judgment Seat of Christ, and, the Great White Throne Judgment. (these will be discussed at length in chapter twenty).

After the Rapture, or "catching away" of the Church, (discussed in chapter one) believers, the only ones taken, will pass through the Judgment Seat of Christ. This Judgment is not only for those living at the time of the "catching away," but also for those believers who have died, for, "we which are alive and remain, shall be caught up together with them (dead in Christ [I Thess. 4:16-17])." Paul calls the dead here, the "dead in Christ." This speaks only of born again Christians (those born of the Spirit).

Another judgment called "the Great White Throne Judgment" is found in Revelation 20:11. This judgment is for the dead, not the dead in Christ. Those judged there are all those who have rejected Christ. They will have died (first death), then, will be resurrected for this judgment (20:11-15), and afterwards cast into the Eternal Lake of Fire (second death).

> And death and hell were cast into the lake of fire. This is the second death. Rev. 10:14. (Ref. pg. 54)

Smyrna Symbolic

Smyrna should inspire us today to stand for Christ no matter how severe the ridicule or abuse. We should always remember that Christ is in control. He is the one who will reward us, even for death. Paul, who was also well-versed in Old Testament writings, knew that death was actually a blessing (Phil. 1:21; Rom. 8:18). It is in the Old Testament that we find that the death of saints is precious in the Lord's sight (Psa. 116:15). These verses in no way substantiate suicide or assisted suicide. (Ref. pg. 57)

In the Background

The persecution brought by the Roman government

during the Smyrna church age caused many to flee to the wilderness for safety. This scattering provided a seed-bed for what was to become, centuries later, a major force against the progressions of religious Rome.

Montanists

Around AD 170, we find a sect of people called Montanists. They may have been followers of a minister named Montanus, or were called such because they were people of the Mountains. The sect's name may have been from the word *"Montane,"* Latin for Mountaineers, always freeman. The origin of the name is uncertain.

The Montanists movement was not a new form of Christianity; on the contrary it was the primitive Christianity which fled from pagan Rome. The movement was not without doctrinal error. The group demanded a moral life, and held sort of a Pharisaical outlook on morality. The reason for such demanding probably lies in the fact that the New Testament was not widespread reading material at the time, thus, they were unlearned to a degree. They did believe, however, in immersion as the form of baptism and in a moral Biblical life afterwards.

Although much of their history comes from their enemies, a Montantist, Tertullian, wrote in their defense around AD 200. Romanism viewed the Montantists as the most vile of men. They were thought of as mystics and, most certainly, as rebels.

Novatians

Around AD 251, we find another sect known as the Novatians, said to be followers of a man known as Novatian. Novatian withdrew fellowship from the Roman religion due in part to differences concerning baptism and the practice of sacrificing to Roman emperors as gods.

This sect believed in local church independence. These people also rebaptized those who had given in to the oppressions of Rome and later returned to the Christian faith. The Novatian movement met with and joined the Montanists in Asia Minor. This merge brought with it an attempt to reclaim doctrinal purity. Both the Montanist and Novatian movements are said to have begun during the Smyrna church age.

To Pergamos

> THE SALUTATION - And to the angel of the church in Pergamos write; These things saith he which hath the sharp sword with two edges; COMMENDATION - I know thy works and where thou dwellest, even where Satan's seat is: and thou holdest fast my name, and hast not denied my faith, even in those days wherein Antipas was my faithful martyr, who was slain among you, where Satan dwelleth. COMPLAINT - But I have a few things against thee, because thou hast there them that hold the doctrine of Balaam, who taught Balac to cast a stumblingblock before the children of Israel, to eat things sacrificed unto idols, and to commit fornication. So hast thou also them that hold the doctrine of the Nicolaitanes, which thing I hate. WARNING - Repent; or else I will come unto thee quickly, and will fight against them with the sword of my mouth. PROMISE - He that hath an ear, let him hear what the Spirit saith unto the churches; To him that overcometh will I give to eat of the hidden manna, and will give him a white stone, and in the stone a new name written, which no man knoweth saving he that receiveth it. Rev 2:12-17

Pergamos Literal

Pergamos sat on top of a mountain arising out of a beautiful valley. This setting gave it an air of royalty and authority to the traveler beholding it from the valley beneath.

Pergamos was one of the most renowned cultural and religious centers of the world. Two of the great boasts of the city were its famous college of medical priests and its library, second only to Alexandria, Egypt. In a friendly gesture, Mark Anthony gave the Pergamos library to Cleopatra. The volumes were later moved to Alexandria.

Pergamos was the imperial and administrative center of Asia and a capital city for four hundred years. Its most elaborate feature was its Acropolis (fortified height) which rose about 1000 feet in the center of the city. Several temples were built there in honor of the gods, one of which was the temple to Asklepios, a Greco-Roman god of healing. (Ref. pg. 59)

Pergamos Spiritual

The salutation comes from "he which hath the sharp sword with two edges." This, at the very onset, gives clue to disfavor. There was a much needed "dividing" and "cutting asunder" (Heb. 4:12) in Pergamos. The name Pergamos means "marriage;" however, it was not a good one, as we shall see.

Christ refers to the city of Pergamos as the seat of Satan. This quite possibly could refer to the worship of heathen gods which was very much present there. But in all probability, it refers to the evil system which brought such false worship (discussed in "Pergamos Historical").

The city had temples built in honor of Athenos, the goddess of wisdom and the arts, Zeus (Cush), the father of other gods, and to mortal heroes. Zeus was the Roman

Jupiter. The church at Pergamos held a loyalty to Christ's name, even in this society polluted with idol worship and imperialism.

Their faith stood fast even at the martyrdom of Antipas. Tradition says that this man was placed inside a brazen bull and slowly roasted to death (A.T. Robertson, *"Word Pictures In The New Testament"*). His death was esteemed highly by Christ, for He calls him "my faithful witness." Even though Church members were faithful in keeping the name and faith of Christ, there was a great complaint against the Pergamos Church. They had members who held to the doctrine of Balaam.

Doctrine of Balaam

The doctrine (instruction and practice) of Balaam is seen in the book of Numbers chapters 22-25. Balak, the king of Moab, wanted Balaam, the soothsayer (Josh. 13:22), to put a curse on Israel. The Lord would not permit Balaam to do so. Balaam then suggested that Balak give a great licentious feast of Baalpeor and invite the men of Israel. The men of Israel fell prey to this tactic. When they saw the "daughters of Moab," they committed whoredoms with them and eventually bowed down to the gods of Moab. The doctrine was thus to seduce and introduce idolatry.

So we see here a practice of seduction to introduce idolatry into the Church. Thus, evidence reveals that some persons of the Pergamos Church began to allow a mixing, of sorts, with the idolatrous practices held by the world, especially the Roman world. What had happened here was that which the apostle Paul had warned the church of

Colossae about (Col. 2:8,9). He had warned of philosophy and tradition. Pergamos was a city having great philosophical, literary and cultural influence. (Ref. pg. 59)

Pergamos Historical

The name Pergamos, as mentioned earlier, means, "marriage." The marriage of the Pergamos Church was not a good one. It was a union of Christianity and paganism. The Church, to this point in history, had lost its first love, fallen into persecution, and had now given in to the persuasion of idolatry. The true Church was on a downward spiral, while a false church began to spiral upward.

Nicolaitanes

A powerful force alongside the philosophies of paganism (introduced here as the doctrine of Baalim) were the over-lording Nicolaitanes. The Nicolaitanes played a great role in the fulfillment of idolatry in the Church and became instrumental in setting up a religious hierarchy to control the people. Ephesus had rejected any attempt of the Nicolaitanes to control the Church, but now, in Pergamos, we find the sect has finally infiltrated and gained a certain amount of control (v.15). Thus, they began to restructure church worship and doctrine.

The Pergamos church age began around AD 312 and extended through AD 606. During this period, the Chaldean hierarchy moved from Babylon to Pergamos. Attalus III was the Priest-King of Chaldea and, in fleeing from the Persians, settled at Pergamos to set up his hierarchy there. This move to Pergamos and the intent, which later sprang to the forefront, would blossom into a false Christianity (false doctrine). This also refers to Satan's seat. At first, Attalus persecuted Christians, but he later changed his tactics to exalt the Church and attempt to unite church and state. This objective was accomplished with the aid of the Emperor Constantine.

The Emperor Constantine (305-337) and Priest-King Attalus wished to unite their Christian and pagan subjects into one people, thus consolidating the Roman Empire. The already existing mix of paganism (doctrine of Baalim) with Christianity had opened the doorway for further corruption through these two entities.

Although it is said that Constantine had become a Christian, his motives were more political than religious. He attempted to gain both Christian and pagan support. In doing so, he gave birth to a polluted sort of Christianity. It was a Roman Christianity, a combination of paganism and Christianity.

This gave the Nicolaitanes ample opportunity to institute greater control over the people, as their practice was one very familiar to Romanism. (Remember that Nicolas [Acts 6:5] was a proselyte who evidently brought with him elements of Romanism)

A sensuous form of worship was introduced to the Church and the character of preaching was changed. Constantine himself used the Baalim method to seduce the bishops of the Church. He imposed buildings called basilicas to be used for conversion into churches. Such tactics would enhance a more paganistic setting and encourage pagans into the Church. The stage was now set for the ultimate take-over. (Ref. pg. 61)

In the Background

God, however, did not leave His Word and truth unattended. The Lord of the sharp two-edged sword was also dividing out those who would cling to gospel truths. The Montanist and Novatian rebellion would now be further supported and reinforced by yet another group of so-called rebels.

Donatists

Around AD 311 a group of dissenters called the Donatists developed in northern Africa (southern Roman Empire). Their doctrine and practice was the same as the Novatians. They stood for separation of church and state and were thus rebels against the Roman government.

Throughout the Empire, these groups, deemed heretics by "Roman Christianity," flourished. The merging of these groups brought more understanding of Scripture and doctrine. As a result, there was a great desire surging, an earnest desire to recover doctrinal purity. As more and more understanding from each group was applied, their individual errors concerning the gospel began to be corrected.

This sincere attempt to return to God's Word would reveal the multiple errors of the newly established Roman Church. Doctrinal purification would continue in the background of Christian history until the God-appointed time was right to flourish again as a contending force. The fulfillment of such a time was not to come quickly, for the darkest time in Christian history was about to unfold (see Thyatira Historical).

Pergamos Symbolic

The Pergamos Church is symbolic in that we are to be faithful and hold fast the faith, even in the midst of martyrdom. In addition, we are to abstain from idolatrous practices. Sadly, this has not been the case. Many church members are given over to paganism through such societies as Freemasonry, the Eastern Star, and ecumenism, to mention but a few of the seducing spirits which have descended from ancient Babylon (See author's book, *"The Masonic-Christian Conflict Explained"*).

In addition, at a time we call Easter is the invasion of the Passover rabbit. Alongside our Passover Lamb, we (Christianity as a whole) teach our innocent little ones to gather up rabbit eggs. A rabbit doesn't even lay eggs. Why not a Passover chicken or duck? Since ancient times, pagans have worshipped rabbits as sex and fertility gods. Likewise, eggs, since ancient times, have been symbols of fertility, sex, and new life. An important feature of pagan springtime celebrations that of new life and fertility, among other things.

Even the greatest of disguises can't hide the hideousness of Halloween. Many Christians (surely ignorant of its true meaning) have parties in churches and fellowship halls encouraging participation in characterizing ghosts, goblins and all sorts of ghastly creatures (demons).

Halloween (All Hallowed's Evening) is actually a festival of death which was venerated some 300 years before Christ. The god of death, Samhain, was worshipped by the Druids in honor of the death of the old year and beginning of a new one. It has nothing to do with Christ at all.

The Druids would dress in peculiar robes with magi-

cal markings on them and go from house to house in
search of particular foods to replenish their strange dietary
restrictions. They carried with them their personal spirit
guide (represented by an oil lamp) inside a hollowed-out
turnip. This spirit was "Jock of the lantern." Immigrants
to the New World used turnips or pumpkins. We now recognize their spirit guide today as "jack-o-lantern." If the
desires of the Druids were not met, a human sacrifice was
to be offered to their god through a "bon fire," known to
them as a "bone fire."

Does all this sound familiar? Many traditions of this
form of paganism are found in modern observances. It is
obvious that such things should not be part of the Church.
Either ignorance or stubbornness prevails.

The church at Pergamos is warned to repent, or else
Christ will come quickly and fight with the sword of His
mouth. Those who do repent and overcome will be given
hidden manna, a white stone, and a new name. These
aspects reveal the care, acceptance and recognition of
those who separate themselves from paganism. (Ref. pg.
68)

To Thyatira

THE SALUTATION - And unto the angel of the church in
Thyatira write; These things saith the Son of God, who hath his
eyes like unto a flame of fire, and his feet are like fine brass;
COMMENDATION - I know thy works, and charity, and service,
and faith, and thy patience, and thy works; and the last to be more
than the first. COMPLAINT - Notwithstanding I have a few
things against thee, because thou sufferest that woman Jezebel,
which calleth herself a prophetess, to teach and to seduce my servants to commit fornication, and to eat things sacrificed unto
idols. And I gave her space to repent of her fornication; and she

repented not. Behold, I will cast her into a bed, and them that commit adultery with her into great tribulation, except they repent of their deeds. And I will kill her children with death; and all the churches shall know that I am he which searcheth the reins and hearts: and I will give unto every one of you according to your works. PROMISE - But unto you I say, and unto the rest in Thyatira, as many as have not this doctrine, and which have not known the depths of Satan, as they speak; I will put upon you none other burden. But that which ye have already hold fast till I come. And he that overcometh, and keepeth my works unto the end, to him will I give power over the nations: And he shall rule them with a rod of iron; as the vessels of a potter shall they be broken to shivers: even as I received of my Father. And I will give him the morning star. He that hath an ear, let him hear what the Spirit saith unto the churches. Rev. 2:18-29

Thyatira Literal

The name Thyatira comes from an uncertain origin and thus carries no distinct definition. This is probably due to the hidden revelation, which will open as our study progresses. Thyatira was a frontier town and the least important of the seven mentioned. Renowned for its trade guilds and unions, it had many business and social functions. The two main industries of the city were wool and dye. The social functions of the city included meals in honor of the gods. (Ref. pg. 73)

Thyatira Spiritual

The announcement to the church at Thyatira was from the Son of God, "who hath eyes like a flame of fire and feet like fine brass." He has, and indeed shall, trod through the fiery trials which this Church represents. These attributes also reveal that He sees all the inner workings of this Church, as if to acknowledge their hidden practices. Christ remains in control despite the condition and influence of its hidden hierarchy. This underlying force in Thyatira is referred to as the "depths of Satan." Some members of the Thyatira Church were unaware of the underlying workings, even though it was open before them (2:24). Those persons, evidently the minority, would not fall into the same plight as those who were capable of perceiving the situation.

Christ knows the works, charity, service, faith, patience and works of this Church (v.19). Note, He says, "the last to be more than the first," yet He begins with works and ends with works. Both times this word is *"ergon"* (Gk) which means "toil, deeds, or labor." It is evident that the church at Thyatira placed great emphasis on works, even above that of love (charity) and faith. They had evidently missed all that the Law and Prophets rested upon and that which Jesus taught (Matt.22:37-40). They were definitely more religious than Christian.

Jezebel

The church at Thyatira permitted the prophesying of Jezebel. This was a great complaint against them. Jezebel taught and seduced the church to commit fornication and to eat things sacrificed to idols. This "fornication" refers to a drawing away from Christ through idolatry, while "sacrificing to idols" refers to setting up idolatrous images.

Many scholars believe there may have been an actual woman by that name in the Thyatira church, probably of noble lineage and very influential. It is evident that Jezebel, whether or not she was an actual person, represented the "system of paganism," and, carried the traits of her Old Testament prototype.

Jezebel Prototype

Ahab, a king of Israel, married Jezebel, a princess of idolatrous Tyre, to strengthen the political ties of his kingdom. Jezebel, however, was steeped in idol worship. She killed the prophets of God and introduced the licentious worship of Baal (sun worship) to Israel. Her daughter, Athaliah, married Jehoram, son of Jehoshaphat and king of Judah, which introduced idolatrous worship into Judah. Thus, Jezebel caused all of Israel to sin (I Kings 16:29-33).

We see then that the church of Thyatira possessed a mixture of pagan and Christian principle. Thyatira would prove to be typical of what was to befall the church world, as a whole, during the progression, or in this case, "digressive stage," of church history. (Ref. pg. 74)

Thyatira Historical

The upward swing of paganism was now outwardly overpowering true Christianity. The church world was now reaching the lowest ebb of Christian character in its history due to both outside and inside influences. Pergamos only revealed Satan's seat, but Thyatira had his depths. The "depths of Satan" were being outwardly revealed. The intermingling of Christian and pagan principles, brought by Attalus and Constantine, had reached its pinnacle through the system of Jezebelism. The outward church was now pagan.

We first saw the Church, as a whole, and after the death of the apostles (except for John in the beginning), as:

1. Losing its first love, yet rejecting the Nicolaitane and Balaam doctrine; the Ephesus church age (AD 70 - AD 170). (See chart, pg. 490)

2. Falling into persecution during the Symrna church age (AD 170 - AD 312).

3. Accepting Nicolaitane and Balaam doctrines during the Pergamos church age (AD 312 - AD 606).

4. Completely saturated by paganism during the Thyatira church age (AD 606 - AD 1520).

A church had been born that would become the most renowned religious machine and political influence of all time. The true Church would be pushed into the background and eventually into hiding through the severest of persecutions.

By this time the Roman Empire had fallen (approx. AD 450) and power had begun to shift from the emperors to the popes. Thus, in all actuality, Rome never fell, but only shifted its power. In AD 1200, the papacy had reached its pinnacle of power. Innocent III (ruled 1198-1216) declared, "As the Vicar of Christ, all power is given to me in heaven and in earth." Kings and nobles alike were subject to the power of the popes for they claimed the power to excommunicate and condemn to Hell the disobedient. Innocent and other popes played nobles, kings, and nations against each other and thus kept civil powers weakened and dependent upon them.

The time-frame of this church age corresponds with

what is known as the "Dark Ages," and gives a distinct picture of the "papal system" which was dominant from around AD 606 until the Reformation of AD 1520. It is a system of works over faith and ritual over commitment. It venerates the worship of the mother, the woman over the child (Christ), a sort of Jezebelism as found in the Thyatira Church.

Degradation Of Christ

When images were placed in church buildings for people to bow down to it became fully idolatrous. This is where the most corrupt and degrading thing that could ever happen to Christ and his mother Mary had happened. Images of the Roman goddess, Venus with baby Jupiter on her lap, were soon replaced with images of Mary and Baby Jesus. Note that statues of Diana (Venus under another name) are seen in dictionaries and encyclopedias as having a rosary about her neck, as is used today to venerate Mary.

This was not a revolution of change, but a resolution to incorporate; not a conversion to Christianity but an adaptation of paganism in order to appear Christian. The rituals and observances remained basically the same as those of paganism, only the names and images were changed to appear Christian.

The paganistic philosophy of previous ages had paved the way for the most degrading form of worship and idolatry the Church world would ever see. This system of worship was the spawning of the Great Harlot religion (17:5) that would later become the seat of the false prophet (13:11-18).

The papal system today is venerated as "Christian" due to the incorporating of Mary in the place of Venus. It is portrayed in movies, in government and in everyday language as Christian. Pagans of other factions have recognized the comparison of this Roman system with paganism. Referring to the "Christian world," (speaking of "Roman Christianity"), Albert Pike, a renowned pagan, writes:

> "The God of nineteen-twentieths of the Christian world is only Bel, Moloch, Zeus, or at best Osiris, Mithras, or Adonai, under another name, worshipped with the old Pagan ceremonies and ritualistic formulas. It is the Statue of Olympian Jove, worshipped as the Father, in the Christian Church that was a Pagan Temple; it is the Statue of Venus, become the Virgin Mary. (*Morals & Dogma,* pg. 295)

To worship the Son of God, and Mary, the chosen vessel of God, with paganism and paganistic ritual, was the most clever and deceptive system of philosophy that Satan could hope for. In fact, it is called the depths of Satan.

In the Background

We must note again, however, that God did not leave His Word and truth unattended during this dark period of church history. We know there were those in Thyatira who did not know the depths of Satan, but on a greater scale were those rebels of Rome who were flourishing in the hills and valleys of the Empire. From home to home and city to city these possessors of true Christianity continued to abound and spread the gospel of Christ.

Paulicians

We have mentioned the Montanists, the Novatians and the Donatists. Now upon the scene, we find the Paulicians (AD 653). These separatists were also known as the Cathari, Bogomils and a variety of other names. They were called Paulicians due to their possession, not only of the gospels, but also of the letters of Paul. For reasons of persecution, religious Rome accused these groups of believing in dualism, but with no success. Dualism is the doctrine that two opposing forces, one good and the other evil, are forever counterposed against each other. Rome, however, could not stay the hand of God from working in these peoples.

The persecution of the Paulicians, along with that of the groups mentioned above, aided greatly the spreading of the gospel, and subsequently, facilitated the further purifying of their teachings. This gave rise to a resurgence toward pure faith and truth.

Paterines

Around AD 750 in Milan, Italy, another group of "rebels" were on the rise. They were the Paterines. Elements of their beliefs and practices ran parallel with that of the Paulicians.

Persecution drove the Paterines into the Alps, especially into the Piedmont Valley, where they met with the spiritual heirs of the Novatians, the Donatists, the Paulicians, and various other peoples. These peoples were now called the Waldenses, possibly because of the fervent and influential evangelist, Peter Waldo. Here the seed for revival was conceived and purified. Fervency among the leaders of this large group of Christians sparked a real spiritual awakening.

This, however, infuriated religious Rome. The awakening was a threat to Romanism. Pope Lucius III in special council (AD 1183-84, later, but still in the Thyatira period) proclaimed, "to bind in the chain of perpetual anathema those who presumed to preach, public or privately, without the authority of the bishop." Pope Innocent III, at the Fourth Lateran Council, in AD 1215, adopted the following decree:

1. All rulers are exhorted to tolerate no heretics in their domain.

2. If any ruler refused to clear his land of heretics, he shall be deprived of his authority and driven from his land by force.

3. Everyone who joins in an armed expedition against heretics is granted indulgence (forgiveness without penance).

The Beast Revealed
Many people were tortured and killed during this great carnage, but none surpassed the tortures of the Waldenses. In all, 36 persecutions were launched. The Catholic Church gave authority to certain monks to wipe out the Waldenses. Many victims were frozen to death, thrown from cliffs and dashed to pieces, driven into caves and burned to death or suffocated, ripped open, disemboweled and left to die or impaled upon prongs of trees and left to

die. The beast of Rome was revealing her true self.

The Catholic Church boasted that the Waldenses had been totally wiped out, but not so. They had been wiped out as an organized body, but not as a Christian people. Their scattering became just another form of spreading the gospel. God can always turn the plight of the Devil into something good. The dispersed Waldenses and their doctrine continued to exist in such offsprings: Henricians, Arnoldists, Lollards, Anabaptists, Mennonites, Dutch Baptists, and on and on.

Cautious Witness

These scattered Christians had to witness with caution. A prospect for the gospel was first asked, quite obscurely, his feelings toward religious Rome. If the answers were favorable, the Christian would choose to give witness of Christ. A poor choice often proved fatal. Many times Christians were turned over to the authorities, losing their lives upon refusing to expose the whereabouts of other Christians. To be a witness for Christ in those days often brought death. Many exposed witnessing Christians to religious Rome seeking forgiveness for sins, and for indulgences. Indulgences, in a nut-shell, are partial remissions of punishment still due for sin after confession and supposed forgiveness.

Again, it must be noted that flourishing Christianity among these so-called rebels and the spreading of the gospel throughout the Roman Empire became the strong driving force behind the Reformation period.

Note: The teaching of each of the aforementioned groups engulfs, in one form or another, most Protestant teaching today, some holding fragments of Romanism, while others are more purified. (Historic - Ref. pg. 77)

Thyatira Symbolic

We have seen that Constantine's form of Christianity was a mixture of Romanism and Christianity. We have seen the progress of the Nicolaitanes and those who taught Balaam. We have also seen, in these united systems, a cloak of Christianity without the truth.

The seriousness of the situation can readily be seen for modern society in the religious situation of the world. The largest and most influential religion in the world (deemed "Christian") is Roman Catholicism. It is headed out by the Vatican, which is none other than the pagan child of Constantine and Attalus, nurtured by idolatry, and matured by ecumenical clout and political power. It is a force to be reckoned with. Even the United States has an ambassador to the Vatican.

Roman Catholicism's system of salvation by works aligns perfectly with Thyatira (v.19) and remains a prominent doctrinal stance today. Repeating prayers in Mary's name, as well as prayers to other saints, is foreign to true Christianity. This is another form of the paganistic prayers to Venus and Jupiter. (Ref. pg. 82)

Headed For Tribulation

The Roman Catholic system is represented by Jezebel. Christ gives her "time for repentance" (v.21) and states that she will go into great tribulation if she does not repent. This reveals the longevity of the system. The church age from around AD 606 to around AD 1520 only depicts the portion of church history best suited to

Thyatira, not that it will cease to exist as an entity. In fact, as our study progresses, we will see that the papal system fits all too clearly Babylon the Great, the mother of Harlots and Abominations of the Earth (Rev. 13:11-18; 17:5), and the seat of the false prophet. This system will be present upon the Earth, and, indeed, be a major force, after the "catching away" of the true Church and will go into the Tribulation Period. During that time, this system and its leader (false prophet) will influence the world to follow the one-world government and its leader, the AntiChrist (one-world government will be discussed later - chapters 6 and 13).

Her children (many denominations and religions) will be killed "with death" (during the Tribulation Period). Some persons of Thyatira, however, do not know of her doctrine (v.24). They are ignorant of the depths of Satan (possibly new converts or unlearned persons). These will be spared the plight of the Tribulation Period and are told to hold that which they do have "till I come."

Those who will overcome are those who will hold to Christian principles and keep the works of Christ, not the works of the system. They will rule with Christ over the nations during the Millennial Age (2:26). They will be given the "morning star," the true Jesus with a pure lineage, due to true acceptance (22:16).

Note About Numbers In Scripture

Generally in Scripture when topics are mentioned in numbers of seven, the number one relates to the number seven, two relates to six, and three relates to five, thus, the number four as the focal point, or center of discussion.

This considered, Thyatira, and that which it represents, will be the religious focal point for the Tribulation Period. This system will play a major role in the formation of the one-world government and one-world religious system (Rev.13:11-18). This will be discussed again, in more detail, toward the end of chapter three.

Ω

The Seven Churches In Asia

Part 2
Chapter 3

Chapter three is a continuation of the messages to the seven churches. It provides the perfect break in our study.

The last chapter ended with Christian history being plagued by the overlording Nicolaitanes, the doctrine of Balaam, and the rule of the papacy. This chapter begins with the salutation to Sardis. Sardis means "the escaping one." We will find out just what Sardis was escaping from and where it was headed.

Seven Spirits, Seven Stars

The message to Sardis comes from the One who has the seven Spirits of God, and the seven stars in his hand. We have seen in chapter one that the seven Spirits of God are the seven horns and seven eyes of the slain Lamb, Jesus Christ (5:6). We have seen also that these seven Spirits are sent forth into all the Earth. Seven is the number of completeness, hence the complete, full, and total omnipotence and omnipresence of the Lord in the personage of the Holy Spirit.

The number seven also indicates a seven-fold ministry of the Holy Spirit. In the upper room, Christ revealed the Holy Spirit to be: 1. the Comforter (Jn.14:16); 2. the Spirit of truth (Jn.14:17); 3. the presence of Christ (Jn.14:18-20); 4. the manifestation of Christ within the believer (Jn. 14:21-22); 5. the abiding presence of the Trinity (Jn.14:23-24); 6. the teacher (Jn.14:25-26) and 7. the peace of Christ (Jn. 14:27).

Not only do we see these attributes, but we also realize the seven-fold ministry of the Holy Spirit sent forth into all the Earth, working through the seven stars or messengers. This is where Ezekiel's providential wheel in a wheel is working to bring about not only the history of the chosen people of the Old Testament, but also the unfolding of Christian history into future fulfillment. This inner working of the seven-fold ministry of the Holy Spirit, through these stars or angels, will bring about the events and proper conditions that lead to the Second Coming of Christ. They are overseers of the purpose and plan of God concerning the church world.

Each church, church age, and all that a given church represents has an overseeing angel or messenger guiding events toward fulfillment. This spiritual guidance is recognized through the ending statement given each church, "He that hath an ear, let him hear what the Spirit saith unto the churches." We will see the further working and ministry of the seven Spirits in this chapter.

This ministry is realized to the greatest potential beginning with the Sardis church age, the age of "the escaping one." The Sardis portion of church history provides an explosion of Christianity resulting in the various denominational forms we see today.

Keep in mind that we are studying these churches in light of the message to the original church under its given name with the addition of applicable traits.

To Sardis

THE SALUTATION - And unto the angel of the church in Sardis write; These things saith he that hath the seven Spirits of God, and the seven stars; INSTRUCTION - I know thy works, that thou hast a name that thou livest, and art dead. Be watchful, and strengthen the things which remain, that are ready to die: for I have not found thy works perfect before God. Remember therefore how thou hast received and heard, and hold fast, and repent. WARNING - If therefore thou shalt not watch, I will come on thee as a thief, and thou shalt not know what hour I will come upon thee. PROMISE - Thou hast a few names even in Sardis which have not defiled their garments; and they shall walk with me in white: for they are worthy. He that overcometh, the same shall be clothed in white raiment; and I will not blot out his name out of the book of life, but I will confess his name before my Father, and before his angels. He that hath an ear, let him hear what the Spirit saith unto the churches. Rev 3:1-6

Sardis Literal

Sardis was a city divided into two sections, the first being on a high ridge, and the other developed at the foot of the mountain. Gold was found in the streams there until depleted. It was a city of wealth and security, virtually untouchable.

The section of the city on top of the ridge was sitting some 1500 feet from the bottom of the ridge and was said to be perfectly safe from the enemy. However, Sardis was captured twice, both times due to a false sense of security. Once, while guarding against Cyrus of Persia, a guard of Sardis dropped his helmet down a crevice and climbed down to get it. A small band of Persians climbed the crevice and took the city. This happened again during the Greek Empire. (Ref. pg. 83)

Sardis Spiritual

The church at Sardis received no commendation from Christ. The problem with the Sardis Church is that its character did not fit its reputation. It had a reputation of being spiritually alive, but in actuality it was dead. Its people had good works, which in all probability included various programs, ministries and activities, yet they were spiritually lifeless. A church bursting with such activity can seldom be convinced that it is dead.

The church knew what it meant to "be watchful," to "strengthen," and to "hold fast." It could also relate to the phrase, "I will come on thee as a thief." These statements would surely remind them of the two times that the city had been taken by the enemy. They would also stand to warn them of the arch enemy of the Church, the devil.

Although they were to be careful (watch) and strengthen the things that were ready to die, that is to say, almost dead, there were those that held to gospel truths and walked according to righteousness. They were the ones of Sardis which had not defiled their garments (robes of flesh) and the only ones worthy to walk with Christ in white. They were evidently few in number.

The individuals (he that overcometh) of Sardis who had not and did not defile their garments would have their name confessed before the Father and the angels. Those who were not overcomers would apparently have their names blotted out of the Book of Life (v.5).

What is the Book of Life?

Some thirty books are mentioned in the Bible. Example: book of curses (Num. 5:23), book of wars

(Num. 21:14), book of cities (Josh. 18:9), and so on. The Book of Life is distinctly mentioned only eight times in the New Testament (Phil. 4:3; Rev. 3:5; 13:8; 17:8; 20:12,15; 21:27; 22:19) and only alluded to in the Old (Exo.32:32-33; Psa. 69:28; Mal. 3:16). It is in these mentions that we gather meaning and explanation for the Book of Life.

In Philippians 4:3, we find that the Book of Life records those men and women who have accepted Christ and share the gospel message. This reveals that the "Book of Life" is only for Christians, those who have been born again into Christ's family (Jn. 3:3,7; I Peter 1:23) including Old Testament saints. Note that the Book of Life, in the present discussion, does not refer to those who have rejected Christ (13:8) and who have never accepted Him, for they do not inherit eternal life. God's foreknowledge reveals that there will continue to be those who reject Him as long as the Earth remains in its present state (17:8). However, the Sardis Church concerns those who have their names written in the Book of Life. (See "Names Blotted")

Judgment Books

Two types of books will be opened at the Great White Throne Judgment (Rev. 20:12-15): the "books," (collection of books into one book) revealing the facts of judgment concerning lost individuals, and "another book," the Book of Life.

What Are The "Books?"

God is just. He would not judge individuals without first offering a guideline to follow or a rule-book to study;

hence, we have the Bible, a book of books. Christ relates in John 12:48 that those who reject Him and His words will be judged in the last day. Paul also expresses the importance of this in Romans 2:16 where he states that there will be a day when God will judge the secrets of men by Jesus Christ according to the gospel (II Tim. 3:16).

These "books" (contained in the Bible) reveal the facts of the life lived, while the Book of Life will validate the facts. The Book of Life will be present as proof, whether or not any given name is recorded at the Great White Throne Judgment (judgment for lost only). Whoever is not found in the Book of Life will be cast into the Lake of Fire (Rev. 20:15).

Names Blotted?

There is another particular note of interest concerning the Book of Life. I don't want to burst anyone's bubble, but there are names that are blotted out of this book.

Moses prayed that God would blot him out rather than doom his fellow Israelites (Ex. 32:32). God replied, "Whosoever hath sinned against me, him will I blot out of my book" (Ex. 32:33). That is a principal of God, not an aberration of emotion. The word "blot" is "machah" which means to "stroke or rub; abolish." This "abolishment" is not limited to Old Testament times as exemplified by Sardis. It is a warning that those who defile their garments will be blotted out of the Book of Life.

Those of Sardis are warned to overcome. This refers to more than just giving one's life to Christ. We must remember that this letter was to the Church at Sardis, those whose names were already written in the Book of

Life. Christ goes on to say that the overcomers, those who watch, strengthen and hold fast are safe from having their name blotted out. Their names will be confessed before the Father.

Moreover, this blotting-out strictly applies to those who tamper with God's Word by which we are to be judged (Rev. 22:19). Many revisions of Scripture have clouded the understanding of our guideline and standard, the Word. Due to such corruption, it appears that we do not have a distinct study guide that we can fully trust. How terrible this is, and how horrendous the results to those who have added to and taken away from God's Word. (Ref. pg. 84) (See "Sealing of the 144,000" concerning blotting of names.)

Sardis Historical

For review, we have seen the church world:

1. losing its first love, yet rejecting the Nicolaitane and Balaam doctrine; the Ephesus church age (AD 70 - AD 170) (See chart, pg. 490)

2. falling into persecution during the Smyrna church age (AD 170 - AD 312)

3. accepting Nicolaitane and Balaam doctrine during the Pergamos church age (AD 312 - AD 606) This was a time during which Attalus III moved his hierarchy to Pergamos and later became a cohort with Constantine to unite church and state. During this period, also, power was shifted from the emperors to religious Rome, that is, what we now know as the Vatican.

4. saturated by paganism on a grand scale during the Thyatira church age (AD 606 - AD 1520) Indeed, the outward church was pagan. A church had been born that would become the most renowned religious machine and political influence of all time.

We have seen the true Church pushed into the background and into hiding. This would last until the right time to blossom forth and once again openly proclaim the gospel. However, proclaiming the gospel would continue to be a struggle.

A Reformation Begins

As seen earlier, chapter three begins with the salutation to Sardis, that is, "the escaping one." The time was right for a breaking away, a separating and escaping from the powers of pagan Rome.

The papal church of the Thyatira church age had become an intolerable force. They claimed power to save from, or condemn to Hell. Kings and nobles alike feared religious Rome. Not only was Roman Catholicism a formidable and political entity, it also claimed power over the very destiny of souls.

During the Sardis period of church history, the Dark Ages began to receive open light. A great religious reformation would now come into play. The providential wheels of history would once again assure the spread of the gospel.

This Sardis church age began around AD 1520 and lasted until around AD 1750. During this time period, people were growing weary of the over-lording papacy. A sense of nationalism was on the rise. Catholic church services were still held in Latin, which was unlearned by most. People thus desired their own national churches.

Another Turning Point

Also during this period, in AD 1455, a man named Gutenberg had finished developing a movable type printing press. This forever changed the availability and spread of God's Word, and subsequently, its understanding for the common man. Before the invention of the printing press, the Bible had to be hand copied, a slow and tedious task. This careful practice, however, left many with no readable Scriptures for extended periods. The time for the printing press had arrived. God's providential timing is awesome!

Reformation Beginnings

There were men within the Roman church who desired to change her. One attempt came in the middle of the fourteenth century when a man named Wycliff (AD 1320-84) attacked the root of the matter, the corrupt popes. He found them to be greedy and to be opposers of education and learning (They opposed independent thinkers). Although this was about 200 years before a real reformation would take place, Wycliff made an immeasurable impact on the process of reform.

His tenants were as follows:

1. No writing whatsoever has any authority except as it is based upon the Scriptures. 2. Transubstantiation is not taught in the Bible and is a papal innovation. 3. There are but two church orders as based upon the primitive church in the New Testament, bishops and deacons. 4. There is no Bible basis for confirmation or

extreme unction. 5. The clergy has no right to interfere in the civil affairs of the state. 6. Indulgences, monks, the use of images and pictures in worship, sainthood, pilgrimages, confessional, and celibacy are papal innovations and should not be taught.

Wycliff also translated the Bible from the Vulgate (Latin) edition into the language of the English people. His translation bore the marks of the editorials and mistranslations of the Vulgate, but even at that, it was greatly welcomed and accepted by the people. The seed for reform in England was planted by Wycliff and others of like belief. This action would sprout many years later into the Reformation. The reformers from within would fail to change religious Rome, but their action later stirred people of the Empire to bolt forth with fervency.

German & Swiss Reform

Another attempt from within came some 200 years after that of Wycliff. On October 31, 1517, a man by the name of Martin Luther nailed his 95 Theses on the church door at Wittenberg, Germany, touching off real Reformation.

In the beginning, this Reformation was more political than spiritual. It all started when the popes began selling indulgences in order to pay soldiers warring against the Turks, who in turn were waging war with Western Europe. These indulgences were basically forgiveness of sin purchased with money. This so infuriated Luther that he posted his Ninety-Five Theses.

From Background To Forefront

About the same time of the German Reformation was

a Reformation in Switzerland. This land, divided into small territorial districts called cantons, supplied a God-honored force that would stagger religious Rome. Remember that it had been to the valleys of the Swiss Alps that the Waldenses had fled. Here elements of the Montanists, Novatians, Donatists, Paulicians, Paterines and others were to be found as well as other parts of the Empire. They came to be called Waldenses.

The Waldenses were given yet another name or title, Anabaptists (AD 1523), due to their particular practice of re-baptizing. What Wycliff, Luther, Zwingi, and a host of other Reformers had stopped short of accomplishing, the fervent Anabaptists and like assemblies would finish: a separation from Rome and an open recognition as separatists. They were Pro-test-ants, Protestants.

Although there were differences between the Anabaptists and other Roman dissenters, they provided enough clout to protest against religious Rome and be recognized as an organized body. Religious Rome, Roman Catholicism, would not change, but would hold to paganism with a tight grip. She was fully of the spirit of Jezebel.

Alongside the persecution from Rome was the strain of diverse leadership within the ranks of the Anabaptists. During this time, we find such men as John Denck, whose views regarding grace later came to be called Arminianism (expanded by Jacob Arminius) and John Calvin, who held the doctrine of predestination and election. Through these men, and others of like interpretation, a division of Baptists (baptizers) arose. Such discrepancies of interpretation has led to the many Christian denominations we have today.

Although organic succession of particular denominations cannot be traced (although many claim it), doctrinal foundations may be traced. This, in brief, gives a run-down of Christian history concerning separation of Christianity from religious pagan Rome, thus a "Re-forming" of Christianity. From the time of the Reformation until the present, true Christianity has not been pushed into hiding or found only in the background. There are still a few countries today where Christians are persecuted as were our forefathers, but not to the extent of that day.

True Christianity is founded on the belief in the virgin birth of Christ Jesus, in His sinless life, His death, burial, physical resurrection, and His literal and physical return. These attributes are then exemplified by the believers' life-style, which, although often ridiculed, may be revealed and proclaimed openly in many countries. (Ref. pg. 88)

Sardis Symbolic

Sardis represents those Christian denominations and peoples who claim total security no matter what their actions. We must know that sin in the life of the Christian is not without penalty. This is seen in I Corinthians 11:27-31 concerning the Lord's Supper. (See author's book, *"The Bridal Feast, the Lord's Supper, Communion"*)

The Sardis Church also reflects that it is possible to have one's name blotted out of the Book of Life. Although improbable, it is not impossible (See authors book, *"Call To Order"*). Those who believe it to be impossible are among the largest Protestant congregations in the world.

Sadly enough, they, as a body, are once again aligning with Rome on current issues. They are swiftly becoming permissive. Sardis reminds us that only those who do not defile their garments will walk with Christ in white, "for they are worthy." (Ref. pg. 95)

To Philadelphia

THE SALUTATION - And to the angel of the church in Philadelphia write; These things saith he that is holy, he that is true, he that hath the key of David, he that openeth, and no man shutteth; and shutteth, and no man openeth; COMMENDATION - I know thy works: behold, I have set before thee an open door, and no man can shut it: for thou hast a little strength, and hast kept my word, and hast not denied my name. PROMISE - Behold, I will make them of the synagogue of Satan, which say they are Jews, and are not, but do lie; behold, I will make them to come and worship before thy feet, and to know that I have loved thee. Because thou hast kept the word of my patience, I also will keep thee from the hour of temptation, which shall come upon all the world, to try them that dwell upon the earth. Behold, I come quickly: hold that fast which thou hast, that no man take thy crown. Him that overcometh will I make a pillar in the temple of my God, and he shall go no more out: and I will write upon him the name of my God, and the name of the city of my God, which is new Jerusalem, which cometh down out of heaven from my God: and I will write upon him my new name. He that hath an ear, let him hear what the Spirit saith unto the churches. Rev. 3:7-13

Philadelphia Literal

Philadelphia was a border town of Lydia, Mysia, and Phrygia. The people of the city were missionary minded, but not to spread the gospel. The mission and original purpose of the city was to spread Greek culture to the surrounding cities.

The city was built on shaky foundations, literally. Sitting on top of a large earthquake fault, it had been rebuilt after being destroyed by an earthquake by the aid of Emperor Tiberius. The city later had its name changed, from "Philadelphia" to "Neocaesarea," the "New City of Caesar." (Ref. pg. 96)

Philadelphia Spiritual

The general atmosphere in Philadelphia was one of caution and insecurity because of the tremors that would periodically shake the city. The church there could thus relate to the hope of becoming "a pillar in the Temple of God" as promised to the overcomers. There was a Jewish synagogue within the city limits of Philadelphia. The Jews there claimed to be the only followers of the one true God. They considered themselves to have the monopoly to the key of David. Thus, there were contentions between the Jews and the church at Philadelphia.

The early church of Philadelphia was strategically located for gospel missions. This afforded for them the perfect outreach. This opportunity was given by the one truly holding the Key of David.

Key of David

The salutation comes from Jesus Christ, the only Holy and True Lord. He holds the key of David. We see in connection with this key, that those things that He opens no man can shut and that which He closes, no man can open. What then, is this key of David?

In Scripture, a key generally symbolizes authority. The prophet Isaiah described a time when Eliakim, the son of Hilkiah, would be elevated as the king's steward

(Isa. 22:20-22). He would be given the authority to act in the king's name, having control over both the precious and base things of the kingdom. We realize from this example that the key of David stands for the authority given. Jesus as Son, the second personage of the triune nature of God, was sent with the authority of the Father, the first person of the three-fold nature and trinity of God (Jn. 5:23, 30; 6:44). He has authority over all things.

Jesus condemned the scribes for taking away the key of knowledge. They claimed to be the only capable authorities to properly expound upon and explain the Law, thus, as with the Jews at Philadelphia, they thought they held the key. Jesus rebuked this self-appointed authority.

> Woe unto you, lawyers! for ye have taken away the key of knowledge: ye entered not in yourselves, and them that were entering in ye hindered. Luke 11:52

We also find a time when Jesus gave authority of the kingdom over to the care of Peter and the other disciples. They were to possess the "keys of the kingdom." This was the authority to loose and to bind, or, following the metaphor of keys, to open and to shut. Peter and the other apostles were stewards of the gospel.

> And I will give unto thee the keys of the kingdom of heaven: and whatsoever thou shalt bind on earth shall be bound in heaven: and whatsoever thou shalt loose on earth shall be loosed in heaven. Matt. 16:19

This verse is an important one in Romanism. The popes claim apostolic succession from Peter so they may possess, according to their interpretation, the authority to bind and to loose. They interpret this binding and loosing as the power to excommunicate and reinstate whoever they wish. The power delegated, however, was that of the spiritual kingdom, not the physical kingdom, for Christ's kingdom is not of this world (Jn. 18:36).

When Christ asked, "Whom do men say that I the Son of man am?" He received various answers (Matt.16:13-20). He then rephrased the question to the apostles, "But whom say ye that I am?" Peter spoke and boldly said, "Thou art the Christ, the Son of the living God." Jesus affirmed that the Spirit of God had revealed this truth. He told Peter that He would build His Church upon that foundation, that is to say, the foundation of Jesus as the Christ, NOT, that he would build His Church upon the foundation of Peter.

> And I say also unto thee, That thou art Peter (petros, a [piece of] rock), and upon this rock (petra [a mass of] rock - Jesus as Christ) I will build my church; and the gates of hell shall not prevail against it. Matthew 16:18.

The rock was the foundation for the building of the Church. The apostle Paul revealed Jesus Christ, not Peter, as the chief cornerstone:

> Now therefore ye are no more strangers and foreigners, but fellow citizens with the saints, and of the household of God; And are built upon the foundation of the apostles and prophets, Jesus Christ himself being the chief corner stone. In whom all the building fitly framed together groweth unto an holy temple in the Lord: In whom ye also are builded together for an habitation of God through the Spirit. Eph. 2:19-22

Although Peter was considered by Paul to be one of the "pillars" of the gospel (Gal.2:9), and Luke tells us that by him the first stones of the Church were laid to both Jew and Gentile (Acts 2; Acts 10), Peter, himself, was not that foundation, nor was he appointed so. Peter knew well who was the foundation of the Church. He knew from Isaiah's prophccy (Isa. 28:16) that Jesus was that foundation and rock. Speaking to the Church, he records:

> Ye also, as lively stones, are built up a spiritual house, an holy priesthood, to offer up spiritual sacrifices, acceptable to God by Jesus Christ. Wherefore also it is contained in the scripture, Behold, I lay in Sion a chief corner stone, elect, precious: and he that believeth on him shall not be confounded. I Peter 2:5-6

The claim of the bishops of Rome to apostolic sucession from Peter is an outright fallacy and a deliberate attempt at power over the Church. They have continued to follow the path and spirit of the Nicolaitanes.

Regarding Philadelphia, Christ is seen as the one having the key of David. He has total authority over the affairs of Heaven and Earth. His kingdom is absolute, irresistible and uncontrollable by anyone but himself. He alone holds the complete authority to open and to close the events of history (Dan. 2:21).

The commendation to the church at Philadelphia is that they had "little strength." This is not to be viewed in light of weakness on the part of the church, but in relation to their small number as compared to the religious world surrounding them. The door of evangelism would not be shut due to their "little strength" ("for," explanatory word. v.8). The very nature of the city was to be that of a missionary and to stand as example to the church. The church was strategically set for the spreading of the gospel. Little is much when God is in it!

The Lord knew the works of the Philadelphians and

opened missionary doors for them. He entrusted this important task to them because of their faithfulness to His Word and to His name. They evidently studied the Word, lived the Word, and proclaimed the Word. Their work for the Lord would not go unnoticed and unrecognized. The opposers of the true gospel, those of the synagogue of Satan, will be made to worship before their feet. This promise will evidently be kept at the Great White Throne Judgment. (See chapter two, "What Constitutes a Jew"). These despisers of the true gospel will not only see the recognition and reward that God has for those who follow Him, but will also realize their mistake of rejection. They will be placed under the authority of those who hold the true gospel. (Ref. pg. 97)

Philadelphia Historical

After the Reformation came a time of great revivals. Christians of the wilderness came forth in droves to proclaim Christ (although small in number as compared to paganism). They certainly came to know what it was to have an "open door" before them. It had been opened by Christ, the one holding the key of David. No one could shut what He had opened, or open what He had shut.

The Philadelphia church age was the coming alive of the "spiritually dead" Sardis church age. This church age is best represented in history as extending from around AD 1750 until somewhere around the mid 1900's. Keep in mind that many of the characteristics of these churches will continue until the catching away of the Church (true believers in Christ) or until the Second Coming of Christ.

The spiritual awakenings that began to form during

the Philadelphia church age have greatly affected our time. These awakenings began around AD 1739, with George Whitefield, who was followed by other great evangelists such as, John Wesley, Charles G. Finney, and D.I. Moody.

Around AD 1793, William Carey sailed to India to perform missionary work. Since his walk through the open door to India, the Lord has opened doors to China, Japan, Korea, Africa, and on and on. The Philadelphia church age was one of open doors, the likes of which had not existed before.

This aspect brings us to verse ten where we find, "I (Christ) also will keep thee from the 'hour of temptation,' which shall come upon all the world, to try them that dwell upon the Earth."

Hour of Temptation

Later in our study we'll see that a terrible time called the Tribulation Period is to come upon the entire Earth. This time is detailed from chapter six through chapter eighteen in the book of Revelation. One of the promises given to Philadelphian Christians, that is, to those who keep the Word concerning Christ's patient continuance, is that they shall be kept from this terrible time, the "hour of temptation."

The word "hour" is used to designate a period of time, not that of sixty minutes. It is a metaphor used to indicate a short span of time much like the word "day" is used. Example: the "day of the Lord" often speaks of a "time" of the Lord, not necessarily of a twenty-four hour period.

The proper length of this hour is revealed by the study

and comparison of God's Word. The prophet Daniel, in reference to the same order of events as those to which John's hour refers, calls it a week. Again, the day of the Lord is a figure of speech relating to a very real time which is to occur. The references to an hour, or week, or day are figures of speech concerning this occurrence, not specifics regarding a length of time. The best reference point to properly equate the length of this hour of temptation is found in the book of Daniel. Remember that Revelation is the "opening" of what Daniel was instructed to "seal up."

Seventy weeks are determined upon thy people and upon thy holy city, to finish the transgression, and to make an end of sins, and to make reconciliation for iniquity, and to bring in everlasting righteousness, and to seal up the vision and prophecy, and to anoint the most Holy. Know therefore and understand, that from the going forth of the commandment to restore and to build Jerusalem unto the Messiah the Prince shall be seven weeks, and threescore and two weeks: the street shall be built again, and the wall, even in troublous times. And after threescore and two weeks shall Messiah be cut off, but not for himself: and the people of the prince that shall come shall destroy the city and the sanctuary; and the end thereof shall be with a flood, and unto the end of the war desolations are determined. And he shall confirm the covenant with many for one week: and in the midst of the week he shall cause the sacrifice and the oblation to cease, and for the overspreading of abominations he shall make it desolate, even until the consummation, and that determined shall be poured upon the desolate. Dan. 9:24-27.

The angel, Gabriel, had told Daniel that seventy weeks (490 yrs. or 70X7) "are determined upon thy people" (the Jews - children of Israel) "and upon thy holy city" (Jerusalem).

From the going forth of the commandment to restore and to build Jerusalem, until the Messiah, the Prince, shall be seven weeks (7X7=49 yrs.) and threescore (60) and two weeks (2) (62 wks X 7 = 434 yrs.). That is to say, 49 + 434 = 483 yrs., or 69 weeks (69 X 7 = 483). From the seventy weeks (490 yrs.) determined upon Daniel's people (the Jews), we have one week left (one seven year period). (Each 7-year period being equal to one week, as estimated from the decree of Artaxerxes Longimanus of Neh. 2:1-8)

At the crucifixion of Christ Jesus, sixty-nine of those weeks (483 yrs.) were fulfilled. This leaves one week (7 yrs.) yet to be fulfilled. Gabriel goes on to say that at the end of the sixty-nine "weeks," Messiah (Jesus) will be cut off (crucified), but not for himself (for others).

Between Jesus' crucifixion and the hour of temptation (Tribulation Period, the last seven years), lies the church age, which refers to the period extending from the day of Pentecost until the Second Coming.

Those persons with the characteristics of the Philadelphia church age, and other overcomers will be kept from the hour of temptation (3:10) which will come upon all the Earth.

As the Church (born-again Christians) is "caught out" from the hour of temptation, the last week (7 yr. period) determined upon Daniel's people (Jews) will begin. All those who have rejected Jesus Christ as Lord during the church age, Jew and Gentile alike, will be left behind to go into this time of "Jacob's trouble" (Jer. 30:7).

As the events of the Tribulation Period (hour of temptation) unfold, the Antichrist (one-world leader - prince that shall come) will be revealed (II Thess. 2:8). The "kings of the earth" represented by the "ten horns" (chp. 17:12) and by the "toes" of Daniel's image (2:42), will have power with the beast one hour (Rev. 17:12). Again, we see the metaphor of Daniel's week.

Some who adhere to the "historical interpretation" claim that the seventy weeks of Daniel's prophecy were fulfilled at Christ's entry into the ministry and ended with the stoning of Stephen three and one-half years after the crucifixion. Dates are severely adjusted to make that assumption. In addition, those who hold to that interpretation also claim that the "prince that shall come" refers to Christ (Dan. 9:26). However, it is the Antichrist, not Christ, who will enable the abomination of desolation (Matt. 24:15).

Temptation Of The Hour

The temptation of this "hour," this "week," or this "day of the Lord" will be to conform to the world system which will prevail during the Tribulation Period. One such temptation would be to accept the one-world religious leader (false prophet) who will tempt people to accept the one-world political system with its leader, the Antichrist. This temptation includes the taking of the mark of the beast in order to keep food on the table or to maintain community or job-related status. (The Antichrist, the one-world system and mark of the beast will be discussed in later chapters.)

The Ending Of Philadelphia

For the sake of prophetic application, the mid-1940's was a turning point for church history. Around 1948, events unfolded that marked the beginning of last-day fulfillments. They align with the predictions of events described by Christ that occur just prior to His return and those pertaining to the Laodicean church age. They began, however, nearing the end of the Philadelphia church age and at the beginning of the Laodicean age. Keep in mind that as one church age fades, another church age is unfolding, thus events overlap (see chart, pg. 490).

Note Israel

The proclamation of Israel as an independent Jewish state on May 14, 1948, was the most significant event to mark a great change in Christian history. Although not being Christian, and after being scattered among the nations of the world for almost two thousand years, the Jewish people have survived as a race. They had to be an established and preserved people before the events of the coming Tribulation Period could unfold.

The Jews (flesh and blood lineage) rejected Christ at His first coming (John 1:11) and will reap the seventieth week that is determined upon them (Dan. 9:24). Thus, they hold great interest to all of Christianity. It is significant because true believers in Christ are to be "caught out" prior to this Tribulation Period. Note again, that Philadelphian Christians are to be "kept from the hour of temptation."

Dead Sea Scrolls

The Dead Sea Scrolls are ancient manuscripts from Palestine which were found in caves near the northwestern shore of the Dead Sea. The first group of these scrolls was discovered in 1947. They are considered the greatest manuscript discovery of modern times.

The significance of these ancient scrolls is that they contain a designated "Temple Scroll," which contains architectural plans for building the temple as well as detailed descriptions of the services and festivals associated with it. Some scholars believe that these finds are a direct link to a command to rebuild the future temple. At any rate, such discoveries have prompted the urgency to rebuild a temple in Jerusalem.

Scripture tells us that there shall be a temple in which the Antichrist will set himself up in authority and demand to be worshipped as God during the Tribulation Period (II Thess. 2:4). Thus, plans for the building of the temple, such as those presented in the Dead Sea Scrolls, are pertinent and very timely.

Computers

Shortly after 1948, computers hit the mass market. The first mechanical digital computer called the analytical engine was designed and tried in 1830. Then in 1930 came the first analog computer, called a differential analyzer, which was a great aid during World War II. In 1944 came the first digital computer called the "Mark I." The most important computer advancement came in the 1940's through the work of John Von Neumann. His was the idea of storing the computer program in the machine's memory. In 1951 the builders of ENIAC developed "UNIVAC I," the first computer to be mass produced. The computer industry was on its way. The computer will play a great role in fulfilling prophecy concerning the Laodicean church age. It is the only means available by which every person on Earth may be numbered and continually monitored. (The mark of the beast and numbering discussed in chapter 13.) (Ref. pg. 99)

Philadelphia Symbolic

Philadelphia Christians are patiently awaiting the shout, the voice of the arch-angel and the trump of God for their "catching away" (I Thess. 4:16-18). They are keeping the word of His patient continuance and holding fast to the name of Christ in a fast-paced world. Those of Philadelphia are told to "hold fast" to that which they have, that no man take "thy crown." What crown?

The Crown Of Life

The crown promised to Philadelphians is undoubtedly the crown of life, a promised reward for those who endure trials (James 1:12). These trials or temptations differ from those of the Tribulation Period (Philadelphians are promised to be kept from the Tribulation Period). These trials refer to the everyday struggles of Christian life. It is an imperishable crown given to the faithful followers of Christ (I Cor. 9:25).

> Jesus said unto him, Thou shalt love the Lord thy God with all thy heart, and with all thy soul, and with all thy mind. This is the first and great commandment. And the second is like unto it, Thou shalt love thy neighbour as thyself. On these two commandments hang all the law and the prophets. Matt. 22:37-40

> Flee also youthful lusts: but follow righteousness, faith, charity, peace, with them that call on the Lord out of a pure heart. II Tim.2:22 (Ref. pg. 105)

To Laodicea

THE SALUTATION - And unto the angel of the church of the Laodiceans write; These things saith the Amen, the faithful and true witness, the beginning of the creation of God; THE COMPLAINT - I know thy works, that thou art neither cold nor hot: I would thou wert cold or hot. So then because thou art lukewarm, and neither cold nor hot, I will spue thee out of my mouth. Because thou sayest, I am rich, and increased with goods, and have need of nothing; and knowest not that thou art wretched, and miserable, and poor, and blind, and naked: THE COUNSEL - I counsel thee to buy of me gold tried in the fire, that thou mayest be rich; and white raiment, that thou mayest be clothed, and that the shame of thy nakedness do not appear; and anoint thine eyes with eyesalve, that thou mayest see. THE CHASTENING - As many as I love, I rebuke and chasten: be zealous therefore, and repent. THE PROMISE - Behold, I stand at the door, and knock: if any man hear my voice, and open the door, I will come in to him, and will sup with him, and he with me. To him that overcometh will I grant to sit with me in my throne, even as I also overcame, and am set down with my Father in his throne. He that hath an ear, let him hear what the Spirit saith unto the churches. Rev. 3:14-22

Laodicea Literal

The city was named after the wife of Antiochus II, Laodice. If her name had anything to do with her character, she must have been of a bitter sort indeed, for the name Laodicea comes from two Greek words, *"laos"* meaning "people," and *"dike"* meaning "judgment." Thus, "people-judgment;" Laodice may have been a gossip.

Laodicea was the chief city of Phrygia, a Roman province now known as modern Turkey. The city is now a deserted heap of ruins the Turks call *"Eski Hisar,"* or "old

Castle."

Laodicea was built on the banks of the Lycus River in the fertile Lycus valley. It was a city of great wealth, with its claim to fame lying in its two main industries, financial and banking centers and the manufacturing of clothing, especially that of black wool. Three main highways of the day passed through Laodicea, which greatly added to the city's wealth and social prosperity. Another great claim was that of Laodicea's medical school, famous for its production of eye salve.

Laodicea Spiritual

The church at Laodicea was the worst church of the seven. There is no commendation from Christ, that is to say, no good thing is said of this church. Paul had sent word to Laodicea's pastor, Archippus, to "Take heed to the ministry which thou hast received in the Lord, that thou fulfill it" (Col. 4:16,17). Evidently, the spiritual condition of the church was not good.

The salutation comes from the Amen, the Faithful and True Witness, the beginning of the creation of God. Scripture reveals that all of creation is attributed to Christ (Jn. 1:1-3,10; Col. 1:12-17).

The church in Laodicea had begun to incorporate within its belief system the philosophy of the world, especially when comparing Paul's message to Archippus with the salutation from Christ. It was still a church, but a sickening one.

Notice the difference in the message to Laodicea from those of the other six churches. It is not to the church *in* or *of* Laodicea as with the others; it is unto the church *of the*

Laodiceans. This is significant in that Christ is not "in" or "of" this church; they are neither cold nor hot, but sickening to him (v.16). In fact, He is on the outside knocking on the door to get in.

The spiritual condition of the church is symbolized by lukewarm water (v.16). Water in Scripture is usually represents the Holy Spirit (John 7:38). The form of water, spoken of by Christ concerning Laodicea, is not that cold ("psuchros," chilly) water of a running stream, or that of an active, icy lake. It is not that of hot (Gk - *zestos,* boiled) water as used for cooking and cleansing. It is lukewarm (Gk - *tepid,*- moderately warm) water. This form of water is found in stagnant ponds and water holes. It is stale and foul. The character of such water is caused by lack of development and activity. The spiritual condition of the Laodicean Church, although rich and increased with goods, is that of a stale and foul waterhole. We have seen in the Sardis Church a deadness, yet there were those who had life in them and did not defile their garments. This is not even said of the Laodicean Church.

Christ knows the character of this church and offers counsel. Because of their material wealth they believe themselves to be rich, increased with goods and needing nothing. Christ says they are wretched, miserable, poor, blind, and naked. What a terrible condition.

This church is one that will be chastened. Christ is not there, but wants to be. He loves those persons of the Laodicean Church. "As many as I love, I rebuke (to tell a fault) and chasten" (admonish, discipline) (v.19).

Laodicea Historical / Prophetic

Many scholars believe we are now living in the Laodicean church age. As previously noted, the dates used in this study are approximate according to the events of Christian history. Thus, the events of the day suggest that we are indeed living in the Laodicean church age, but not completely, not totally. After all, Christ is on the inside of the true Church today. The Laodicean church age will come to its fulness when true believers, those of the character of the Philadelphian Christians, are taken out (caught away, the Rapture). Those left behind will inherit the chastening of the Tribulation Period.

Again, concerning the seven churches in Asia and their historical relevance, we view the church world as:

1. losing its first love, yet rejecting the Nicolaitane and Balaam doctrine; the Ephesus church age (AD 70 - AD 170) (See chart, pg. 490)

2. falling into persecution during the Symrna church age (AD 170 - AD 312)

3. accepting Nicolaitane and Balaam doctrine during the time of the Pergamos church age (AD 312 - AD 606)

4. completely saturated by paganism (outwardly) during the Thyatira church age (AD 606 - AD 1520)

5. coming out and escaping from the over-lording papal religious system during the Sardis church age (AD 1520 - AD 1750)

6. opening missionary doors during the Philadelphia church age (AD 1750 - AD 1948)

Numbers And The Tribulation Focal Point

At the end of chapter two is a number comparison concerning the seven churches. The number one relates to seven, two relates to six, and so on. This comparison, I believe, is the best way to introduce the religious focal point of who and what the church of Laodicea represents.

Note again that when topics are mentioned in numbers of seven, the number one will relate to the number seven, two will relate to six, three will relate to five, thus, the number four being the focal point, or center of discussion.

Using the number comparison, we see that Ephesus (1) represents the beginning church and Laodicea (7) represents the church of the end.

Symrna (2) represents the persecuted church and Philadelphia (6) represents the church that is promised the removal from persecution occurring during the Tribulation Period.

In comparison, Pergamos (3) represents the mixing of paganism with Christianity and Sardis (5) represents separation from paganism.

This considered, Thyatira (4), or that which Thyatira represents, will be the religious focal point for the consummation and fulness of the age. This is not because of numbers only, per se, but because the whole of Revelation aligns with such comparison. Again, this system will play a major role in the formation of the one-world government. It will be the one-world religious system (Rev.13:11-18) of the Laodicean church age, Roman

Catholicism (represented by Thyatira), that will be the religious focal point for the culmination of the church age, that is to say, the Laodicean church age. It is Thyatira in her fulness.

The Fulness Of Thyatira

Revelation chapter 13 reveals that a false religious system will thrive during the Tribulation Period, the seven-year period known as the time of Jacob's trouble (Jer. 30:7). A religious leader known as the false prophet will head this massive one-world religious system. This false prophet will cause all the world to come under the power of the one-world government and its leader, the Antichrist (first beast of Revelation chapter 13). During this time, the judgment of the Tribulation Period will fall upon everyone left behind at the "catching away" of true believers in Christ. Remember that the name Laodicea means "people-judgment," hence, a time of a "judgment of the people."

There are many religions in the world today but none have polluted the name of Christ, even deifying His mother Mary, like the system which thrived during the Thyatira church age. The Thyatira Church was the culmination of paganism and Christianity, and serves as the focal point and center of attention for the Laodicean age.

It is said that the Thyatira Church (the Jezebel religion) would go into great tribulation (trials). These great trials will be realized during what is known as the Tribulation Period. However, before the unfolding of the Tribulation Period, she would first be given space to repent (2:21). Pagan Rome has had time to repent, especially since the time of Christ, indeed much longer, but has not done so. To the contrary, she has grown into the most influential, wealthy and largest religious denomination in the world. In addition, she has seduced many religions of the world into joining with her.

We see today the fulness of Thyatira coming to the forefront as the harlot religion of Jezebel, Roman Catholicism. Many Protestant denominations are now returning to her captivating arms. The freedom which many reformers fought for and died for is being discounted by their very offspring. Many of these Protestant denominations, are taking their blood-bought heritage before the feet of Jezebel in the name of Christian unity.

Jezebel and her cohorts will go into great tribulation (2:22) unless they repent. We know by Scripture that pagan Rome, as a whole, will not repent, but will suffer great trials and tribulations during the Tribulation Period. Thus, she and her children, those who fall under her seductive "care," will be killed. We will briefly study this again in chapter seventeen (v.15,16).

Sadly, this tells us that multitudes will miss the "catching away" of the Church. Only those with characteristics of the Philadelphian Church and other overcomers will be taken.

The Knock At The Door

Many ministers have used verse 20 as a metaphor concerning the desire of Christ to come into man's heart. "He stands at the door of your heart, knocking to come in." This represents more than just a catchy phrase and carries more than just spiritual application. It is a direct plea to

those who will have missed the "catching away," or
"Rapture of the Church." It is a statement reaching out to
those who are involved in anti-Christ systems which will
suffer great trials during the Tribulation Period. Those
who realize their plight and cry out for Christ will have
the opportunity to open the door of salvation, but at a
great price.

The Price of Tribulation Salvation

Yes, people will be saved during the Tribulation
Period (those who accept Christ). Their salvation, however, will come at a much greater price than many Christians
today will ever have to pay. One cannot miss the open
door provided today (before the "catching away") and
wait until the Tribulation Period and expect Christ to personally catch him or her away at whim. There will be a
distinct difference in accepting Christ now and putting it
off in hopes of salvation at the last moments of church history.

Notice in verse twenty the statement, "if any man hear
my voice, and open the door, I will come in to him, and
will sup with him, and he with me." This is a statement
about partaking of those things which Christ experienced.
Notice also, that one will not go to Christ, but Christ
(through the Holy Spirit) will come and dine with him.
They stay; He comes. Thus, they must partake of the terrible things of the Tribulation Period, particularly death.

Death?

Today, during the church age (Pentecost to Rapture),
we are to give our bodies as a living sacrifice (Rom.
12:1,2). During the Tribulation Period, people will give

their lives literally, by beheading (Rev. 20:4). The question is, if you can't live for Christ now, how will you then? This, in essence, is what the prophet Jeremiah said:

> If thou hast run with the footmen, and they have wearied thee, then how canst thou contend with horses?.... Jer. 12:5

Example Of James And John

We see an example of dining with Christ in Salome's sons, James and John. John is the scribe for the book of Revelation. Salome had asked Jesus to allow one of her sons to sit on His right hand and the other on His left hand in His kingdom (Matt. 20:20-23). Jesus asked them if they were able to drink of the cup that He was to drink of and be baptized with the baptism He was to be baptized.

James, John, and their mother, at this point, were looking to an earthly kingdom and did not yet grasp the kingdom of which Jesus was speaking. Jesus, in essence, asked them if they were able to drink of the cup of suffering and be baptized with suffering. Upon their affirmation, Jesus told James and John they would indeed drink of the cup and be baptized, that is, they would bear ridicule, affliction, persecution, heartbreak, and all that comes with being a true witness.

James became the first apostle to die by martyrdom at the hand of Herod (Acts 12:2). John lived a long life, and, as far as we know, he died a peaceful death. John, however, witnessed the death and persecution of the other apostles. He witnessed in the Revelation vision the suffering, death, plagues, famines, and so on, of multitudes of people living during the Tribulation Period. Both James and John did, indeed, drink of the cup of Christ.

To Sit On His Throne

Jesus told James and John that they would indeed drink of the cup and be baptized with the baptism, but to grant them to sit on His right and left side would be given to whom it is prepared for by the Father. Here (3:21), we see that it is prepared for those who give their lives literally during the Tribulation Period. The overcomers (of the Laodicean church age - the age of the false church) will be granted to sit with Christ on His throne. Why? "Even as I also overcame, and am set down with my Father in his throne."

Laodicea Symbolic

Laodicea symbolizes those individuals who boast in their wealth and social status who are without Christ. They attend church on occasion, but receive little because they apply themselves very little. They are lukewarm individuals, neither dedicated nor hardened against religion. Such individuals are in need of eyesalve, for they cannot see clearly. Laodicean individuals are not seekers, for they have no clue where to begin; neither are they knocking, because they can't see the door clearly (Matt. 7:7-8). Jesus is knocking and they have ears to hear, but do not hear. Religion has blinded these people to the point that they may be touched by truth, but not reached with truth.

Laodicea represents the sad condition of the end-time church. It is a religious institution having no Holy Spirit motivation, no dedicated Christians sold out to Christ. Its spirit is one of habit and religious reverence. It is a false church with a false leader. The colors of Constantine's political church shine within its corridors. It is defiled. It is corrupt. It is pagan. This church, with all its tentacle religions, will be headed by the papacy, the seat of the false prophet. How sad this is.

Ω

The
Open Door
In Heaven
Chapter 4

What would you think if you saw a door opening in an unexpected place, out of nowhere, especially in the heavens? At the very least, you would be anxious as to who or what's about to come out. Such a door was opened in Heaven before John.

John, however, had no time for curiosity, fright, or questions. Instead he was prompted to "come up hither" and was immediately taken through this door. This was no ordinary door, for it was the door to Heaven. Not to the atmospheric heaven, or the universal heaven, but the third Heaven, the one into which the apostle Paul had been caught up (II Cor. 12:2). The door had opened for John to pass into the Heaven where God dwells.

John's first vision or revelation in chapter one occurred while he was on the Isle of Patmos, on Earth (John hears a voice and turns to see); now he is caught up into Heaven.

In the next two chapters of Revelation (4-5), John sees and hears things instrumental in opening up and prompting the day of the Lord, the Tribulation Period. These two chapters are thus "introductory chapters" for that terrible time.

Come Up Hither.

After this I looked, and, behold, a door was opened in heaven: and the first voice which I heard was as it were of a trumpet talking with me; which said, Come up hither, and I will shew thee things which must be hereafter. Rev. 4:1

Upon seeing the door opened in Heaven, John hears a voice saying, "come up hither." This was the first of many voices John would hear in Heaven. The voice was as a trumpet talking. The announcement of this trumpet-voice revealed an opening up of the things hereafter, that is, things future.

John's ascent into Heaven is a type (forerunner, example) of the "calling out" of the Church (born-again believers). John heard the sound of a trumpet and was immediately taken (v.2). Likewise, the first sound we will hear will be the trump of God, and we will immediately be taken (I Cor. 15:52; I Thess. 4:16).

Chronological Order?

Although this is an example of the "catching away," or Rapture, it is not to be thought that the Rapture of the Church will occur after the completion of all seven of the church ages.

The "after this" in verse 1 reflects only what John saw after receiving the messages to the churches, not that a complete chronological order of events is maintained. Keep in mind that reading the Bible straight through often does not produce a chronological order of events. More frequently, a straight-through approach reveals a retelling, retracing, and overlapping of events. This is often called "repetition and expansion." Concerning the overall picture, the proper method to place events in chronological order is by compiling and comparing Scripture (II Tim 2:15).

Overlapping Events

This overlapping, retracing, backing-up and rehearsing of events is a common literary style in Scripture. Sometimes it occurs from verse to verse, chapter to chapter, or book to book, and it particularly applies to the book of Revelation, after all, chapters 6 through 19, some 245 verses, cover a relatively short period of time (7 yrs.). Many times John retraces particular time-frames within that period. This is done so that additional events, occurring within that same time-frame, might be explained more thoroughly without losing the progress and intent of the message. Again, it is "repetition and expansion."

The same event is sometimes presented in greater detail in different chapters. Thus, a given subject may appear to refer to more than one event when in fact various references point to the same event. Overlapping, backing up and retracing would then be the proper measure for John to take when placing so many events into the same time-frame.

Due to this overlapping and to John's literary style (as instructed by Christ - 22:16), many events of Revelation are found out of chronological order. Collectively, however, they support the overall progression of events which brings the entire book to its proper end and intent. As we will see later, key verses keep such style in check.

The Throne and Its Occupant

And immediately I was in the spirit; and, behold, a throne was set in heaven, and one sat on the throne. And he that sat was to look upon like a jasper and a sardine stone: and there was a rainbow round about the throne, in sight like unto an emerald. And round about the throne were four and twenty seats: and upon the seats I saw four and twenty elders sitting, clothed in white raiment; and they had on their heads crowns of gold. And out of the throne proceeded lightnings and thunderings and voices: and there were seven lamps of fire burning before the throne, which are the seven Spirits of God. Rev. 4:2-5.

Immediately John was in the spirit and caught up into the third heaven. Here, "in the spirit" marks the second major vision of Revelation. The first thing John sees is a throne and its occupant. The one sitting upon the throne had the likeness of a jasper and a sardine stone, evidently a combination of these two elements.

The common link between these two stones, other than that they are both of the chalcedony family (a translucent variety of quartz), is the similarity of the color brown. Although jasper is usually red, it may also be brown, yellow, green, or crystal clear. Jasper is mentioned only four times in the book of Revelation, two of which describe jasper as crystal clear (4:3; 21:11,18,19) while two give no reference to a particular shade.

The sardine stone is a reddish brown color. Thus, the likeness of the one on the throne was a reddish-brown illumination. This is realized due to the jasper having either a brownish color or being crystal clear. This would allow for the sardine stone to give off the reddish-brown appearance. This was his likeness, not his image. An image is a representative figure or physical likeness, while a likeness is a portrayal of that image. They are distinguished in Genesis 1:26. Thus, this reddish-brown color has significance.

Red

The color red symbolizes God's divine providence and the abundant life He has given to mankind, especially at the crucifixion (Acts 20:28). Several attributes of God's provision are described by the color red, such as Jacob's stew (Gen. 25:30), and the sacrificial heifer (Num. 19:2). Isaiah 1:18, however, reveals red (scarlet) as applying to sin. Christ not only provided the perfect sacrifice for man, but He became sin for us (II Cor. 5:21).

The reddish color in Heaven, then represents God's care and provision toward man through his redemptive plan.

Brown

The color brown is mentioned only four times in Scripture and applied only to sheep (Gen. 30:32, 33,35,40). They were the sheep chosen by Jacob that were to be distinguished and set apart from those of his father-in-law Laban. Many Biblical comparisons are made between sheep and human beings. The Church is referred to as the sheepfold (John 10:1). The color brown as seen by John in the throne-room represents those who have accepted God's provision. They are of the sheepfold, born-again believers.

The likeness of the one sitting on the throne was that of a brilliant, reddish-brown, translucent crystal, revealing God's provision for His people. The jasper and sardine denotes the attributes and presence of our Saviour Jesus Christ there in the throne-room. He is the second personage of the threefold divinity of God. He is God. (compare

Isa. 43:11; Lu. 2:11; Acts 20:28). He now sits at the right hand of the Father (Acts 2:32,33; Rom. 8:34), the first personage of the divinity of God.

Note that Christ is later seen standing in the midst of the throne. This also verifies His presence (Chp.5). This is an important factor as we will see later.

The Bow of Promise

God keeps his promises. He is faithful. His Word is sure. This is emphasized by the presence of the rainbow "round about" the throne. God had set the bow in the sky as a covenant with Noah, indeed with mankind and the Earth, that it would never again be destroyed by flood (Gen. 9:13-17). The rainbow in Heaven is a token of that pledge, a symbol of the covenant. This covenant symbol is continually present before God.

The rainbow is compared to the emerald, the fourth foundation stone of the new Jerusalem. Four is the number of the world: There are four seasons, four elements, four divisions in the Eden river, four world powers revealed to Daniel, and so on.

The emerald is a deep green variety of beryl, the eighth foundation stone of the new Jerusalem. The number eight stands for the "new order of things." The eighth day is the beginning of a new week; God commanded Abraham to circumcise every male child on the eighth day; Noah's family consisted of eight persons; Noah was the eighth person (II Peter 2:5).

Green represents the regenerative life of Earth vegetation. This emerald rainbow represents the preservation of the Earth, until the "new order of things," particularly, a time when the covenant will be fulfilled. This fulfillment is depicted by the use and color of the foundation stones. It is also realized in the word "everlasting" of Genesis 9:17, which concerns the rainbow. It is *"owlam,"* which means, "a vanishing point," coming from the Hebrew *"alam"* which means "hidden."

We know that this present Earth is reserved unto fire (II Peter 3:10,11) and then there will be a new heaven and a new Earth, thus, a "new order of things." On the new Earth will be the new city, new Jerusalem. The foundation stones of the new city carry significance concerning the knitting together and understanding of the book of Revelation. These will be explored in chapter 21.

Indeed A Bow

It is evident that John sees the reflection of a rainbow in the Sea of Glass beneath the throne (v.6), where it appeared as a complete circle (round about). This rainbow was not, then, an actual circle revealing an eternal continuance, or eternal covenant, but it was indeed a bow, a semicircle as those seen on Earth. This would reveal the continuance of the covenant concerning the Earth "until its time of fulfillment" as seen in the number four and a time of a "new order of things" as seen in the number eight.

Four And Twenty Seated Elders

John also sees twenty-four elders seated, clothed in white raiment, and wearing crowns of gold upon their heads. Who are these elders? They are not angels because the title of elder is never applied to angels. Neither do angels have crowns or sit on thrones. These things are not said of angels, but they are said of men. These elders are thus redeemed men who represent redeemed mankind.

These elders are twenty-four in number, the double of twelve. Twelve is the number of "eternal perfection," representing eternally redeemed mankind. The elders could only be representatives of both Old and New Testament saints. Twelve is the product of the divine number three (as in the Trinity) multiplied by four, the number of the world. There were twelve stones in the High Priest's breastplate; twelve cakes of shewbread; twelve wells of water at Elim; and twelve spies sent into Canaan.

Twelve Tribes - Twelve Apostles

There were twelve tribes designated by the names of the twelve ancestors from whom they descended. These twelve ancestors represent Old Testament saints (particulars in names discussed later). The twelve apostles represent the New Testament saints. Their white raiment and golden crowns also suggest that they represent redeemed men. These make up the twenty-four elders.

In the prophetic vision of the future, John saw these twenty-four seats occupied. The seats, at the present, are empty. The elders are now under the Sea of Glass awaiting the "catching away." John, himself, will be one of those elders after the resurrection. Remember that this is a vision of the future, after the "catching away," or Rapture, and involves saints of both the Old and New Testaments. (See "Keys of Death & Hell," chapter one, and "Sea of Glass" later in this chapter)

Soul Sleep?

The above thought concerning the apostles and others

who are asleep in Jesus is not to be confused with "soul sleep," a theory held by many that denies man a conscious existence between death and the resurrection based upon the condition of his body. According to the theory, the soul is a combination of body and soul. When the body dies, so does the soul. In retrospect, nothing is left to actually rest, for the soul ceases to exist. What, then, is called a resurrection to those adhering to soul sleep would really be a re-creation.

The "soul sleep" theory is completely unscriptural and is not to be confused with the Biblical truth of those who sleep in Jesus.

And the very God of peace sanctify you wholly; and I pray God your whole spirit and soul and body be preserved blameless unto the coming of our Lord Jesus Christ. I Thess. 5:23

At death we do not cease to exist as with "soul sleep" theology. Scripture relates that:

1. The body goes back to the dust of the Earth (Gen. 3:19; Job 34:15; Psa. 104:29). The body ceases to function as a living, thinking being.

His breath goeth forth, he returneth to his earth; in that very day his thoughts perish. Psa. 146:4

The word for "thoughts" here is *"eshtonah"* and means "thinking." The Greek word for "perish" is *"abad"* which means "to wander away." This reveals that the thoughts leave the body when the spirit leaves. However, the seat of human emotion and thought, the soul, continues to exist. It contains within its make-up all the feelings, thoughts, and presence of the body. Concerning the lost, after the resurrection of the "dead" (without Christ) the souls from Hell will also be re-united with the body, judged at the White Throne Judgment (Rev. 20:11-15), and both soul and body cast into Gehenna Hell (Matt. 10:28).

2. The spirit or life-force of the body goes back to God who gave it (Eccl. 12:7). This spirit or life-force is temporary. We have Scripture as witness (Gen. 6:3). We also have cemeteries as witness. The spirit here is the life-force and separate from the Holy Spirit.

3. Concerning the Christian, the soul is redeemed by God (Psa. 49:15) and taken to the place of perfect peace and rest directly beneath the throne of God (see section "Sea of Glass" in this chapter). To the Christian, death is referred to as sleep (I Cor. 11:30; 15:51; I Thess. 4:14; 5:10). Sleep is not only a symbolic term for death, but is also given as a rest (Heb. 4:8-11). This rest may be of a total or partial unconsciousness. The soul, in its rest, is aware of the perfect peace and contentment of its surroundings, but is unaware of the passage of time as it generally is with earthly sleep.

The awareness of the soul, of those who die not having accepted Christ as Saviour, is quite different from that of the Christian. Theirs is not a condition of rest, but of torments. The conditions of both the Christian and the unsaved man are clearly seen in the narrative of the rich man and Lazarus (Lu. 16:19-31).

Thus, the "soul sleep" theory is a heretical and false

doctrine concerning the true nature of the soul.

Lightnings, Thunderings & Voices

John saw great sights (v.5). He also heard thunderings and voices coming from the throne. These lightnings were *"astrape,"* bright shining lightning. This reveals the awesome power which proceeds from the throne of God. More than just flashes of light, they were powerful illuminations coming from the throne of God. His great power illuminates even from the seated position.

All those in the throne room of Heaven proclaimed the glory of God by responding with thunderings, that is, *"bronte,"* roarings. Imagine the overwhelming power that John witnessed. The voices heard were *"phone',"* which means, "tones that disclose" (to articulate sounds whether bestial or artificial). Thus, all the representatives of heaven beckoned a call upon John's arrival. How awestruck John must have been!

The Seven Spirits of God

Here we find representatives of the seven churches in the seven lamps of fire burning before the throne (v.5). They are the seven lampstands or candlesticks seen earlier. They are now lit and burning, for they are "lamps of fire."

These lamps are presently burning. They are the seven Spirits of God. Remember that John's catching away is a type of the Church. This representation of the church world is realized because these lamps are "lamps of fire." These lamps, familiar to the people of John's day, were fed by oil. In Scripture, oil is a type of the Holy Spirit. We have already discussed earlier other aspects of the seven

Spirits of God. In this instance, however, these seven lamps of fire represent the progression of the Church through time from Pentecost until the Rapture or "catching away," during which is the outpouring and presence of the Holy Spirit. These lamps began to burn on the day of Pentecost.

The Sea Of Glass

> And before the throne there was a sea of glass like unto crystal: and in the midst of the throne, and round about the throne, were four beasts full of eyes before and behind. Rev. 4:6

It was to the paradise side within the Earth that Christ had taken the thief on the cross who had accepted him, as seen in chapter one. When Christ arose from the dead, He led captivity captive. That is, those in paradise were taken out and transported to the "Sea of Glass" directly beneath the throne of God (v.6). That was when Christ moved paradise from within the Earth to Heaven. He led those captive in paradise within the Earth to captivity in the paradise of Heaven, a place of perfect tranquility.

Contrary to fanciful belief, those who die in the Lord are not seen in Scripture as praising God, jumping, running and enjoying a mansion. They are at rest, at peace; they are awaiting the resurrection. I do believe they are aware of the most blissful rest and peace imaginable, but they are asleep in Jesus. They are at rest (Heb. 4:9-11). At the Rapture of the Church, this sea will be emptied. This is for the uniting of these souls with their new bodies at the resurrection (I Thess. 4:16-17). Afterward, the Sea of Glass will be used for the keeping of the souls of those martyred during the Tribulation Period. They will be restless souls yet at rest (discussed further in chapter 6:9-11).

The Four Beasts

> And the first beast was like a lion, and the second beast like a calf, and the third beast had a face as a man, and the fourth beast was like a flying eagle. And the four beasts had each of them six wings about him; and they were full of eyes within: and they rest not day and night, saying, Holy, holy, holy, Lord God Almighty, which was, and is, and is to come. And when those beasts give glory and honour and thanks to him that sat on the throne, who liveth for ever and ever, Rev. 4:7-9

Around the throne, John sees four beasts full of eyes before and behind (v.6). These beasts represent untamed beasts (lion), domesticated beasts (calf), mankind (man), and fowls (eagle). These beasts represent all created beings and praise God day and night without ceasing. They are continually present around the throne of God.

The intelligence of these beasts is realized in the "face of the man" and in the eyes which were round about and within. This reveals their intelligence to carry out missions. In the "face of the lion," we realize their power and majesty. In the "face of the ox," we see that of patient service. In the "face of the eagle" we see a symbol of swiftness to execute judgment.

These beasts are "*zoon,*" living creatures and are to be distinguished from "*therion,*" dangerous untamed animals, the beasts of chapters eleven, thirteen, and seventeen. They are the living creatures of Ezekiel's wheel in a wheel vision (Ez. chpt.1) and protect the throne of God. They are the cherubim which go wherever the throne goes and vice versa (Ez. chpt.1). They are four in number, which reveals their work also has to do with the world.

The noted difference in the beasts of Ezekiel and those which John sees is that in Ezekiel's vision, they have four wings, while John's vision reveals each one has six. These wings are seen as used for worship and service. Four reveals their service on behalf of the Earth while six, the number of man, reveals their service on behalf of man. Part of their worship is their service. It is the four beasts which prompt John to look upon the events occurring on Earth as the first four seals are opened (6:1,3,6,7).

The manifestation of the living creatures in Ezekiel's vision reveals the providential work of God. This overseeing aspect as carried out by these beings concerns the progression of world history as seen in the providential wheel in a wheel. The recurring revolution of the larger wheel represents the move through the ages and suggests the changes to which men and nations are subject (Eccl. 1:4-7). The wheel in the middle of the larger wheel suggests the inner workings of history whether in politics, church history, or the phases of human life. These progressions are not in confusion, for the rings are full of eyes, revealing intelligent purpose. In John's vision, there are no wheels, as they are fixed around the throne in Heaven.

John is witness to yet another aspect of their function. They give glory, honor, and thanks to God continually. As these beasts have to do with the Earth (four) and man (six) their glorious praise is echoed by the four and twenty elders (4 X 6 = 24).

> The four and twenty elders fall down before him that sat on the throne, and worship him that liveth for ever and ever, and cast their crowns before the throne, saying, Thou art worthy, O Lord,

to receive glory and honour and power: for thou hast created all things, and for thy pleasure they are and were created. Rev. 4:10-11

The four and twenty elders, in reply to the beasts, fall down before God and cast their crowns at his feet, saying, "Thou art worthy, O Lord, to receive glory and honour and power: for thou has created all things and for thy pleasure they are and were created" (See Col. 1:12-18).
Ω

The Book
With
Seven Seals
Chapter 5

God gave Adam dominion over Earth, including every one of its creatures (Gen. 1:26). In a moment of weakness, Adam lost that dominion to the arch-enemy of God, the Devil (Gen.3:1-19). This was a serious matter.

This shift of dominion is clearly seen in the wilderness temptation of Christ. The Devil tempted Christ by offering Him the power and glory of the kingdoms of the world - "for that is delivered unto me" (Luke 4:5-6). Christ did not submit to the wiles of the Devil, but caused him to flee by quoting Scripture (Matt. 4:1-11).

The Devil, in the Garden of Eden, in the form of a serpent, won a major battle against mankind. The lost dominion of Adam is like the Old Testament law concerning the surrender or sale of land. The loss of dominion and control was part of such a transaction (Lev. 25:25-27). This law also afforded the opportunity to redeem the lost possession, as we will see later.

Adam's disobedient act involved more than just eating forbidden fruit. It was a surrendering, a selling-out to the Devil. Adam had not lost ownership of the Earth, for it was not his to lose. He did, however, lose access to the Garden, and he lost the dominion entrusted to him. Adam's sin of disobedience not only severed man's fel-

lowship with God (Rom. 5:12), it was a surrendering of
Earth dominion as well.

We have the great privilege of restoring fellowship
with God by personally accepting Christ as Lord and
Savior (I Tim. 2:5; Rom. 10:13). This is wonderful; however, if Earth dominion is not redeemed and restored we
will never receive our promised inheritance.

Possession Redeemed

The apostle Paul tells us that the possession of our
inheritance "shall be redeemed." It is a promise from God.
The redemption of our inheritance is seen in the word
"until" of Ephesians 1:13-14:

> In whom ye also trusted, after that ye heard the word of truth, the
> gospel of your salvation: in whom also after that ye believed, ye
> were sealed with that holy Spirit of promise, Which is the earnest
> of our inheritance until the redemption of the purchased posses-
> sion, unto the praise of his glory. Ephesians 1:13-14

The inheritance of this purchased possession is for
those who have heard and believed the gospel. These are
the ones who have accepted salvation and are thus sealed
(stamped) with that Holy Spirit of promise. This seal is
the promise, the pledge of an inheritance yet to come
(pledge - earnest, Gk.). Again, our inheritance will be
redeemed. God has promised it.

God Stakes A Claim

This possession was purchased at Calvary, but it has
not yet been redeemed. This word "purchased" (Eph.1:14)
does not mean that Christ paid a price and bought back
Earth dominion (Christ wouldn't bargain with the Devil,
nor would the Devil sell). The word "purchased" is

"peripoiesis," the act of "preserving or saving."

Redemption of the soul was bought at Calvary (I Cor. 6:20; 7:23), however, Earth dominion was not. The cross was also a physical statement from God to show ownership of the Earth. God owned it already, for He created it. The Earth was not born under sin as was man. Thus, as with the prospector of the Old West who "staked his claim," the cross was the "staking of a claim" to the Earth and to the control of it.

God does not have to buy back what is already His, all that has to be done is to redeem what has been lost. As God is proper in all His ways, He shall redeem Earth dominion by the proper method. As a lamb was commanded for a sacrifice to represent the coming sacrifice of Christ (Gen. 22:7,8; Lev. 1:10; 3:6,7), a method was set in motion under the law for the redemption of a lost possession (Lev. 25:25-27).

The Title Deed

And I saw in the right hand of him that sat on the throne a book written within and on the backside, sealed with seven seals. And I saw a strong angel proclaiming with a loud voice, Who is worthy to open the book, and to loose the seals thereof? And no man in heaven, nor in earth, neither under the earth, was able to open the book, neither to look thereon. And I wept much, because no man was found worthy to open and to read the book, neither to look thereon. Rev. 5:1-4

Still in Heaven's throne room, John sees a book in the right hand of the one sitting on the throne. It is a peculiar book with writing on the outside and on the inside. This book was *"biblion,"* a roll or scroll. John evidently recognized the type of document that it was, for it was written on the inside, yet sealed up. It was an apparent title deed.

Such documents, those written without and within, were usually property deeds. If the inside became full, the outside would then be used. These documents also contained a concise description of the contents on the outside. Thus, one did not have to break the seals in order to know the nature of the document. In fact, the seals were not to be broken unless proper representatives were there to validate the claim to property.

The Search For A Worthy Man

Suddenly there appears a strong (forcible) angel, who asked loudly, "Who is worthy to open the book, and to loose the seals thereof?" This angel had great authority to oversee the opening of the document. He was to verify the credentials of the claimant. There must be a man found worthy to open this sealed book. No action of transfer could properly occur without such a man.

It is interesting that the search would be for a man to redeem the lost possession (v.3). But, according to the manner of redeeming a lost inheritance in the Old Testament, the one losing the possession, if able, could redeem the lost possession at an appointed time after the sale or loss. If a man was not able to redeem it, a kinsman must be found to redeem it (Lev. 25:25). There are two illustrations of such a kinsman redeemer in the Old Testament, Ruth 4:1-12, and Jeremiah 32:6-12.

The man, Adam, had lost Earth dominion, thus, a man —someone born of the human race— must redeem it.

John witnesses a search for the proper man (v.3). There was no man, either sitting in elders' seats in Heaven or under the Sea of Glass. There was no suitable man alive on Earth. Hades was also searched. This was to show that every man, wherever he might be, was examined.

Man, as we know, does not have the ability to save himself, much less redeem Earth dominion (Eph. 2:8,9). The search for a worthy man, left John in despair. He wept much (v.4). All was not hopeless, however, for there came a proclamation from one of the elders. Someone had been found.

Behold The Lamb Of God

> And one of the elders saith unto me, Weep not: behold, the Lion of the tribe of Juda, the Root of David, hath prevailed to open the book, and to loose the seven seals thereof. And I beheld, and, lo, in the midst of the throne and of the four beasts, and in the midst of the elders, stood a Lamb as it had been slain, having seven horns and seven eyes, which are the seven Spirits of God sent forth into all the earth. Rev. 5:5-6

"Weep not," John is told, for one has prevailed and is worthy. Note again that the search had been for a worthy man (Rom. 3:10). The lost possession could not properly be redeemed until this person or a kinsman was found. The possession was lost by man and must be redeemed by a man, or a kinsman.

The worthy person was the "lion," the strong one of Judah (Gen. 49:10). He was of the "root of David," also referred to as the "root of Jesse," David's father (Isa. 11:10; Rom. 15:12).

In the midst of the throne, and in the midst of the four beasts, and in the midst of the twenty four elders, John

sees a Lamb as it had been slain. This lamb was standing,
a sure witness to the resurrection of the slain Lamb. The
elder had just called him a Lion, but John sees a Lamb. It
is Jesus, the one whose earthly heritage came through
King David and the tribe of Judah. He, also, is to take the
throne of King David (Luke 1:32).

This is a picture of Jesus, the Lamb of God. It was He
who was sacrificed for the sin of the world. He was
acknowledged as such by John the Baptist, "Behold the
Lamb of God which taketh away the sin of the world"
(Jn.1:29,36). The Lamb is a picture of Jesus' humanity
(for men are referred to as sheep). It is also a picture of
His sacrificial death on the cross (the slain lamb). He was
our Passover Lamb.

Jesus is our kinsman redeemer in that He came as a
man (God became flesh - Jn. 1:10), lived as man (Jn.
1:14), and died as a man (Rom. 5:15). He was fully man
and fully God, born of a virgin and conceived of the Holy
Ghost. He alone is worthy to open the title deed.

Jesus is often called the "son of man" referring to His
entitlement to the Earth and the world. He is also called
the "son of David," which reveals His right to the throne.
He is called the "son of Abraham," revealing His title to
the land of Israel and all the royal grant to Abraham. He is
called the "Son of God" as He is heir to all things. These
attributes reveal His inheritance as well as ours (Rom.
8:17).

Christ is the only one with the proper credentials, also
the only one worthy to take the title deed and break the
seals (Col. 1:13-20). "Thou art worthy to take the book,
and to open the seals thereof: for thou wast slain, and hast

redeemed us to God by thy blood..."

> And, having made peace through the blood of his cross, by him to reconcile all things unto himself; by him, I say, whether they be things in earth, or things in heaven. Col. 1:20

Not until chapter 10 do we see Christ Jesus standing with one foot upon the land and one foot upon the sea redeeming the lost possession. Then He cries "There shall be time no longer;" that is, "no more delay." Thus, there is no formal redeeming of the lost possession until the proper steps are taken to secure it, hence, the Tribulation Period.

Our Inheritance

The Hebrews related to Canaan land as their inheritance. It was promised to Abraham and his descendants (Num. 33:53). The land of Canaan is a picture of the heavenly land promised to believers. This likeness is often seen in such hymns as "I am bound for the promised Land," "I'm on my way to Canaan Land," and many others. The concept of such an inheritance springs from Jewish roots:

> For ye are all the children of God by faith in Christ Jesus. For as many of you as have been baptized into Christ have put on Christ. There is neither Jew nor Greek, there is neither bond nor free, there is neither male nor female: for ye are all one in Christ Jesus. And if ye be Christ's, then are ye Abraham's seed, and heirs according to the promise. Galatians 3:26-29

Those who have faith in Christ Jesus are God's children and thus are Abraham's descendants. This is not by flesh and blood lineage, except for those of Jewish descent, but by a spiritual lineage of faith (Gal. 3:7).

Christ is heir to the throne of David (Lu. 1:32) and to the earthly kingdom over which He shall reign, thus the Millennial Reign. The fulfillment of this prophecy will begin at the Second Coming of Christ, after which He shall set up this kingdom. He will literally sit upon the throne of David during that time. At that point, the Christian will have been caught up at the Rapture (before Trib.) and will rule and reign with Christ. (See chart, pg. 483)

Believers of the church age are promised that we will rule and reign with Christ (II Tim. 2:12; Rev. 20:6), thus joint-heirs (Rom. 8:17), and will inherit this kingdom and the dominion of it. Christ will one day return to reclaim and redeem this lost possession and set up this kingdom.

This inheritance also applies to those who help the Jews (brethren) during the Tribulation Period (Matt. 25:40). This kingdom was prepared for this purpose (inheritance) from the foundation of the world (Matt. 25:34). So a portion of our inheritance will be the Earth and the dominion over it (for wherever Christ is, there shall we be [I Thess. 4:17]).

Our purchased possession is to rule and reign with Christ. This will bring with it the dominion and control of the Earth. We will also inherit the new heaven, the new Earth and the new city (Rev. 21:1). What glories await the believers in Christ Jesus!

Jesus Takes the Book

And he came and took the book out of the right hand of him that sat upon the throne. And when he had taken the book, the four beasts and four and twenty elders fell down before the Lamb, having every one of them harps, and golden vials full of odours, which are the prayers of saints. And they sung a new song, saying, Thou art worthy to take the book, and to open the seals thereof: for thou wast slain, and hast redeemed us to God by thy blood out of every kindred, and tongue, and people, and nation; And hast made us unto our God kings and priests: and we shall reign on the earth. Rev. 5:7-10

Jesus stands as the slain Lamb, reflecting His sacrifice for man. He stands because of his apparent resurrection. Upon taking the book in His hand He expresses the characteristics of the Lion of the tribe of Judah, to rule with kingly power.

There is a grand and glorious celebration in Heaven upon the taking of the book (vs.8-14). The time has come to redeem the lost possession. The worthy one has taken the title deed. Note that the prayers of the saints are present before God in the golden vials (v.8). They are of a sweet smelling savor to God. The prayer of "thy kingdom come" is now in sight.

The Majestic Worship Of Christ

And I beheld, and I heard the voice of many angels round about the throne and the beasts and the elders: and the number of them was ten thousand times ten thousand, and thousands of thousands; Saying with a loud voice, Worthy is the Lamb that was slain to receive power, and riches, and wisdom, and strength, and honour, and glory, and blessing. And every creature which is in heaven, and on the earth, and under the earth, and such as are in the sea, and all that are in them, heard I saying, Blessing, and honour, and glory, and power, be unto him that sitteth upon the throne, and unto the Lamb for ever and ever. And the four beasts said, Amen. And the four and twenty elders fell down and worshipped him that liveth for ever and ever. Rev. 5:11-14

When Christ takes the title deed, the innumerable host of heaven proclaim His worthiness, His power, and His glory. All of Heaven and Earth will experience and express the power of God as Christ stands and takes the book in hand. These expressions of praise will doubtless be the most frightful sounds the lost world will experience this side of Hell, for every creature on Earth will become vocal and noisome.

We will witness the taking of this title deed, for the event will occur after the "catching away." We will not only witness all this wondrous praise which John witnessed, but we will also have the privilege of joining in.

The taking of this title deed, however, will usher in the most dreaded of times for the world. The events of the Tribulation Period will begin to unfold as Christ Jesus begins to break the seals of the title deed (Matt. 24:21).
Ω

The Lamb Breaks The Seals
Chapter 6

When the seven seals are broken and all the subsequent events have occurred, the title deed will be fully unrolled, or opened. This will be the time when Christ returns to reclaim the lost possession. First, however, a time of Earth cleansing and redemption must be completed. The breaking of the seals to the title deed will bring the most terrible time in Earth's history.

The time-frame which the opening of the seals covers is called the "time of Jacob's trouble" (Jer. 30:7). It will be the time of the pouring out of God's wrath, the most terrible time that the Earth and its inhabitants will ever experience (Matt. 24:21). There will be volcanoes, meteoric blasts, plagues, famines, and so on. Such events, in years past, have been only mere shadows of trouble as compared to this terrible time.

It is the Tribulation Period, the seventieth week of Daniel's prophecy (one week = 7 yrs. - Dan. 9:27). Not only is the Tribulation Period given for Earth cleansing and Earth redemption, it is also a time prepared for those who have rejected Jesus as Messiah. It is determined upon Daniel's people (the Jews, Dan. 9:24), but not exclusive ly. This terrible period will fall upon all of those left behind at the "catching away" of the true Church (born again believers - I Thess. 4:16).

Seal No. 1 - White Horse Rider

> And I saw when the Lamb opened one of the seals, and I heard, as it were the noise of thunder, one of the four beasts saying, Come and see. And I saw, and behold a white horse: and he that sat on him had a bow; and a crown was given unto him: and he went forth conquering, and to conquer. Rev. 6:1-2

Many have concluded that this white horse rider is Christ himself. This cannot be Christ. He is in Heaven holding the title deed and breaking the seals. He is not seen riding a white horse until chapter nineteen at His Second Coming. That is also a time when the armies of the world will be gathered at the battle of Armageddon. They are not gathered here; they won't be until the end of the Tribulation Period.

Christ is not seen here with a diademed crown and a vesture dipped in blood. Again, that is the Second Coming. He is also seen then with a great weapon, a sharp sword which proceeds from His mouth. This white-horse rider, as pictured in verse one, reveals this rider as having a simple bow with no arrows. These evidences reveal that this is not Christ, but someone else. Who, then, is this white horse rider?

New World Order

In chapters two and three we saw the formation of a one-world religion. That system is already forming and will be in place immediately prior to the Tribulation Period. We know, according to chapter thirteen of

Revelation, that the false prophet (head of the one-world religion) will support a one-world government and its leader (13:11-18). It only stands to reason that such a system and person must be in place before this will be possible. In chapter six we are first introduced to this one-world government and New World Order.

The white-horse rider is the head of this New World Order, the one-world government. He is the "prince who is to come" of Daniel's seventieth week (Dan. 9:27), the "little horn" that rises among nations (Dan. 7:8), and ruler of the ten kingdoms of the end-time political world (Rev. 17:12). He is the "mouth" speaking great things of Revelation 13:5. He is the Antichrist.

The Antichrist is seen as having a bow, but no arrows. He has no crown until one is given to him. The picture is that of a conqueror who conquers by means of peace, as symbolized by the white horse and an empty bow. He will dazzle the world with his strategical and governmental intelligence. This flatterer, an arch manipulator, will gain the trust of the world's political leaders.

The Antichrist first comes in as a man of peace (white horse rider with peaceful bow). He conquers by means of peace. He will be promoted as head of the one-world government, thus the "crown" which will be "given to him." He will continue to appear as a man of peace until he establishes complete power and control over world governments. (See chart, pg. 484)

The Hour Of Antichrist

We know that Christians will be saved from the "hour of temptation" which shall come upon all the world (chpt.

3). This "hour," as we have seen, aligns with Daniel's seventieth week, thus a seven-year period (one week = 7 yrs.). The "crown" (kingship) given the Antichrist will come from the governments of the world, particularly a group of ten. These "ten" are the "ten horns" of Daniel's vision concerning the fourth beast (representing both the first Roman Empire and the revived Roman Empire; Dan. 7:7-8). They refer to the same entities as the "ten toes" of the image of Nebuchadnezzar's dream (Dan. 2:41-42). They are the "ten horns" and "ten kings" of Revelation 17:7-12 (discussed later).

Interestingly, these "ten kings" receive power (gain complete world domination) through the Antichrist for "one hour" (Rev. 17:12). By giving leadership (a crown) to the Antichrist (who has dazzled world governments) they in turn receive world dominance (Rev. 17:12-13). The complete rule of the Antichrist will last for seven years, the "hour of temptation" (Rev. 3:10; See also chapter three, "Hour Of Temptation"). This "hour" is the same time-frame given to the kings who rule with the Antichrist (Rev. 17:12). It is also the Antichrist and his government who will enforce the "mark of the beast" (discussed under the "Temptation of the Hour").

From the beginning, the Antichrist's goal will be that of self-exaltation. Underneath his dazzling brilliance and influence for good will be a heart of lawlessness. This lawless heart will make way for the most evil, demonic activity since the expulsion of angels from Heaven at the fall of Lucifer. These fallen angels will play an important role in the book of Revelation (discussed later).

The apostle Paul mentions the rise of this "lawless"

individual and the condition of the church world immediately prior to the "catching away" of the Church:

> Let no man deceive you by any means: for that day shall not come, except there come a falling away first (During Philadelphian and Laodicean overlap), and that man of sin be revealed, the son of perdition (the Antichrist); Who opposeth and exalteth himself above all that is called God, or that is worshipped; so that he as God sitteth in the temple of God, shewing himself that he is God (after receiving world dominance). Remember ye not, that, when I was yet with you, I told you these things? And now ye know what withholdeth that he might be revealed in his time. For (explanatory word) the mystery (secret workings) of iniquity (Sin) doth already work: only he who now letteth will let (Holy Spirit), until he be taken out of the way (Rapture of Church at which time the Holy Spirit and His protective work leaves). And then shall that Wicked (lawless one, Gk.) be revealed (given his crown), whom the Lord shall consume with the spirit of his mouth (at Armageddon), and shall (Christ shall) destroy with the brightness of his coming (Second Coming): Even him (Antichrist), whose coming is after the working of Satan with all power and signs and lying wonders,...II Thess. 2:3-9 (Parenthetics my emphasis)

The presence of the true Church is the force holding back the onslaught of Satan. This is due to the inner presence of the Holy Spirit. The world may try to wipe us out, but such martyrdom would only enhance the popularity of Christianity (as with the Waldenses). It will take the removing of Christians by Christ himself (I Thess. 4:16) before the Tribulation Period can begin and the Antichrist be revealed.

Introduced By Lion-beast

This white horse rider, the Antichrist, is introduced by the first of the four beasts which John had seen earlier (chpt. 4). The first beast was like a lion. Who better to introduce kingly power than the representative of the king of beasts. This first beast, as seen earlier, represents untamed beasts. This certainly fits the character of the Antichrist. This individual possesses the characteristics of Lucifer (Isa. 14:12-15), the light bearer become the adversary, Satan. He is a deceiver. He shall later become possessed by Satanic forces, virtually Satan incarnate (discussed in chapters forthcoming).

The Term Antichrist

Little children, it is the last time: and as ye have heard that antichrist shall come, even now are there many antichrists; whereby we know that it is the last time ... Who is a liar but he that denieth that Jesus is the Christ? He is antichrist, that denieth the Father and the Son. Whosoever denieth the Son, the same hath not the Father: (but) he that acknowledgeth the Son hath the Father also.... And every spirit that confesseth not that Jesus Christ is come in the flesh is not of God: and this is that spirit of antichrist, whereof ye have heard that it should come; and even now already is it in the world. I Jn. 2:18,22,23; 4:3

According to the above Scriptures, the term antichrist not only describes the one-world leader, but also those who deny that Jesus is the Christ (anointed one, Messiah). This term also applies to every spirit (movement) which denies that Jesus is of God. Being "of" God means more than just believing that Jesus held godly principles, but that Jesus, the second personage of the three-fold embodiment of God, is God (See Chapter One, "Answer").

Aligning Prophecy Of Jesus

The six seals of chapter six fulfill the prophecy Jesus had given on the Mount of Olives. Six of the seven seals aligns in Scriptural order as recorded in Matthew's gospel.

Jesus first set the stage for this prophecy after He departed from the temple. Jesus had just proclaimed, "Behold your house is left unto you desolate." The disciples wanted to show Him the buildings of the temple, perhaps in an attempt to change the prophecy concerning it. He told them that the temple would be thrown down. They later came to Him privately upon the Mount of Olives and asked "When shall these things be? and what shall be the sign of thy coming, and of the end of the world (age)?"

The first set of verses to fulfill Jesus's prophecy and fall in line with the first seal are found in Matthew 24:4-5:

> And Jesus answered and said unto them, Take heed that no man deceive you. For many shall come in my name, saying, I am Christ; and shall deceive many. Matt. 24:4-5

Seal No. 2 - Red Horse and Rider

> And when he had opened the second seal, I heard the second beast say, Come and see. And there went out another horse that was red: and power was given to him that sat thereon to take peace from the earth, and that they should kill one another: and there was given unto him a great sword. Rev. 6:3-4

Everything will appear peaceful as the Antichrist subtly secures his position of leadership. However, political powers (nations) on Earth will oppose this New World Order. And certain religious factions will also oppose and resist the new government. The one-world "new age" dream, the long-awaited utopia, will be in danger due to these opposing powers. Thus, they must be dealt with.

This means war. These wars will quite possibly be the result of the implementation of the mark of the beast. It is evident that this mark will be implemented early in the first part of the Tribulation Period. (discussed under "Seal No. 5").

Red

As we discussed earlier, the color red is a picture of God's divine providence and His gift of abundant life (chpt. 4), especially that of the crucifixion (Acts 20:28). That was its representation as viewed by John in Heaven. The color red here is not associated with the sacrificial death of Christ, but with the death of those left on Earth after the Rapture of the Church. It is a symbol of the shed blood of many under the direction of the new government and the Antichrist.

Introduced By The Calf-like Beast

The second beast, the representative of domesticated creatures (calf-like appearance), introduces this horseman (I Thess. 5:3). War means that innocent persons will be killed as peace is taken from the Earth (Matt. 24:6-7).

The Rider

Notice that power was given to the rider of the red horse to take peace from the Earth. This tactic is yet another stepping stone toward personal and complete world dominance by the Antichrist. World dominance, at this point, is complete, but through the efforts of the one-world government. Thus, the rider of this red horse is the dominant leader of the unified government, the Antichrist, but has not yet received his "crown." War is his characteristic although it is accomplished for the ultimate "good" of the New World Order. This man of peace will doubtless have avenues through which to protect his reputation.

Aligning Prophecy Of Jesus

> And ye shall hear of wars and rumours of wars: see that ye be not troubled: for all these things must come to pass, but the end is not yet. For nation shall rise against nation, and kingdom against kingdom:... Matt. 24:6-7

Seal No. 3 - Black Horse And Rider

> And when he had opened the third seal, I heard the third beast say, Come and see. And I beheld, and lo a black horse; and he that sat on him had a pair of balances in his hand. And I heard a voice in the midst of the four beasts say, A measure of wheat for a penny, and three measures of barley for a penny; and see thou hurt not the oil and the wine. Rev. 6:5-6

The black horse signifies famine. Many able-bodied men will have been drafted to war against the opposers of the New World Order. War automatically means that many industries will prosper. However, the farming industry will suffer because acres of farmland will be destroyed. The result will be a shortage of food supplies. Presently, we depend on others for our food supplies. We have "super-centers" and vast chain-distributors of food and various other products. Widespread war will affect such food industries, causing widespread famine.

A day's wage at the time of John's writing was a penny, a *denarius*, which would buy a *"choenix"* (2 pints) of wheat. This is a meager supply of food for a day's work, but is just a foreshadowing of the overwhelming inflation which will occur during the Tribulation Period.

Oil & Wine

The olive trees and the grapevine may not be affected by this outbreak of war. Their crops are not harvested until some time after wheat. However, because the world's orchards and plantations will suffer (8:7), the oil and wine mentioned in this passage must refer to something else. Oil and wine symbolize abundance, indicating that those of wealth and political power will not be affected by the famine. They, of course, will be protected by "the system." The inflation will not affect them as it will the general public.

Rider

The black horse rider is also the Antichrist, the dominant head over the democratic one-world government which will instigate wars. This famine is merely another characteristic of the power-hungry Antichrist brought to light.

There will be no true, heart-felt sympathy for those endangered by famine. A great distress cry will undoubtedly be launched by the new government; however, this action, again, will be for the sake of appearance.

Introduced By The Man-like Beast

The black horse of famine is introduced by the third beast. He represents mankind, the one having the face of a man. Many men, women, and children will die in this famine.

Aligning Prophecy Of Jesus

...and there shall be famines,... Matt. 24:7

Seal No. 4 - The Pale Horse And Rider

And when he had opened the fourth seal, I heard the voice of the fourth beast say, Come and see. And I looked, and behold a pale horse: and his name that sat on him was Death, and Hell followed with him. And power was given unto them over the fourth part of the earth, to kill with sword, and with hunger, and with death, and with the beasts of the earth. Rev. 6:7-8

The rider is here given a name. His name is Death, the opposite of Life.

Jesus Is Life

Jesus said this of Himself in John 14:6, "I am the way, the truth, and the life: no man cometh unto the Father, but by me." Jesus is also called the Bread of Life (Jn. 6:35,48), the Light of Life (Jn. 8:12), the Resurrection and the Life (Jn. 11:25), the Prince of Life (Acts 3:15), the Justification of Life (Rom. 5:18). The list could go on and on revealing that Jesus is Life.

Antichrist Is Death

It would only stand to reason that the Antichrist, the false Christ, is the opposite of life. The Antichrist is death. He is the symbol and representative of death. The true nature of the Antichrist is seen in these verses (7-8). He is death.

Not only is the Antichrist death, but Hell follows him. His very nature breeds violence and destruction. The world will fall for his deceptive practices and reap the results. The plight of the world is to reject Christ and follow such an individual. "I (Christ) am come in my Father's name, and ye receive me not: if another shall come in his own name, him ye will receive" (Jn. 5:43). In addition, the "and Hell followed him" refers to the very beings of Hell that will possess the Antichrist and trail him in order to gain control of the Earth (See trumpet judgment no. 5).

Legal Murder Increased

We see here the culmination of the effects of pushing the New World Order upon the world. The personal pronoun "him" is used of the Antichrist in verse eight. However, power was given to "them" over one-fourth of the world's population, to kill by either war, famine, or mercy killing (v.8). This reveals the rule of the Antichrist and his allies, hence, the one-world government. They will enforce control by any means.

Animals will also be affected by this famine (v.8). Their beastly nature is totally unleashed. These animals not only roam hills and valleys killing and ravaging other beasts, but they also prey upon people. The homeless and others found unprotected will fall prey to these beasts. This is yet another bit of evidence revealing the travail of animals for the Lord's return (Rom. 8:19-21), which shall be fulfilled at the end of the Tribulation Period.

Aligning Prophecy Of Jesus

...and pestilences, and earthquakes, in divers places. All these are the beginning of sorrows. Matt. 24:7-8

Seal No. 5 - Souls Of The Slain

And when he had opened the fifth seal, I saw under the altar the souls of them that were slain for the word of God, and for the testimony which they held: And they cried with a loud voice, saying, How long, O Lord, holy and true, dost thou not judge and avenge our blood on them that dwell on the earth? And white robes were given unto every one of them; and it was said unto them, that they should rest yet for a little season, until their fellowservants also and their brethren, that should be killed as they were, should be fulfilled. Rev, 6:9-11

At the opening of the fifth seal, John sees souls under the altar. These are not physical bodies, but soulish bodies. They are under the altar before the throne of God in the Sea of Glass. (That quickly refutes the theory of "soul sleep.") "But I thought the Sea of Glass was emptied immediately before the catching away of the Church?!" True. The Sea of Glass was emptied immediately prior to the Rapture of the Church (as discussed in chapter four). This was done so that those dying in Christ might be united with their new bodies at the resurrection (I Thess. 4:16-17). The Sea of Glass, having been emptied for the Rapture, will be used again for keeping the souls of those who die for the cause of Christ during the Tribulation Period.

They will have been martyred (Rev. 20:4). This is where the Sea of Glass is seen as "mingled with fire" (red, as blood). They are those martyred individuals who had gained victory over the beast by taking death instead of denying Christ (Rev. 15:2). Their martyrdom was due to their refusal to take the mark of the beast.

Mark Of The Beast

These souls under the altar cry with a loud voice, "How long, O Lord, holy and true, dost thou not judge and avenge our blood on them that dwell on the earth?" The answer is that they should rest for a little season "until their fellowservants also and their brethren, (that) should be killed as they were, should be fulfilled" (v.11). Note that only those brethren sealed of God will escape this slaughter (See chapter seven).

It is evident that the mark of the beast has, at some point, been issued as law. For between seal number six and seal number seven there are 144,000 sealed in response to the worship and allegiance to the government (See chapter seven, "Angel From The East"). This event is before the blowing of the first trumpet of seal number seven and pouring out of the first vial. The pouring of the vials are but detailed descriptions of the blowing of the trumpet judgments (one of those retelling or retracings mentioned earlier). In the detailed account of the vials, we find a noisome and grievous sore coming upon them who had (past tense) the mark of the beast and who had worshipped his image.

This is also seen in the words "fellowservants" which is "*sundoulos,*" a co-slave, and "brethren" which is "*adelphus,* the womb, a brother." These will reap the same plight as those souls under the altar. They are the ones left behind after the Rapture, Gentiles (co-slaves) and Jews (the womb, brethren).

Here the souls cry for vengeance (v.10). They were killed for the word of God and the testimony which they held. These are those who had, after the "catching away," believed the Word of God. They testified to the gospel and vindicated the message of the Church (born-again believers have already been caught away). They subsequently refused the mark of the beast and were martyred. We must keep in mind that one must be wise to the mark of the beast. It is a subtle occurrence (13:18 - "Here is wisdom").

Timeframe

Seal five is a testimony to the character of the one-world government, with the Antichrist dominating the decisions. At this point, he has not yet set himself up as God in the temple, but is well on his way to achieving world dominance. The evidence points to the mark of the beast being implemented by the government early during the first half of the Tribulation Period. This plan will be stubbornly refused by the Jews, many of whom will be killed (Seal 5). However, this outward expression of domination by the government will play directly into the hands of the Antichrist, eager for complete world dominance. He does not gain complete control until midway through the Tribulation Period. However, he will be instrumental in constructing a plan to execute the mark. This plan will exclude the Jews (for a time) and will doubtless be a part of the signing of a covenant with them (Dan.9:27). The previous stand against the mark (souls under the altar) will appear to be a victory for the Jews and will cause them to agree to separation and complete independence. This will last for only three and one-half years.

Aligning Prophecy Of Jesus

Then shall they deliver you up to be afflicted, and shall kill you: and ye shall be hated of all nations for my name's sake. And then shall many be offended, and shall betray one another, and shall hate one another. And many false prophets shall rise, and shall deceive many. And because iniquity shall abound, the love of many shall wax cold. But he that shall endure unto the end, the same shall be saved. Matt. 24:9-13

Seal No. 6 - A Great Earthquake

And I beheld when he had opened the sixth seal, and, lo, there was a great earthquake; and the sun became black as sackcloth of hair, and the moon became as blood; And the stars of heaven fell unto the earth, even as a fig tree casteth her untimely figs, when she is shaken of a mighty wind. And the heaven departed as a scroll when it is rolled together; and every mountain and island were moved out of their places. And the kings of the earth, and the great men, and the rich men, and the chief captains, and the mighty men, and every bondman, and every free man, hid themselves in the dens and in the rocks of the mountains; And said to the mountains and rocks, Fall on us, and hide us from the face of him that sitteth on the throne, and from the wrath of the Lamb: For the great day of his wrath is come; and who shall be able to stand? Rev. 6:12-17

When Christ opens the sixth seal, great physical changes will take place directly related to the Earth, its atmosphere, and the universe. The opening of seals one through five have had to do with mankind. The breaking of seal number six spawns astronomical events such as have not occurred since God spoke the universe into existence.

Earthquake

The first event listed in the sixth seal is a great earthquake. Today earthquakes are not uncommon; however, this earthquake will be "great" (*megas,* Gk), reaching an intensity and power beyond any earthquake presently known to man. This earthquake, prophesied for many years, will occur just prior to the last half of the Tribulation Period (Ez. 38:19; Jer. 4:24; Amos 8:8; Joel 2:10; Hag. 2:6; Matt. 24:7).

Sun, Moon & Stars

The great earthquake, no doubt, will cause volcanic eruptions as well as many other disasters. The smoke and dust from these effects will cause the sun to turn to darkness and the moon to blood. The prophet Joel also describes these "wonders":

> And I will shew wonders in the heavens and in the earth, blood, and fire, and pillars of smoke. The sun shall be turned into darkness, and the moon into blood, before the great and the terrible day of the LORD come. Joel 2:30-31

John reveals that meteor showers will plunge through the atmosphere, causing added calamity. Dust and gas will form into murky clouds of smoke and ash that will darken the sun and tinge the moon blood-red.

The sun itself will not actually turn black and the moon will not actually turn to blood. These effects will be seen as likenesses. This is clearly seen in Joel's prophecy (pillars of smoke) and in John's account. John uses the small word "as," which is a word of description. The combined upheaval of earthquake, volcanic eruptions, fire, smoke, and ash results in the blackening of the sun from clear view (black "as" sackcloth, or mohair, worn as a sign of grief). A smog-like screen will cause the moon to appear blood red ("as" blood). If the sun itself actually became black, its rays would cease and the Earth would quickly freeze. There is no record of such an occurrence during the Tribulation.

The Heavens Roll Back

Notice in verse four that the heaven departed (separated) like a tightly rolled scroll when let loose. This is the atmospheric heaven surrounding the Earth. The effects of the earthquake and the falling meteors will separate the atmospheric heaven. Such commotion will cause "every mountain and every island" to move out of its place. Not just one or two. The destruction of the earthquake and the meteoric blasts will indeed be great ("*megas*"). These events will get the attention of man. However, as great as it will be, it is not "the big one" recorded under the seventh vial (16:17-20).

Unrepentant Men

Seven categories of men will be affected by these catastrophes (v.15). The descriptions of these categories covers every man, whether rich or poor, bond or free. They are kings, great men, rich men, chief captains, mighty men, bondmen and freemen. It is a complete coverage (number seven). Every human on Earth will apparently be aware that God had something to do with these calamities, for they affirm such awareness (vs.16-17). Thus, this seal serves as a wake-up call, a last chance for repentance before the trumpeters appear to announce the wrath of God for the last half of the Tribulation.

Instead of repenting to God, these people have a different prayer. They cry for the mountains and rocks to fall upon them and hide them from "the face of him that sitteth on the throne, and from the wrath of the Lamb." They are not ignorant of this day of wrath, but they still refuse to repent. Instead, they wish to hide. How often God pleads for man to repent and man tries to hide!

Wake-Up Call To God's Wrath

Seal number six ushers the beginning of the Great

Tribulation period (last half). It is an awakening to the pouring out of God's wrath which is about to unfold. The people's cry not only affirms their awareness that the events are of God's doing, but that the "great day of his wrath is come; who shall be able to stand?"

The last half of the Tribulation Period is referred to as the Great Tribulation, a time when multiple judgments will be unleashed upon the Earth and its inhabitants. Seal number six calls the people to repent before this "Great day of God's wrath" is poured out (Joel 2:30,31).

Certain events will occur just before the Great Tribulation. Chapter six ends with only six of the seven seals having been broken or opened. Before the seventh seal is broken (chpt. 8), there is a proclamation given concerning God's chosen people, the Jews (discussed in chapter seven). The proclamation not only concerns God's chosen people, but also the message of Christ's Coming and promised kingdom (Matt. 6:10)

Ω

Parenthesis To Seal 144,000

Chapter 7

Have you ever had to stop what you were doing in order to fit something else into your already busy schedule?

There is such a break in the busy schedule of the book of Revelation. The opening of the seals is halted in order to reveal another aspect of the Tribulation Period. Thus, chapter seven is like a parenthesis. It is an interval between seal number six (6:12) and seal number seven (8:1). This interval is for the sealing of 144,000 persons from the twelve tribes of the children of Israel.

The events covered in chapter seven are not limited to a time-span lasting between seals six and seven only. They only begin there. John's interval includes his seeing four angels at the four corners of the Earth, hearing the number of those who are to be sealed, and seeing those who respond to the proclaimed message. He also sees those who have a positive response around the throne of God in the new Jerusalem on the new Earth. Thus, chapter seven reveals the message, the message bearers, the respondents, and the eternal reward of those who are faithful during the Tribulation Period. These aspects will be discussed as we progress through the chapter.

The Preparation For Sealing

> And after these things I saw four angels standing on the four corners of the earth, holding the four winds of the earth, that the wind should not blow on the earth, nor on the sea, nor on any tree. And I saw another angel ascending from the east, having the seal of the living God: and he cried with a loud voice to the four angels, to whom it was given to hurt the earth and the sea, Saying, Hurt not the earth, neither the sea, nor the trees, till we have sealed the servants of our God in their foreheads. Rev. 7:1-3

The effects of the calamities of the atmosphere from seal number six (6:12) must be calmed before the sealing of the 144,000 can occur. Thus, after seeing the first six seals opened and the subsequent occurrences, John sees four angels standing on the four corners of the Earth— the north, south, east, and west. The four angels are seen holding the winds so that there is no movement of the atmosphere. A dead still falls upon the Earth immediately prior to the sealing of the 144,000 children of Israel.

Another Angel

John beholds another angel ascending from the east. This angel proclaims, "Hurt not the earth, neither the sea, nor the trees, till we have sealed the servants of our God in their foreheads," to the other four, who possess the authority to launch terrible destruction upon the Earth, the seas, and the trees, but are instructed to abstain from doing so by this "sealing" angel. The proclamation of the angel is heeded until the blowing of the first and second trumpet judgments of seal number seven (8:7,8).

The Hope Of Healing

The ascension of the angel from the east is significant. There will be those of Israel who are looking to the east for the "Sun of righteousness with healing in his wings" (Mal. 4:2). Their gaze will not only be due to the catastrophes of seal number six, but because of grief. They grieve for all those who had taken the mark of the beast, especially for those who had refused the mark and were slaughtered. Those murdered loved ones are those who had refused to align with the New World Order, that is, those who refused the mark of the government (as a beast). They are the souls (previously discussed) who cried out from under the altar of seal number five. The grieving aspect is seen in the Old Testament type of the man with the Inkhorn.

The Man With An Inkhorn

The grieving Israelites will be recognized by God, as was the case in Ezekiel's vision concerning the man with an inkhorn (Ez. 8). Ezekiel saw in a vision the officials of Israel who were worshipping Baal in secret observances. Ezekiel saw a company of Israelites who were greatly grieved because of that abomination. God commanded a man with an inkhorn to go through the city and mark in the forehead those who were grieving over such idolatry. Those who were sealed (marked) were spared the great slaying that followed (Ez. 9:1-7). In like manner, the 144,000 with the "seal of the living God" will be protected, not only from the mark of the beast, but also from the events of the Great Tribulation (last 3 1/2 yrs.) which soon follows.

The angel from the east is typified by the man with the inkhorn. The seal of the inkhorn man was the seal or mark of God. Likewise the angel from the east has the "seal of the living God." He directed the other four angels to hold the winds until "we" (which included himself - like the inkhorn man) have sealed the servants of our God in their foreheads. Those who are grieved for taking the mark of the Beast are as those who worshipped Baal, for to worship any other system or acknowledge any other than Christ Jesus (such as the Antichrist) is idolatry (I John 2:23).

Not The Mark Of The Beast

The seal of the 144,000 is NOT the mark of the beast, but the "seal of the living God." This seal or mark is placed in the foreheads of those Israelites who fear the name of the Lord (Mal. 4:2) (note that "born-again believers" have long since been taken out in the Rapture of the Church). To this point (during the Tribulation), these 144,000 have escaped the mark of the beast, for they are sealed in contrast to those who have already taken the mark (a foreshadowing of this is found in Ezekiel 3:8). It is possible that a part of the covenant between the Antichrist and the nation of Israel is that of suspending the mark for the Jews. The 144,000 are of the children of Israel. The seal of the living God is a stamp for security. It is NOT the mark of the beast! The mark of the beast will be discussed in detail in chapter thirteen.

Note: The Antichrist will grow weary of those who stubbornly refuse to take the economic mark of the beast. Secret forces will be employed to take care of these rebels. Some, however, cannot be forced to take the mark, neither can they be slaughtered, for they (the 144,000) have the protection of God. The Antichrist will set himself up in the temple of God proclaiming himself as God (II Tim. 2:4), outwardly demanding obedience. At that time he will break the covenant with Israel and begin to enforce the taking of the mark for all individuals. However, instead of obeying this false messiah, multitudes will accept the message of the 144,000.

Thus, a terrible onslaught of force will be directed once again at the Jews as a nation. This will fulfill Matthew 24:14-22:

> And this gospel of the kingdom shall be preached in all the world for a witness unto all nations (witness of the 144,000); and then shall the end come (last half of Tribulation Period). When ye therefore shall see the abomination of desolation (Antichrist setting himself up as God), spoken of by Daniel the prophet, stand in the holy place, (whosoever readeth, let him understand:) Then let them which be in Judaea flee into the mountains (fleeing of Jews): Let him which is on the housetop not come down to take any thing out of his house: Neither let him which is in the field return back to take his clothes. And woe unto them that are with child, and to them that give suck in those days! But pray ye that your flight be not in the winter, neither on the sabbath day: For then shall be great tribulation (last 3 1/2 yrs), such as was not since the beginning of the world to this time, no, nor ever shall be. And except those days should be shortened, there should no flesh be saved: but for the elect's (Jews) sake those days shall be shortened. Matt. 24:14-22

Compared to this terrible time, Hitler's Holocaust will seem like training school. There is going to be another holocaust of God's chosen people, the Jews. (This "fleeing" will be discussed further in chapter twelve.)

What Is This Seal Of God?

We are told in chapter fourteen just what this seal is:

the "Father's Name" (14:1). In Scripture, many names are given to the Father. Which name is to be used?

The Father is called *Jehovah-jireh* - "The Lord will provide;" *Jehovah-nissi* - "The Lord is my banner;" *Jehovah shalom* - "The Lord is peace;" *Jehovah-shammah* - "The Lord is there;" *Jehovah-tsebaoth* - "The Lord of Hosts;" *Jehovah-elohe-israel* - "Lord God of Israel;" as well as a host of other names. These appellations, as that of "Christ" given to Jesus, are descriptive titles and not the actual name. What name is to be on the seal? (The list above is by no means conclusive.)

When God appeared to Moses in the burning bush, He revealed himself as "I AM" (Ex. 3:14). God is thus called Jehovah or Yahweh, a derivative of the Hebrew "I AM." Usually Jehovah or Yahweh is translated "Lord" in the English Bible. This translation is due to a practice of late Old Testament Judaism, which taught that Yahweh was the sacred name of God and not to be mentioned. Instead "my Lord" (*Adonai*) was used.

The name on the seal is quite possibly "I AM," the name which God himself revealed; however, this is but a guess. The name may well be the name with which Jesus returns, which no man knows but He himself (Rev. 19:12). Those 144,000 marked with the "seal of the living God" will know its source, if not its total significance.

The 144,000 Who Are Sealed

And I heard the number of them which were sealed: and there were sealed an hundred and forty and four thousand of all the tribes of the children of Israel. Of the tribe of Juda were sealed twelve thousand. Of the tribe of Reuben were sealed twelve thousand. Of the tribe of Gad were sealed twelve thousand. Of the tribe of Aser were sealed twelve thousand. Of the tribe of Nephthalim were sealed twelve thousand. Of the tribe of Manasses were sealed twelve thousand. Of the tribe of Simeon were sealed twelve thousand. Of the tribe of Levi were sealed twelve thousand. Of the tribe of Issachar were sealed twelve thousand. Of the tribe of Zabulon were sealed twelve thousand. Of the tribe of Joseph were sealed twelve thousand. Of the tribe of Benjamin were sealed twelve thousand. Rev. 7:4-8

John does not witness the sealing of these 144,000, but only hears the number and ancestry of those sealed. It is unmistakable that they are descendants of the twelve tribes of the children of Israel. There is not one Gentile among them. There are 12,000 out of each of the twelve tribes listed, thus 144,000 (12,000 X 12).

Note: The Jews (or Israel collectively) refused Jesus and His Messiahship. Jesus told them that Jerusalem would be destroyed and that they would be scattered throughout every nation. Jerusalem was destroyed in AD 70 under Titus and the Jews were dispersed among the nations. However, it was also prophesied that they should, in the last days, be gathered again from the nations. In AD 1948, after nearly two thousand years, Israel once again became a nation. They would, by necessity, have to be brought back as a people before there could be 144,000 from which to choose. They are still gathering in.

Names Blotted Out

There is a remarkable difference in the twelve tribes listed in Genesis as compared to the list in chapter seven. The names of Ephraim and Dan are omitted and replaced by Joseph and Levi. Why is this?

We must remember that after the Egyptian bondage,

the tribe of Joseph was honored through his two sons, Ephraim and Manasses. In addition, the tribe of Levi was not to be numbered among the tribes, particularly for war (Num. 1:47). They were to be set apart for tabernacle duties. Nor did the tribe of Levi receive territorial inheritance due to these duties. Considering the recognition of Joseph through his sons (two tribes), particularly Manasses, thus subtracting the name Joseph and setting-apart the tribe of Levi for tabernacle duties, Manasses and Ephraim would make up the eleventh and twelfth tribes.

Manasses is mentioned in chapter seven, but Ephraim is omitted. The tribe of Dan is also omitted. They are respectively replaced by Joseph and Levi. What would cause the blotting out of Ephraim and Dan?

We find the answer in Deuteronomy 29:18-21:

> Lest there should be among you man, or woman, or family, or tribe, whose heart turneth away this day from the LORD our God, to go and serve the gods of these nations; ..... The LORD will not spare him, but then the anger of the LORD and his jealousy shall smoke against that man, and all the curses that are written in this book shall lie upon him, and the LORD shall blot out his name from under heaven. Deu. 29:18,20-21

The tribes of both Dan and Ephraim permitted Jeroboam to set up "golden calves" to be worshipped. One was set up at Dan in the "tribe of Dan" and the other at Bethel in the "tribe of Ephraim" (I Kings 12:25-30). This idolatry resulted in their names being blotted out of mention in chapter seven of Revelation. Due to this blotting out, the descendants of Dan and Ephraim, if there are any, will go through the Tribulation Period unprotected.

Twelve tribes listed in Genesis: Reuben, Simeon, Levi,

Judah, Dan, Naphtali, Gad, Asher, Issachar, Zebulun, Joseph, Benjamin.

Twelve tribes of Revelation: Juda, Reuben, Gad, Aser, Nepthalim, Manasses, Simeon, Levi, Issachar, Zabulon, Joseph, Benjamin.

We read in chapter three the statement of the Lord concerning the blotting out of names (Ex. 32:33). We have also seen those of the Sardis Church who were warned to overcome or else a "blotting out" would occur. It was also mentioned that this blotting out of names strictly applies to those who tamper with God's Word (Rev. 22:19). It is here, in chapter seven, that we find example of such blotting.

Character Of The 144,000

The 144,000 are further described in chapter fourteen (vs.1-6). They are those not having been defiled with women. This defiling is *"moluno"* which means "to soil" coming from the word *"melas"* or black. This simply refers to the overshadowing or mindful responsibility of having a household to take care of, especially a wife (*"gune"* - women, spec. a wife) (I Cor. 7:33). Thus, they are unmarried. This concept is made clearer by the teachings of the apostle Paul concerning family responsibility (I Cor. 7).

Virgins

These 144,000 are also chaste. They are referred to as "virgins." Not only are they unmarried, but they are pure from all sexual conduct or practice. The word "virgins" is *"parthenos."* Although origin is unknown, *"parthenos"* is referred to as "a maiden." Thus, these 144,000 will undoubtedly consist of both male and female witnesses.

> And it shall come to pass in the last days, saith God, I will pour out of my Spirit upon all flesh: and your sons and your daughters shall prophesy, and your young men shall see visions, and your old men shall dream dreams: And on my servants and on my handmaidens I will pour out in those days of my Spirit; and they shall prophesy: And I will shew wonders in heaven above, and signs in the earth beneath; blood, and fire, and vapour of smoke: The sun shall be turned into darkness, and the moon into blood, before that great and notable day of the Lord come (see seal number six): And it shall come to pass, that whosoever shall call on the name of the Lord shall be saved. Acts 2:17-21

Many believe they are not necessarily virgins in the sense of sexual conduct, but that this refers to their chastity in being separated from any corruption by the Antichrist government. This too, is possible.

No Guile In Them

The 144,000 also have no guile in their mouth. They have a purpose that supersedes faultfinding. They are not there to proclaim the wickedness of the one-world government or its leader, but to proclaim a message of greater importance. This message will no doubt spur an explanation of their living under a totalitarian government, and its evils; however, they do so without the blaspheming of individuals. There is a great difference between explaining a situation which involves individuals and that of bashing the character of the individual. It is an art which few have mastered. They, however, will have mastered such character. They carry their message without fault before the throne of God.

Purpose Of The 144,000

Man has had a choice in every dispensation of time since the Garden of Eden. That choice is to accept or reject the plan and principles of God. The Tribulation Period will be no different. A message will go out by the 144,000 witnesses concerning the coming Messiah. It will be the message familiar to Jews, one that was proclaimed by the Old Testament prophets. It is the message of the kingdom. The proclaiming of the coming kingdom and the gathering of believers will be the primary purpose for the sealing of the 144,000.

The Kingdom Message

Matthew records a prophecy concerning the message which the 144,000 proclaim.

And this gospel of the kingdom shall be preached in all the world for a witness unto all nations; and then shall the end come. Matt. 24:14

These "sealed ones" proclaim a message for the entire world. It is the kingdom message. The fulfillment of this message is the Millennial Reign. It is the answer to the "thy kingdom come" of Jesus's model prayer (Matt. 6:9-13). It is the kingdom over which Jesus, the Messiah, shall reign, thus fulfilling Luke 1:32-33. This message will reach all the world and be a witness to all nations. It has nothing whatsoever to do with those who call themselves "Jehovah's Witnesses" today.

The New Testament preaching of the kingdom began with John the Baptist, followed by Jesus and the disciples. However, Jesus was rejected.

The kingdom message, that is to say, the message of

the earthly kingdom, for the most part, ceased. This message will resume after the "catching away" of the Church, hence, during the Tribulation Period.

The gospel or "good news" proclaimed today is the gospel of the grace of God. The focal point of the Tribulation Period message will not be that of salvation, per se, although the essence of salvation remains, but that of the "good news" of the coming kingdom.

The gospel (good news) of the kingdom will be a message of the coming reality of an earthly rule as opposed to the "New World Order" and earthly rule of the Antichrist. The kingdom message will prompt a great refusal of both the mark of the beast and allegiance to the established one-world government. This will infuriate the Antichrist and his utopian cohorts. At that time, particularly, one will have to give his life in a literal sense (be killed) for the witness of Christ.

These Are They

After this I beheld, and, lo, a great multitude, which no man could number, of all nations, and kindreds, and people, and tongues, stood before the throne, and before the Lamb, clothed with white robes, and palms in their hands; And cried with a loud voice, saying, Salvation to our God which sitteth upon the throne, and unto the Lamb. And all the angels stood round about the throne, and about the elders and the four beasts, and fell before the throne on their faces, and worshipped God, Saying, Amen: Blessing, and glory, and wisdom, and thanksgiving, and honour, and power, and might, be unto our God for ever and ever. Amen. And one of the elders answered, saying unto me, What are these which are arrayed in white robes? and whence came they? And I said unto him, Sir, thou knowest. And he said to me, These are they which came out of great tribulation, and have washed their robes, and made them white in the blood of the Lamb. Rev. 7:9-14

This great multitude will be a class of saved persons of the last days, especially the last 3 1/2 years of the Tribulation Period. Their salvation will differ from the salvation of our present time, the church age. We, now, are to be "living sacrifices" (although many are persecuted and killed) for Christ (Rom 12:1) and are awaiting to be "kept from the hour of temptation" (Rev. 3:10). During the Tribulation Period, persons will have to give their lives literally for Christ. They will be beheaded (Rev. 20:4). There has recently been a renewed interest in cutlery. This would indicate that beheading in a literal sense could quite possibly be the main form of execution during that time.

Here (vs. 9-14) we see a foreview of victory even though these message respondents were killed. These are they which are the "brethren and fellowservants" who were killed as those souls under the altar of seal number five (6:9) were killed. They are those martyred (20:4) during the Tribulation Period for refusing the mark of the beast, thus fulfilling the answer to those souls who cried from under the altar (6:11). They will live and reign with Christ during the Millennial Reign, as does the previously resurrected Church (20:4).

The Heavenly Response

John has a wondrous foreview of the glories that await the respondents to the kingdom message. All of Heaven forwards a glorious tribute to those martyred for the cause of Christ and of His kingdom. It is glorious. All the angels stand in reverence. The elders (able to sit in seats due to the resurrection of the Church) and the four beasts fall on their faces and worship God saying, "Amen: Blessing, and glory, and wisdom, and thanksgiving, and honour, and power, and might, be unto our God for ever and ever. Amen."

The honored multitudes are arrayed in white robes as were their brethren and fellowservants of seal number five. They have washed their robes and made them white in the blood of the Lamb. To wash something in blood would normally turn the object red; however, this washing is that of taking a stand for Christ, even unto death, and proclaiming Him as the Messiah. This will bring their martyrdom, thus, a washing in the blood of the Lamb (Rom. 8:17).

The Duties Of The Redeemed

Therefore are they before the throne of God, and serve him day and night in his temple: and he that sitteth on the throne shall dwell among them. They shall hunger no more, neither thirst any more; neither shall the sun light on them, nor any heat. For the Lamb which is in the midst of the throne shall feed them, and shall lead them unto living fountains of waters: and God shall wipe away all tears from their eyes. Rev. 7:15-17

We have seen earlier that these multitudes will rule and reign with Christ during the Millennial Reign. To what, then, do these verses refer?

Here we find a picture of the eternal duties of those who are martyred for Christ's sake during the Tribulation Period. They are not the bride, but will reign with Christ during the Millennial Reign, as will the Church, and will inhabit the new city, new Jerusalem, as will the Church. They will serve in God's temple. But there is no temple in Heaven! Right?

God's Temple

Several temples are mentioned in Scripture: Solomon's temple (II Sam. 7:13); Zerubbabel's temple (Ezra 3:12); Herod's temple (Matt. 21:12-14); the spiritual temple (Jn. 2:19; I Peter 2:4,5); the Tribulation temple (II Thess. 2:4; Rev. 11:2); and the millennium temple (Acts 15:16; Ez. chpts. 40-43). However, the temple mentioned here (7:15) is "his" temple, that is, God's temple. In God's temple the martyrs of the Tribulation period will serve him day and night (7:15). What is this temple?

A temple is generally a building in which a god or gods is worshipped, a place where the god manifests his presence. Thus, temples are considered holy or sacred. There is no earthly temple in the new city, new Jerusalem, but there is a temple: The Lord God Almighty and the Lamb are the temple of it (21:22).

The presence of the one and only true God will completely overwhelm the perfect city, new Jerusalem. God's holiness will permeate everything from the most minute pebble in the bottom of the River of Life to the utmost height of the city. It is His temple. It is His overwhelming presence.

God's temple will be in the new city, new Jerusalem, on the new Earth, for he shall dwell among them (7:15). The redeemed of the Tribulation Period will dwell in the presence of the Eternal God forever. There they (and we) will hunger no more, for they will be fed by the Lamb of God. They shall thirst no more, for Christ will lead them unto living fountains of waters and wipe away all their tears. These are heavenly characteristics and can only refer to conditions found within the new city, new

Jerusalem.

Servants In The Temple

Those Tribulation saints become servants in God's temple. This is clearly seen in Chapter 22:3,4. They are there identified as those who will also have His name in their foreheads.

> And there shall be no more curse: but the throne of God and of the Lamb shall be in it; and his servants shall serve him: And they shall see his face; and his name shall be in their foreheads. Rev. 22:3-4

They Serve Day And Night

They will serve God day and night in His temple. This appears odd at first, for there are those who believe there is no night and no sunlight on the new earth at all (22:5). Neither shall the light of the sun be upon them, nor any heat (7:16).

> And there shall be no night there; and they need no candle, neither light of the sun; for the Lord God giveth them light: and they shall reign for ever and ever. Rev. 22:5

We must remember that this refers to the city, not to the world outside the city, for we know that there will be nations outside the new city, new Jerusalem, whose kings bring their honor and glory into it (21:26). The gates of the city shall not be shut at all by day (*"hemera,"* the whole 24 hours): for there will be no night there (in the city). It is here we must understand somewhat of the future of the Earth, of the sun, and of the moon. In addition, just what or where is the new Earth on which the new city rests?

Perpetual Earth

We must know that this Earth, although it is to be purified by fire (II Peter 3:10), is established forever (Psa. 78:69, 104:5; Eccl. 1:4).

And he built his sanctuary like high palaces, like the earth which he hath established for ever. Psa. 78:69 .... Who laid the foundations of the earth, that it should not be removed for ever. Psa. 104:5

One generation passeth away, and another generation cometh: but the earth abideth for ever. Eccl. 1:4

The Earth is to be purified by fire, a purification which will occur after the Millennial Reign of Christ. However, the Earth was created to exist forever and to perpetuate itself. That is to say, it will continue to grow vegetation and spring forth in its appointed times. The new Earth on which the new city, new Jerusalem sits will be the same Earth we now inhabit, only purified. The landscape, however, will doubtless be changed, due to the events of the Tribulation Period and its purification by fire. (See chart, pg. 485)

The heavens and the Earth will melt with fervent heat during its purification. The "heavens" refers to the atmospheric heaven, although plural, due to the reference of the various elements found within it. The word "Earth" is "*ghay,*" and refers to the Earth's surface and the works upon it, not that the heavens and Earth will melt into oblivion. John tells us they will "pass away." However, this term is "*parerchomai,*" which means "to change from one condition to another." (For more information, see the author's book, "*The Jurassic Mark.*")

As far as day and night are concerned, both the sun and moon will continue to exist. The sun's light will shine through a new atmosphere upon a newly purified Earth. However, it will not shine in the new city, new Jerusalem, for the brightness of the glory of God will outshine the sun, even at midday (Acts 26:13).

> And the city had no need of the sun, neither of the moon, to shine in it: for the glory of God did lighten it, and the Lamb is the light thereof. Rev. 21:23

Note that this verse does not say that there was no sun or moon at all, only that there will be no need of the sun or moon to shine in the new city, for God's glory, Christ, is the light of it (Matt. 17:1-2; Jn. 8:12; Acts 9:3-5; I Jn. 1:5). For more on this, see chapter twenty one, "Sunshine On The New Earth."

The Earth has been established forever. As long as there is an Earth, day and night will exist. This thought comes from the heart of God:

> While the earth remaineth, seedtime and harvest, and cold and heat, and summer and winter, and day and night shall not cease. Gen. 8:22

As discussed at the beginning of the chapter, the events of chapter seven are not limited to a timespan lasting between seals six and seven only. We have seen that they extend from the sealing of the 144,000 into the eternal realm of the new Earth. This we will continue to see as our study progresses.

Ω

The Seventh Seal

Chapter 8

In chapter eight, the opening of the seals resumes with the opening of the last seal, seal number seven. The opening of the seventh seal is not conclusive in itself. It contains seven trumpet judgments, seven thunders, seven vials, and the events which occur upon their implementation.

Chapter eight covers only four of the seven trumpet judgments. These four judgments prompt the opening of the last half of the Tribulation Period. This is the time of which Christ specifically stated that there should be none the like (Matt. 24:21). This timeframe will be further revealed beginning with trumpet number five.

The seals have revealed thus far: 1. the rise of the Antichrist; 2. war against those nations which oppose the authority of the one-world government; 3. great famine which follows destructive wars; 4. death which occurs due to famine and war; 5. the souls from under the altar which cry out to be avenged; 6. seal number six is seen as a wake-up call to repentance before the great and terrible day of the Lord. And now, after the interval and sealing of the 144,000, comes the opening of the seventh seal.

Silence In Heaven

And when he had opened the seventh seal, there was silence in heaven about the space of half an hour. And I saw the seven angels which stood before God; and to them were given seven trumpets. And another angel came and stood at the altar, having a golden censer; and there was given unto him much incense, that he should offer it with the prayers of all saints upon the golden altar which was before the throne. And the smoke of the incense, which came with the prayers of the saints, ascended up before God out of the angel's hand. And the angel took the censer, and filled it with fire of the altar, and cast it into the earth: and there were voices, and thunderings, and lightnings, and an earthquake. And the seven angels which had the seven trumpets prepared themselves to sound. Rev. 8:1-6

The opening of seal number seven causes a silence in Heaven for about half an hour. The word *"hemiorion"* is the Greek here and means "half an hour." There is no reason to believe that it refers to anything other than about thirty minutes. We have seen that the Tribulation Period is referred to as the "hour of temptation;" however, it is not reasonable to think that this silence in Heaven refers to one half of the Tribulation Period, but rather just what the first impression gives, about thirty minutes. The silence is due to the last seal being broken to the "title deed." Complete ownership is clearly verified as all of Heaven is silent.

Every created being in Heaven is silent: the angels, the four beasts, and the elders. It is a silence of awe, a gasp before the exhaling, the anticipation of what is about to follow. No doubt the anticipation made the short time-span seem as though it lasted for hours.

During this "silence in heaven," John sees seven

angels standing before the throne of God. They were given seven trumpets and silently stand in reverence, ready to do God's bidding. However, before they are summoned to act, John sees another angel stand before God at the altar.

The Golden Censer

This angel holds a golden censer. A censer is thought to be a ladle or shovel-like container used for carrying live coals of fire on which incense was to be burned (Num. 16:6, 17-18, 37-39, 46). The censers of the tabernacle were made of bronze (Ex. 27:3; Lev. 16:12) while the censers of the temple were of pure gold (I Kings 7:50; II Chron. 4:22). The censer was used in the purification ritual on the Day of Atonement (Lev. 16:12-14) and here, likewise, it is used for the purpose of forging toward the Great Tribulation (last half).

Much Incense

The angel was given much incense, a sweet-smelling substance burned as an offering to God on the altar in the tabernacle and in the temple. It was a symbol and expression of the Hebrews' prayers. The angel with the golden censer is given much incense to offer with the prayers of all saints. This incense is offered with the prayers of the Tribulation saints, and especially of those slaughtered during that time (6:9).

> And the smoke of the incense, which came with the prayers of the saints, ascended up before God out of the angel's hand. Rev. 8:4

The Preparation For Judgment

The angel takes the golden censer, fills it with coals of

fire from the altar, and casts them to the Earth. This is the silence-breaker for all of Heaven. The casting of the fire to the Earth is followed by voices, thunderings, lightnings, earthquake and hail. Although mentioned several times in Revelation, there are only three places where all five of these aspects are mentioned together or closely related (8:5-7; 11:19; 16:18-21). These summon the first steps toward the beginning of the Great Tribulation (vials are detailed aspects of the trumpets, discussed later) and to its ending. The voices, thunderings, lightnings and earthquake signal the seven angels who are standing before God to prepare to sound the seven trumpets. These are seven trumpet judgments which shall be unleashed upon the Earth, four of which are recorded in chapter eight.

Trumpets

What is the significance of blowing trumpets? We know that trumpets were used to rally troops on the battlefield (Josh. 6:4; I Cor. 14:8). They could apparently be regulated and were thus used for musical instruments (Psa. 98:6; II Chron. 5:12).

However, trumpets were also used in the Old Testament by priests during services of sacrifice, especially to announce the Day of Atonement (Lev. 25:9). The Day of Atonement was the only day required by Law for public fasting and humiliation. On that day, the nation of Israel was to publicly reveal atonement for its sins (Lev. 23:27; 16:29; Num. 29:7). It was a solemn, holy day celebrated with elaborate rituals (Lev. 16; Heb. 10:1-10).

The Hebrews also had a Feast of Trumpets, which was a large part of the celebration of the Passover. Strangers and native-born people alike were punished if they did not observe this feast. Only unleavened bread was to be eaten during this feast, commemorating the haste with which Israel left Egypt. In like manner, as the blood was drained from the sacrificial animal for the Passover, so the life or the power of leaven was removed from the bread offered to God.

Atonement And Trumpet Type

In likeness, or type, the blowing of the seven trumpets typifies the Day of Atonement and the Feast of Trumpets. In type, this Day of Atonement is not a twenty-four hour day, but an extended span of years during the Tribulation Period. It is the call for atonement, the cleansing of God's chosen people in order to present them to himself. Ezekiel states that God doesn't do this because of the people, but because of His name's sake (Ez. 36:22-23). God has promised to carry out the promise of Israel's restoration for the Millennial Period and it will be done.

The Feast of Trumpets is also a type. The blowing of the trumpets witness that the Messiah, Jesus, the true Passover Lamb, was rejected. Thus, the true Passover (of which all other Passovers are but shadows), was discarded and counted as nought (Jn. 1:11). The earthly penalty for discarding the ultimate sacrifice (Jesus's death on the cross and spiritual kingdom) is the Tribulation Period, in particular, the last half of the Tribulation. It will take such a time for Israel to accept Jesus, the Messiah.

Trumpets will be sounded as a token of remembrance. They are a testimony before God of the rejection of the ultimate Passover Lamb. God's people must be brought back. This is why the judgments of the Great Tribulation must be executed.

Trumpet No. 1: Hail & Fire

> And the seven angels which had the seven trumpets prepared themselves to sound. The first angel sounded, and there followed hail and fire mingled with blood, and they were cast upon the earth: and the third part of trees was burnt up, and all green grass was burnt up. Rev. 8:6-7

To this point, the 144,000 witnesses have been sealed and are spreading the gospel of the kingdom. As we saw earlier, John saw four angels holding back the winds from the four corners of the Earth for the sealing of these witnesses. The four angels John saw are no longer restrained from hurting the Earth, the sea and trees (7:2-3). With the blowing of the first trumpet, God's wrath falls upon the Earth, evidently through the operation of these four angels.

Here we find that one-third of the trees and all green grass are burned up. Earth's vegetation is greatly affected.

The judgment prompted by the sounding of the first trumpet parallels the seventh plague of Egypt. Moses had gone to Egypt under God's direction to free the children of Israel from Egyptian bondage. The sad difference is that the trumpet judgments are directed toward Israel, whereas the plagues were directed at Egypt and the Pharaoh.

Trumpet No. 2: Volcanic Eruption

> And the second angel sounded, and as it were a great mountain burning with fire was cast into the sea: and the third part of the sea became blood; And the third part of the creatures which were in

the sea, and had life, died; and the third part of the ships were destroyed. Rev. 8:8-9

This great mountain, no doubt, refers to a large volcanic mass of molten rock which is cast into the sea. Note that it says "the sea," which usually refers to the Mediterranean Sea (Gen. 49:13; Psa. 80:11), as opposed to seas or bodies of waters. The effects of this volcanic mass are devastating. One-third of the sea is turned blood red. No doubt it is a mixture of lava and the blood which flowed from the one-third of the sea creatures which are killed. A great tidal wave caused by the plunging volcanic mass will destroy one-third of the ships.

Here again, we find that the sea is affected. This is a portion of the power given to the four angels who previously held the winds at the four corners of the Earth (7:1-3).

Trumpet No. 3: Meteoric Mass

And the third angel sounded, and there fell a great star from heaven, burning as it were a lamp, and it fell upon the third part of the rivers, and upon the fountains of waters; And the name of the star is called Wormwood: and the third part of the waters became wormwood; and many men died of the waters, because they were made bitter. Rev. 8:10-11

Upon the sounding of the third trumpet, a great meteor blazes through the sky and pollutes one-third of Earth's waters. This flaming torch produces toxic gases which pollute the rivers as it explodes, spreads, and falls to Earth. The fountains of waters, that is, the underground streams, are also poisoned by this meteor as the rivers interact with them. Many men die from these poisoned waters.

This blazing star is called "Wormwood," which is *"apsinthos,"* a type of bitterness. Wormwood is a very bitter perennial herb used to produce a very intoxicating beverage in some countries. It is more destructive than other liquors.

The third trumpet judgment is a fulfillment of a prophecy of Jeremiah:

> And the LORD saith, Because they have forsaken my law which I set before them, and have not obeyed my voice, neither walked therein; But have walked after the imagination of their own heart, and after Baalim, which their fathers taught them: Therefore thus saith the LORD of hosts, the God of Israel; Behold, I will feed them, even this people, with wormwood, and give them water of gall to drink. Jer. 9:13-15

Here we find effects upon the water systems of Earth, another effect of the four angels who previously held the four corners of the Earth (7:2-3).

Trumpet No. 4: Sun, Moon & Stars

> And the fourth angel sounded, and the third part of the sun was smitten, and the third part of the moon, and the third part of the stars; so as the third part of them was darkened, and the day shone not for a third part of it, and the night likewise. Rev. 8:12

Again, as seen under the discussion of the sixth seal, the sun, moon, and stars are affected. This is more of the same effects that Christ prophesied in Luke 21:25-28.

One Third?

We have seen a third part of things affected by the trumpet judgments thus far. They are: one-third of the trees, of the sea to blood, of sea creatures killed, of ships destroyed, of water systems, and one-third of the heavenly bodies darkened. Why one-third?

We have seen that the Tribulation Period is determined upon Daniel's people, hence, the Jews. The Jews did not reject God, that is, the God of Abraham, Jacob, and Isaac. Nor did they reject the Holy Spirit on the Day of Pentecost, for the early Church was primarily Jewish. However, they did reject Jesus (Jn. 1:11), thus one-third of the Triune Personage of the one and only Eternal God. He was rejected as the only way (they would continue to cling to the Law). We know that the Tribulation Period is directed toward bringing the children of Israel (also referred to as Jews) to the Messiah, Jesus. It would be reasonable that these "one-thirds" listed are due to the rejection of one-third of the personage of God, particularly, of Jesus.

The Three Woes That Follow

> And I beheld, and heard an angel flying through the midst of heaven, saying with a loud voice, Woe, woe, woe, to the inhabiters of the earth by reason of the other voices of the trumpet of the three angels, which are yet to sound! Rev. 8:13

Although men have died during the first four trumpet judgments, these judgments have been directed primarily toward the Earth. This is for purification purposes. However, in verse thirteen, an angel announces that the last three trumpet judgments are directed toward Earth's inhabitants: "Woe, woe, woe, to the inhabiters of the earth." Three woes and three trumpet judgments are yet to come. A woe ("*ouai*") is an exclamation of grief. Thus, three more periods of great grief will be launched.

The last three trumpet judgments are the three woes

directed at humanity, "Earth's inhabitants." As we will see, John clearly marks these woes. It is with these woes that the "Great Tribulation" (last half) begins in full force. That is to say, that the breaking of the seventh seal and the first four trumpet judgments are the primary steps which lead directly up to the beginning of the Great Tribulation. The evidences for this thesis are clearly marked also.

Ω

Two
Woes
Chapter 9

Chapter nine opens with trumpet number five, the first woe directed toward Earth inhabitants. A woe, as seen earlier, is an exclamation of grief, in this case, great grief. It marks the beginning of the Great Tribulation (last half).

Two of the three woes— the fifth and sixth trumpet judgment— are dealt with in this chapter. The subsequent effects of these trumpets will be poured out upon the inhabitants of the Earth. It will be a very grievous time. "Woe, woe, woe, to the inhabiters of the earth by reason of the other voices of the trumpet of the three angels, which are yet to sound" (8:13).

Woe No. 1: Trumpet Five

And the fifth angel sounded, and I saw a star fall from heaven unto the earth: and to him was given the key of the bottomless pit. And he opened the bottomless pit; and there arose a smoke out of the pit, as the smoke of a great furnace; and the sun and the air were darkened by reason of the smoke of the pit. Rev. 9:1-2

At the sound of the fifth trumpet, John sees a star falling from heaven. This star is not a literal star, but an intelligent being, an angel. This is not only seen by the use of the personal pronouns he and him, but also because of the fact that he has a particular task to carry out. Note that angels are often referred to as stars (Job 38:7; Rev. 12:4).

Some scholars believe this star-angel to be Christ himself, others say he is Satan. Needless to say, there is quite a difference in opinion. We must first look into the situation and responsibility given him before we can identify this angel.

Bottomless Pit

The star-angel is given the key to the bottomless pit. This is the first clue to the identification of the angel. But what is the "bottomless pit"?

Many scholars believe that the bottomless pit is a completely separate abode from that of Hades, Tartaros or Gehenna Hell, the three stages of Hell revealed in the Hebrew and Greek. It must be noted, however, that Scripture does not identify any other abode for torment than these three distinctions of Hell. The only other abode mentioned for holding fallen angels is the Euphrates River (discussed later).

Thus, in order to find just what or where this bottomless pit is, we must examine the three Hells of Scripture. Remembering that when the Hebrew texts (O.T.) and Greek texts (N.T.) were translated into English, the one English word, Hell, was used for Hades, Tartaros and Gehenna. In reality these Hells are different stages and/or divisions of one place of torment. They are explained as follows:

1. Hades. This is the same as the Old Testament "Sheowl," the place where those individuals of both Old and New Testaments are found who have died (and

are dying) without accepting God's plan of escape. They are to be held there until the Great White Throne Judgment (20:12). We know that Hades is a place of torment (Luke 16:19-31) within the Earth, for we know that Jesus descended into Hell before ascending into Heaven (Acts 2:24-27; Eph. 4:8-10; I Peter 3:18-20) (See chapter one - "Keys of Death and Hell").

2. Tartaros. Tartaros is from the Greek *"Tartaroo"* and is found in II Peter 2:4. Tartaros is the lowest abyss of Hades. Peter informs us that this is where the fallen angels are kept. These fallen angels are those of the spirit world (demons) who were cast out with Satan (12:4; Jude 6). They are evidently locked in this abyss and restrained from roaming the higher elevation of Hades. This lowest abyss of Hell, Tartaros, is no doubt the bottomless pit. It is called the "bottomless pit" simply because it has no bottom. If one could do so, one could descend to the very center of the Earth, but would have to merely stop, for there is no bottom. To continue to move in any direction, one would immediately begin to ascend (as the Earth is round). The very title "bottomless" gives reference to the downward direction of this place. In addition, when Christ cast the demons out of the man at Gadarene, the demons besought Him not to cast them into the deep (Lu. 8:26-36). This "deep" is *"abussos,"* which means "abyss (bottomless) pit."

Note: These beings of Luke 8:26-36 were not cast into the abyss at the same time as those fallen angels who were cast out with Satan (then called Lucifer). They were the spirit-flesh beings, or offsprings, of the sons of God (angels as sons - Job 1:6; 2:1) and the daughters of men (Gen. 6:2-5). They were the offsprings of fallen angels. They became disembodied spirits upon the death of the flesh (Gen. 6:3). These disembodied spirits are ever searching for new bodies to inhabit. They do not die when the bodies of their victims die. This is why so many who tend toward the occult, through psychics, mediums, familiar spirits, and so on, believe in reincarnation. Upon opening themselves up to the occult, that is, the world of "familiar" spirits, they become possessed by these immortal beings who have lived in previous bodies. The re-embodied spirit, having the thoughts and memories of previous victims, conveys those thoughts and memories to the new victim. The new victim is convinced that he or she has lived before in a previous life. This is a very deceptive tactic of Satan.

3. Geenna Hell. *"Gehenna,"* the Everlasting Hell, will be the eternal abode of those dead who are judged at the Great White Throne Judgment (Matt. 5:22; 23:33; Rev. 20:11-15). It will also be the eternal dwelling place of Satan, all other fallen angels (Matt. 25:41; Rev. 20:10), and all who have rejected God's plan of escape (Heb. 2:3). As the White Throne Judgment does not occur until after the Millennial Reign, this eternal state of Hell has not yet begun. Its eternal nature will begin when the beast and the false prophet are cast there (discussed later). Geenna (gehenna) is the Lake of Fire of Scripture (Rev. 19:20; 20:10,14,15).

The Star-Angel

It is unreasonable to think that this star-angel is Satan for a number of reasons. First, it is difficult to believe that Satan would be given the key to the bottomless pit. Further, this star-angel is the same one who binds Satan with a great chain and casts him into the pit of chapter 20:1-3. Satan would not bind himself and cast himself into the pit! (Many believe the star-angel to be Satan due to the locust king of 9:11, discussed shortly).

We also know that the star-angel is not a "fallen angel" although he is seen falling from Heaven. John simply means that this angel quickly descends from Heaven. Christ Jesus, the One who has the key to Hell (1:18), would not entrust this key to a fallen angel, a creature that has proven unworthy of trust time and again.

Evidence also reveals that this star-angel is not Christ. We discussed in chapter one how Christ descended into Hell (Hades) and led captivity captive (Eph. 4:8-9), and that He is the one who has the keys of death and Hell (Rev. 1:18). Thus, Christ is the one who gives the key to the descending angel. The star-angel is not Christ.

This star-angel, then, is an angel of rank and authority, a powerful angel assigned the duties of binding and loosing, opening and closing. He is a heavenly angel not named here. He is the one who later binds Satan with a great chain and casts him into the bottomless pit, locking and sealing him up for one thousand years (during Millennial Reign - 20:1-3). Note that the Lord has angels which do His bidding. They hold particular authority, responsibilities and duties.

Angels

Lately, interest in angels has soared, as evidenced by the many bracelets, lapel pins, tie-tacks, ceramic and crystal figurines, depicting the heavenly beings. Angels are most often displayed in the feminine gender; however, Scripture always reveals them as males. They are a great part of all that has occurred, is occurring and shall occur, however, they are not to be worshipped (19:10), for only One is to be worshipped and that is God. In fact, we, one day, shall judge angels (fallen angels - I Cor. 6:3).

Angels play a great role in the affairs of Heaven and Earth. They are immortal (Lu. 20:36), of high order (Psa. 8:5), high in power (II Peter 2:11; II Thess. 1:7; Rev. 18:1; Psa. 103:20) and wise (II Sam. 14:20). They are holy (Mrk. 8:38), innumerable (Heb. 12:22; Job 25:3; Lu. 2:13,14), and desire to look into and understand salvation (I Peter 1:12). They are invisible (Num. 22:22-31). They do not marry in Heaven (Matt. 22:30).

In rank, there are: cherubim, who guarded the Tree of Life (Gen. 3:22) and the mercy seat (Ex. 25:20); seraphim, who proclaim God's holiness (Isa. 6:1-2); the four beasts, who watch over the throne of God and worship Him (Rev. 4:8). The arch-angel, Michael, is the most prominent angel ("*arch*" means "chief"), who fought for the passage of God's Word (Dan. 10:13) and is the prince and overseer of Israel (Dan. 10:21). In Jude (v.9), Michael is recorded as having fought for Moses' body. Gabriel, the "mighty one of God," who serves as messenger to Daniel (Dan. 8:15,16; 9:21), to Zacharias, announcing the birth of John the Baptist (Lu. 1:11-25), and to Mary announcing the birth of Jesus (Lu. 1:27,31,32). Holy ones and watchers decree the downfall of nations (Dan. 4:13,23). Lucifer was the anointed cherub that covereth (Ez. 28:14). He became Satan, the adversary (Isa. 14:12-15). And the list goes on.

The Tormenting Locusts

And there came out of the smoke locusts upon the earth: and unto them was given power, as the scorpions of the earth have power. And it was commanded them that they should not hurt the grass of the earth, neither any green thing, neither any tree; but only those men which have not the seal of God in their foreheads. And to them it was given that they should not kill them, but that they should be tormented five months: and their torment was as the torment of a scorpion, when he striketh a man. And in those days shall men seek death, and shall not find it; and shall desire to die, and death shall flee from them. Rev 9:3-6

When the angel opened the bottomless pit, smoke came out as the smoke of a great furnace. This is the smoke of Hades, particularly a stream of smoke from Tartaros, Hades' lowest abyss. So much smoke ascended that the sun was once again darkened as in the days of the sixth seal and the fourth trumpet judgment.

Out of the smoke came locusts. It is quite evident that these locusts are not literal. The reasons are obvious: They are intelligent beings, for they take commands (v.4); they have a king over them, which ordinary locusts do not have (Pro. 30:27); they are commanded not to hurt the vegetation, as ordinary locusts do (Ex. 10:3-20); neither are they stifled by the smoke or burned with the fire of the pit. These creatures are much more than ordinary locusts; they are demonic beings.

Their command is to torture all those who do not have

the seal of God in their foreheads. Thus, the 144,000 witnesses (chpt. 7) are protected, while those having taken
the mark of the beast are the targets. The inflicted pain
will be as that of a scorpion, an excruciating pain, yet
rarely fatal. Men will seek death, but death will flee from
them. The locusts are commanded only to torment, not to
kill. The length of this torturous time is five months.

The Appearance Of The Locusts

And the shapes of the locusts were like unto horses prepared unto
battle; and on their heads were as it were crowns like gold, and
their faces were as the faces of men. And they had hair as the hair
of women, and their teeth were as the teeth of lions. And they had
breastplates, as it were breastplates of iron; and the sound of their
wings was as the sound of chariots of many horses running to battle. And they had tails like unto scorpions, and there were stings
in their tails: and their power was to hurt men five months. Rev.
9:7-10

It must be noted that John describes these locusts in
terms that would be familiar to readers during his time.
They are descriptive, not literal, terms. This is seen in
phrases, such as: "were like;" "were as;" "like;" "as;" "as
it were;" "was as;" and "like unto."

These locusts, however, are literal. God has always
sent literal plagues. They are commanded to restrain from
hurting things that are literal. They have a literal command. The smoke, the fire and the pit are literal, so they
also must be literal. It will be literal torture which they
inflict upon men.

Joel also gives description of these beings:

The appearance of them is as the appearance of horses; and as
horsemen, so shall they run. Like the noise of chariots on the tops

of mountains shall they leap, like the noise of a flame of fire that
devoureth the stubble, as a strong people set in battle array. Before
their face the people shall be much pained: all faces shall gather
blackness. They shall run like mighty men; they shall climb the
wall like men of war; and they shall march every one on his ways,
and they shall not break their ranks: Neither shall one thrust
another; they shall walk every one in his path: and when they fall
upon the sword, they shall not be wounded. They shall run to and
fro in the city; they shall run upon the wall, they shall climb up
upon the houses; they shall enter in at the windows like a thief.
The earth shall quake before them; the heavens shall tremble: the
sun and the moon shall be dark, and the stars shall withdraw their
shining: And the LORD shall utter his voice before his army: for
his camp is very great (144,000): for he is strong that executeth his
word: for the day of the LORD is great and very terrible
(Tribulation Period); and who can abide it? Joel 2:4-11

The picture is that of demonic creatures, for horses do
not run upon walls or climb upon houses. They do not
enter windows. Neither do horses fall upon swords and
escape harm.

John's picture is a war-like, attacking creature
(armored horse), successful in mission (crowns) and intelligent in execution (faces of men). The accomplishments
of these creatures are their glory (hair of women). They
are indestructible (breastplate of iron) and devouring in
character (teeth of a lion). They are frightening (sound of
wings) which go about greatly torturing (sting of tails).
This woe will bring a fear much greater than the sting of
death, for men will desire to die but cannot.

Demons From The Bottomless Pit?

If these creatures are indeed demons from the bottomless pit, how did they get there and why are they there?
Jude gives us the answer to this puzzle.

And the angels which kept not their first estate, but left their own habitation, he hath reserved in everlasting chains under darkness unto the judgment of the great day. Jude 1:6

Jude, in exhorting the brethren to earnestly contend for the faith concerning the common salvation, was warning of ungodly men who creep into congregations and attempt to turn the grace of God into ungodliness. He then used the example of the Israelites whom God saved out of Egypt, but later destroyed for unbelief. He also used the example of those of Sodom and Gomorrah, who, after being saved, suffered the vengeance of eternal fire. Then Jude used the example of the angels who kept not their first estate (being in God's service), but left their own habitation. These angels (fallen angels - demons) are held (reserved) in everlasting (everduring) chains under darkness, that is, under Hades in Tartaros, unto (until) the judgment of the great day. The great day mentioned here is the Great Tribulation. These locusts are those fallen angels cast out with Lucifer (12:4).

The apostle Peter also speaks of those who creep in unawares. He too, uses examples and mentions those fallen angels:

For if God spared not the angels that sinned, but cast them down to hell, and delivered them into chains of darkness, to be reserved unto judgment;... II Peter 2:4

The Locust King

And they had a king over them, which is the angel of the bottomless pit, whose name in the Hebrew tongue is Abaddon, but in the Greek tongue hath his name Apollyon. Rev. 9:11

Note again that these locusts are not ordinary locusts,

for ordinary locusts do not have kings over them (Pro. 30:27). The name of the locust king in the Hebrew is "Abaddon" which is "a destroying angel." In the Greek it is "Apollyon" or "Apolluon" which is "a destroyer." Doubtless, he is a great destroying angel released when the star-angel unlocks the bottomless pit. It is not Satan, for he is now, at the present, the prince of the powers of the air and not locked up in Hell. He and his minions are presently free to roam about and do their evil bidding. In addition, the names Abaddon and Apollyon are never used of Satan in the Bible.

Why mention this locust king at all? The answer becomes obvious when considering the time-frame of events. The first woe (trumpet five) begins the last half of the Tribulation Period called the "Great Tribulation." At that time the Antichrist becomes most vicious, he breaks the covenant with the Jews and begins to slaughter them. He also sets himself up in the temple claiming to be God and demanding complete worship. Note also that those who have taken the mark of the beast are at this time tormented by the locusts and are in great need of help. They, in turn, call out to their leaders for a solution. The Antichrist will no doubt summon help from the occultists (like Nebuchadnezzar did in times past).

This will open up Antichrist's soul for possession. At that time, the Antichrist will doubtless have an assassination attempt upon his life and will subsequently appear as dead. Abaddon, the locust king, shall take possession of the Antichrist and resurrect his wounded body for demonic use. The Antichrist, until that point, will have had world domination in mind and personal aspirations of power;

however, this man of sin will get more than he bargained for when attempting such control. It is not Satan who will incarnate the Antichrist, because Satan would not put all his eggs in one basket, so to speak. However, it will be a mockery of Father and Son. Separate, yet one in operation. This possession by Abaddon is realized due to the fact that the Antichrist (called beast) is said to have ascended from the bottomless pit (11:7; 17:8).

Some claim that the Antichrist will be a man resurrected from the dead because of statements about the beast "from the bottomless pit" being a "man" of sin. This is not feasible because the bottomless pit is the lower abyss of Hell (Tartaros) used for fallen angels only, not for unrepentant dead men.

> One woe is past; and, behold, there come two woes more hereafter. Rev. 9:12

Woe No. 2: Trumpet Six

> And the sixth angel sounded, and I heard a voice from the four horns of the golden altar which is before God, Saying to the sixth angel which had the trumpet, Loose the four angels which are bound in the great river Euphrates. And the four angels were loosed, which were prepared for an hour, and a day, and a month, and a year, for to slay the third part of men. Rev. 9:13-15

Upon hearing the sixth angel sound the trumpet, John hears a voice from the four horns of the golden altar. This particular altar is the golden altar of incense, the only altar mentioned in the heavenly tabernacle (Isa. 6:6; Rev. 8:3). Note that altars of the Old Testament were not restricted to offerings of animal sacrifices. They were also used to remind the Israelites of their heritage (Josh. 22:26-29) or to "call attention to a major event."

Four Horns Of The Altar

Horns are metaphorically used in Scripture as emblems of strength and power. They are the chief source of attack and defense of the animals which have them. The budding, or sprouting of horns, is a figurative way of referring to the rise of a nation or individual power (Psa. 132:17; Ez. 29:21). They are also figuratively used to indicate a "bringing down" or "degradation," as seen in Job 16:15. The projections on the four corners of the altar of sacrifice (brazen altar - Ex. 27:2) and on the altar of incense (golden altar - Ex. 30:1-3) were called "horns."

The four horns of the golden altar of incense are mentioned here in Revelation to bring to mind the requirement of shed blood for the remission of sin. The Old Testament priests would sprinkle the blood of an unblemished animal on the four horns of the altar to signify that an impurity had been recognized and then cleansed (Ex. 29:12). The shedding of blood was the requirement for the cleansing of man's sinful heart and for the strength and power which was necessary to take the sin away.

The Old Testament practice of sacrificing animals was a forerunner, a type or shadow of the innocent blood that was to be shed on Calvary for man's sins. That innocent sacrifice was Jesus (II Cor. 5:21), the only One having the power to take away the sin of the world (Jn. 1:29).

The Voice From The Four Horns

John hears a voice from the four horns of the altar. Although the speaker is not identified, John's attention is drawn there in order that he might recognize and record the presence of this altar in the heavenly tabernacle. The golden altar and the four horns are presented there to call attention to the major event which is about to follow. The next major event is yet another plague of the Tribulation Period. It is, as with the other plagues, due to the Jew's rejection of the ultimate sacrifice for sin, Jesus Christ. The four horns also draw attention to the power, strength, and wrath of God issued because of their rejection of Christ.

Euphrates River

The sixth trumpet angel is told by the voice from the four horns of the altar to loose the four angels bound in the Euphrates River. Before identifying these four angels, it is necessary to first probe the question of their whereabouts. Why are they bound in the Euphrates River?

The Euphrates is where Satan's seat was in ancient times, particularly Babylon (See chapter two - "Pergamos Historical"). Babylon was erected along the Euphrates River. In this particular mention, the Euphrates stands for both the river and the city of Babylon, for they are intertwined in reference.

Babylon is one of the oldest cities of the ancient world (Babel - Gen. 10:10) and was the model for paganism and idolatry. The sixth trumpet judgment of the Tribulation Period befalls the inhabitants of Earth due to such idolatry. This is seen in 9:20. (Idolatry is discussed in chapters two and three. See the series, "In The Background")

During the time of Nebuchadnezzar, Babylon was expanded. Huge walls were built which extended to both sides of the Euphrates River. Although Babylon was oftentimes used as God's battle-ax (Ez. 32:11), its people would not repent of their worship of graven images and idolatry. This and other such practices led to their fall as a world empire.

Book Of Babylon

The Lord had given Jeremiah a prophecy concerning all the evil that should come upon Babylon because of their idolatry. He was told to "write it in a book" (Jer. 51:60). After being read to the people, the book was to be tied to a stone and cast into the Euphrates River. This was not only a sign that Babylon would sink, but that the evil that was to befall her, in its fulness, was to be bound there until the time the prophecy was loosed.

Although much of Jeremiah's prophecy was fulfilled at the fall of ancient Babylon, portions of the prophecy remain unfulfilled. However, Babylon will flourish once again. It will be a symbolic Babylon, the literal one-world government and intertwined one-world religion of the end-times (both are already in the making). These systems will be in full force during the Tribulation Period.

Identity Of The Four Angels

The four angels bound in the Euphrates River are not "good angels," for good angels are never bound. These angels are four in number, the number of the world. This reflects that their vengeance will spread throughout the entire world during the Tribulation Period, to the north, south, east, and west.

These angels are four spirits (evil spirits - fallen angels) which are to execute the complete fall of the end-time Babylon. They were evidently bound at the time that Jeremiah's book (that book concerning Babylon) was tied to a stone and thrown into the Euphrates River. This belief is based on the overseeing spirits of four major attacks and captures of the historic city of Babylon.

Four Major Attacks

Historically, four major attacks were launched against the city of Babylon, each apparently overseen by an evil spirit or fallen angel. These four assaults were direct, victorious attacks against the city, not mere transferring of control, because different kings and regional powers often seized control. The city of Babylon would be destroyed time and again only to be resurrected again and again. The notable attacks and plunderings are as follows:

1. The attack and capture of Babylon by the Hittite King, Murshilish I, in B.C. 1595.

2. The attack from the Assyrians in B.C. 1250, when Babylon was captured and plundered.

3. The great attack by Sennacherib in B.C. 689 when Babylon was completely destroyed. Sennacherib's successor, Esarhaddon, rebuilt it in B.C. 680-689.

4. The fourth attack by the Medes and the Persians. Afterwards, when the Medo-Persian Empire was overthrown by the Greek Empire under Alexander the Great, Alexander set out to make Babylon his capitol. He died before accomplishing that goal. After his death, one of his successors founded a new capital at Seleucia. Babylon thus fell into insignificance.

It would stand to reason that these four major attacks were overseen by four destructive military-type angels. These bad angels (evil spirits) are those bound in the Euphrates River, in the area of Babylon. They are still bound there because the prophecy of the coming evil on Babylon is still bound. They will be loosed when the sixth trumpet angel sets them free. They are loosed: 1. that they may fulfill the prophecy; 2. to issue a portion of the second woe; and 3. to aid in the final undoing of the end-time Babylon. The fall of the revived Babylon will completely fulfill Jeremiah's prophecy (fall of Babylon discussed in chapter eighteen). These military angels, as we will see, are commanders of a great army.

The Four Angels Loosed

The character of the four angels is also seen in that they were prepared for the specific hour, day, month and year for a particular task, a task of killing. They will be provided (prepared - *"hetoimazo"*) an exact time to be loosed, not loosed for 391 days, as some suppose. The reference reveals that they must remain bound (restrained) until the specific time that they are loosed by the trumpet angel. Evil angels are always ready to do evil. All that is necessary is that they be loosed. They, being military angels, will automatically fulfill the duty to which they are accustomed. They are angels of battle. All four evil angels, which have overseen the previous and major attacks, were bound together and shall be loosed together. These four angels will accomplish their goal.

Demonic Activity In Governments

There is such a thing as demonic activity in the governments of the world. The secular world sees only the visible human agent, the king, the ruthless dictator, the tyrants of history, but there are evil workings behind the scenes. Paul calls this inner working the "mystery of iniquity" (lawlessness - II Thess. 2:7). It is such an inner working of governments that will produce the Antichrist, the "that wicked" of II Thess. 2:8. "Even him, whose coming is after the working of Satan with all power and signs and lying wonders,..." (II Thess. 2:9).

Governments do not just come and go by chance, nor is any human activity independent of spiritual forces (Eph. 6:12). In many places, the word *"kosmos"* ("orderly arrangement") is used for "world" to depict the whole mass of unregenerate men who are against Christ and organized governmentally (Jn. 7:7; I Cor. 1:21; I Peter 5:9; I Jn. 3:1, 13). The head over this orderly arrangement is Satan. He is the prince of this world (Jn. 12:31; 14:30; 16:11). Isaiah depicts Satan as the one "that didst weaken (bring low) the nations" (14:12). God, however, intervenes in human history and overrules as necessary to assure the fulfillment of prophecy (Dan. 2:12). This necessitates spiritual warfare.

Likewise, as God has angels who do His bidding, so are demonic agents fulfilling the evil workings of Satan. They are the "principalities," the "powers," the "rulers of the darkness of this world," the "spiritual wickedness in high places" of Ephesians 6:12.

Demons
Although the word "demon" is not found in the King James Bible, it is referred to some sixty times as *"diamo-*

nion" which is translated "devil" (s), and means "a demonic being." Thus, the existence of demons is not foreign to Scripture. The preferred reference by most scholars is "demon" rather than "devil," in order to avoid confusion when speaking of the Devil, Satan, or his agents. Satan is the "Devil" or *"diabolos"* which is a title which means "traducer, false accuser."

Demons took part in the wickedness at the time of the flood of Noah's time (Gen. 6:1-4). Pagan worship is attributed to demons (Lev. 17:7; Psa. 106:37). They are called "unclean spirits" (Matt. 10:1; Mrk. 6:7), "wicked spirits" (Lu. 7:21; Acts 19:12-13) and "deceiving spirits" (I Tim. 4:1). They are referred to as the "spirit of evil" (I Jn. 4:6), "spirits of devils" (Rev. 16:14) and the "spirit of divination" (Acts 16:16). The primary purpose of Jesus was to be victorious over Satan. This included overthrowing the demonic realm (Matt. 12:25-29; Lu. 11:17-22; Jn. 12:31; I Jn. 3:8). Jesus was falsely accused of being the prince of demons, Beelzebub (Mrk. 3:22; Jn. 8:48).

We must not forget that we are involved in a spiritual warfare with the realm of darkness (Eph. 6:12). Thus we must be aware of our weapons with which we are to fight. These weapons are found in the acronym for "weapons." W: the Word of God (Heb. 4:12); E: the "Effectual" fervent prayer (James 5:16); A: the whole "Armor" of God (Eph. 6:11-18); P: "Praising" the Lord (I Chron. 16:25; Psa 150); O: "Obedience" toward God (I Peter 1:13-16); N: lifting up the "Name" of Jesus Christ (Acts 4:11-12); S: being filled with the "Spirit" (I Jn. 4:1; Eph. 5:18) .

(For the weapons of our warfare are not carnal, but mighty through God to the pulling down of strong holds;) Casting down imaginations, and every high thing that exalteth itself against the knowledge of God, and bringing into captivity every thought to the obedience of Christ;...II Cor. 10:4-5

A Supernatural Army

And the number of the army of the horsemen were two hundred thousand thousand: and I heard the number of them. And thus I saw the horses in the vision, and them that sat on them, having breastplates of fire, and of jacinth, and brimstone: and the heads of the horses were as the heads of lions; and out of their mouths issued fire and smoke and brimstone. By these three was the third part of men killed, by the fire, and by the smoke, and by the brimstone, which issued out of their mouths. For their power is in their mouth, and in their tails: for their tails were like unto serpents, and had heads, and with them they do hurt. Rev. 9:16-19

The four angels are evidently the commanders of a supernatural army of two hundred million (two hundred thousand thousand - 200,000,000). It is possible that they each command forces of 50,000,000 each and are spread toward the north, south, east and west, thus covering the entire globe. As the commanding angels are four in number (the number of the world), their spiritual army (whatever divisions or ranks) will affect the Earth greatly.

This great spiritual army is not fighting against the men of Earth. It is a spiritual battle in the heavens against the arch-angel Michael (discussed further in chapter twelve). The effects of this spiritual battle, however, will affect the men of Earth. Fire, smoke and brimstone will stream from this battle. Although spiritual, it will be a literal battle having literal effects. One-third of humanity will be annihilated during this sixth trumpet judgment (v.15). This is but a portion of the second woe which is directed at humanity.

John describes these demonic creatures, as he did with the locusts, in terms familiar to those of his day. The horsemen are no doubt a demonic hoard of bad angels, while the horses are seen as their mode of transportation or motivating force. Their forces are devouring, as symbolized by the "heads of lions." Their power is in their mouth and represents the forward initiation of fire, smoke and brimstone, while their tail represents the effects which follow.

Disturbing Results

And the rest of the men which were not killed by these plagues yet repented not of the works of their hands, that they should not worship devils, and idols of gold, and silver, and brass, and stone, and of wood: which neither can see, nor hear, nor walk: Neither repented they of their murders, nor of their sorceries, nor of their fornication, nor of their thefts. Rev. 9:20-21

Two-thirds of the Earth's inhabitants are left to face other judgments, for they continue to be non-repentant. How stubborn to repent are those who are wrapped in the blankets of idolatry!

Woe Number Two Continues

Chapter nine ends with only a portion of woe number two expired. Woe number two continues into the next two chapters. It is not until woe number two ends (11:14) that the seventh angel sounds his trumpet. Meanwhile, before the sounding of trumpet number seven, other occurrences take place. We will discuss these in the following chapters.

Ω

The Mighty Angel & The Great Announcement
Chapter 10

Certain spices may be added when cooking a particular meal to make the end result more satisfying and rewarding. Such is the case with this chapter. It is another "parenthesis chapter" which adds spice to an already desirable end.

Chapter ten is out of chronological order concerning the flow of events; however, it was planned that way. It concerns aspects of a great event which are very important to the overall picture of Revelation. We must remember that various Scriptures often refer to the same event while supplying added ingredients. This is part of the "repetition and expansion" of Scripture. Such a literary style as we discussed in chapter four, supplies the much-needed space for explanation which would otherwise be overshadowed by the more spectacular.

In this chapter, John gives a glimpse of a major event which is discussed in more detail later. That major event is the Second Coming of Christ. Thus, this chapter can be considered as a "preview" of that great event. John mentions that the events of chapter ten occur at a later time (v.7). However, one wonders, why the preview?

We must note that chapter ten carries particulars not found in later accounts of the Second Coming. We must also keep in mind that the book of Revelation is the "book of the Revelation of Jesus Christ" (1:1). It should come as no surprise that this "revealing" is mentioned, or at least alluded to, more than just one or two times. In respect to that thought, this chapter adds "power to the punch" for the mind of the reader. It will greatly enhance the overall view and appreciation of the Second Coming.

Kinsman Redeemer

John does not yet give the picture of Christ as King of kings and Lord of lords in this chapter, but reveals the aspect of His role as Redeemer, our Kinsman Redeemer, as seen in chapter five. This chapter, then, is also a follow-up and preview of the fulfillment of chapter five.

Note: It may be beneficial to briefly glance over chapter five before continuing. This will aid in forming a mind-set for the next few chapters of the book.

The Mighty Angel

> And I saw another mighty angel come down from heaven, clothed with a cloud: and a rainbow was upon his head, and his face was as it were the sun, and his feet as pillars of fire: Rev. 10:1

This "Mighty Angel" can be none other than Jesus Christ himself. In the Old Testament, the Son of God is referred to as an angel of the Lord (Exodus 3:2-18). We know that whether in the Old Testament or New, Jesus is the visible manifestation of the invisible God (Col. 1:12-16). An Old Testament appearance of Christ, such as the "fourth man in the fire" (Dan. 3:25), is referred to as a Christophany.

Another reason to ascribe to Jesus the appellation of "Mighty Angel" is seen in chapter eleven. There the Mighty Angel calls the two witnesses "my two witnesses" (11:3). The word for "mighty" is *"ischuros"* meaning "forcible." This, too, reveals that this "Mighty Angel" is Christ, for He is the "Lion of the Tribe of Judah," mighty, powerful, forcible, the only one worthy to open the book (5:5). He speaks with a lion-like voice (10:3). The description given in verse one of chapter ten, corresponding with chapter one, also affirms Him to be Christ. All these evidences confer that this "Mighty Angel" is none other than Jesus Christ. In addition, common angels are never seen in Scripture with a rainbow, apart from God.

The Little Book Open

And he had in his hand a little book open: and he set his right foot upon the sea, and his left foot on the earth, Rev. 10:2

The "Mighty Angel" here has a little book opened in his hand. What is this little book?

Some suppose this "little book" to be the opened version of what Daniel was told to seal up (Revelation) until the "time of the end" (not the "end of time"), thus synchronizing with Daniel's seventieth week. However, for this to synchronize with the seventieth week suggests that it would remain a mystery until that time, that is, the time of the end, the Tribulation Period. If that be the case, we could not know of its contents today, because the book of Revelation would presently be sealed up and its knowledge concealed. That would contradict its very existence and message. In addition, the Tribulation Period does not begin until after the Church (born again believers) is "caught away."

The proper conclusion is that this "little book" is the "seven-sealed book," the title deed to the Earth (chpt. 5). It appears to John as "little" due to the bigger-than-life vision of the Mighty Angel, standing with one foot upon the sea and one foot upon the Earth. This stance indicates a larger view of Christ than normally portrayed. His feet were upon the Earth and upon the sea. The book thus appeared to John as small. Note that the book is now open, again a reference to the Second Coming of Christ. It denotes that the title deed is fully opened and fully ready for inspection concerning proper ownership of the Earth and dominion over it. It is the time of redeeming the Earth-dominion which Adam lost (chpt. 5).

The Seven Thunders

> And cried with a loud voice, as when a lion roareth: and when he had cried, seven thunders uttered their voices. And when the seven thunders had uttered their voices, I was about to write: and I heard a voice from heaven saying unto me, Seal up those things which the seven thunders uttered, and write them not. Rev. 10:3-4

When the Mighty Angel positions his feet upon the sea and upon the Earth he cries out with a loud, lion-like voice. With this tremendous kingly voice he gives a great announcement (discussed later). At that point, we find the seven thunders of Revelation. Although we do not know what the seven thunders uttered, for John was told to leave that out, the very mention of the seven thunders is not without significance.

The common thought of thunder is the sound which immediately follows a flash of lightning. To estimate the significance of thunder, we must review some events in which God used it.

God sent thunder and rain when Samuel called upon Him during the dry wheat harvest (I Sam. 12:17-18). The seventh plague upon Egypt revealed thunder and hail as Moses stretched his rod toward Heaven (Ex. 9:23-34). The Lord sent thunder when giving the law at Mount Sinai (Ex. 19:16; 20:18). David's victory over the Philistines was acknowledged by thunder (II Sam. 22:14-15). These few examples reveal that thunder is "a sound of confirmation exclaiming God's powerful and over-whelming presence." This is yet another reason for this revelation of Christ as the "Mighty Angel." The thunders are seven in number, again, the number of completeness.

Thus, the picture and presence of the Mighty Angel standing with one foot upon the land and the other upon the sea, along with his proclamation, is confirmed by the seven thunders. It is quite possible that their utterance has something to do with Christ's victory at the battle of Armageddon (discussed later). We will not know just what these thunders uttered until we hear them first-hand (at Christ's return when we appear with Him).

It is evident that immediately after the battle of Armageddon and subsequent victory, that Christ then stands upon the sea and upon the Earth. At that point, the complete and powerful Second Coming of Christ will be confirmed by the expression and presence of the seven thunders.

The Great Announcement

And the angel which I saw stand upon the sea and upon the earth lifted up his hand to heaven, And sware by him that liveth for ever and ever, who created heaven, and the things that therein are, and the earth, and the things that therein are, and the sea, and the things which are therein, that there should be time no longer: Rev. 10:5-6

It is here that the Mighty Angel, Christ, who is standing upon the sea and upon the Earth, lifts his hand to declare a most solemn truth. The great announcement is "that there should be time no longer."

This does not mean the "end of time" as some claim, but that "Time's Up, NO MORE DELAY!" We know that time will not end at that point because the 1,000-year Millennial Reign has not yet occurred. What this statement reveals is that the long awaited redemption of Earth-dominion has finally arrived. There is no more delay in redeeming the lost possession. The redemption of the Earth is fulfilled, as seen by His placing one foot upon the sea and one upon the Earth after the battle of Armageddon, and proclaiming, "Time's up (so to speak); I'm here to claim what is mine."

Confirmed By An Oath

The great announcement is confirmed by an oath. This is not the kind of oath or swear which binds one under penalty, for that is a forbidden practice (Matt. 5:34-37; James 5:12). It is the kind of oath of declaring or making a statement of fact with witness (as the seven thunders). An example of such an oath is found in Hebrews 6:13-14:

For when God made promise to Abraham, because he could swear by no greater, he sware by himself, Saying, Surely blessing I will bless thee, and multiplying I will multiply thee. Heb. 6:13-14

This is exactly what Christ does in verse six. Because He could swear by no greater, He swore by Himself. His statement is witnessed by John and the hosts of Heaven and confirmed by the seven thunders. He swore by Himself, for it is He who lives forever, and who created Heaven and Earth, and indeed, all things:

> Giving thanks unto the Father, which hath made us meet to be partakers of the inheritance of the saints in light: Who hath delivered us from the power of darkness, and hath translated us into the kingdom of his dear Son: In whom we have redemption through his blood, even the forgiveness of sins: Who is the image of the invisible God, the firstborn of every creature: For by him were all things created, that are in heaven, and that are in earth, visible and invisible, whether they be thrones, or dominions, or principalities, or powers: all things were created by him, and for him: And he is before all things, and by him all things consist. Col. 1:12-17

The Time of This Event

> But in the days of the voice of the seventh angel, when he shall begin to sound, the mystery of God should be finished, as he hath declared to his servants the prophets. Rev. 10:7

Here we find the time-frame of which the previous verses speak. It will be in the days of the voice (or sounding) of the seventh trumpet. It is a time when the mystery of God will be finished. This brings us back to the question at the beginning of the chapter, "Why the preview?"

In addition to the reasons given at the beginning of the chapter, this preview of the Second Coming is given that John's commission would not lose its significance amidst the grandeur of the Armageddon victory and glorious record of the Second Coming as seen in chapter nineteen. The "little book" aspect, seen separately, brings to mind the great significance of redeeming Earth-dominion back to Himself.

John's Commission

> And the voice which I heard from heaven spake unto me again, and said, Go and take the little book which is open in the hand of the angel which standeth upon the sea and upon the earth. And I went unto the angel, and said unto him, Give me the little book. And he said unto me, Take it, and eat it up; and it shall make thy belly bitter, but it shall be in thy mouth sweet as honey. And I took the little book out of the angel's hand, and ate it up; and it was in my mouth sweet as honey: and as soon as I had eaten it, my belly was bitter. And he said unto me, Thou must prophesy again before many peoples, and nations, and tongues, and kings. Rev. 10: 8-11

In order for John to receive and recant the events of the Tribulation Period, and also the particulars of Earth ownership, he would first have to consume and digest the contents of the "Little Book." He could "eat the book" for it is in vision that he does so. He could do so at this point due to its fulfilled usage (in the vision). To "eat a book" was a metaphor for consuming the contents of a given document.

In this vision, John recalls the taste of the book and the effects of it in his stomach. It was in his mouth as sweet as honey. This speaks of the glorious Second Coming of Christ and the glorious things which await the Christian. How wonderful it shall be! However, in his stomach it was sickening. This speaks of the bitterness which must come before the glories can appear. As with the present gospel message, the message was both sweet and bitter. The present message is sweet in that a way has been made by which man may enter Heaven. The bitter side of that story is that many will reject that way and reap everlasting punishment.

John is then commissioned to prophesy and carry witness of the Revelation of Jesus Christ before many peoples, nations, tongues and kings. We continue to have that witness today through God's Word. We have seen earlier how God's Word is incomplete without the Revelation witness, and how that inspired Scripture is verified by its presence. Praise God for His Word!

> I will worship toward thy holy temple, and praise thy name for thy lovingkindness and for thy truth: for thou hast magnified thy word above all thy name. Psa. 138:2

Ω

The
Two Witnesses
And
The Third Woe
Chapter 11

As the pieces of the puzzle begin to come together, we see more and more of the final picture, the Revelation of Jesus Christ.

Note that chapter eleven continues the parenthesis that began in chapter ten. Although the events mentioned in this chapter are found recorded between the sixth and seventh trumpets, they are not limited to that time-frame. The time-frame for the events recorded in this chapter, with the exception of verses fifteen through nineteen, is stated as 1260 days, or 42 months or three and one-half years. These all refer to the same period, the last half of the Tribulation Period. Also in this chapter we find the end of the second woe (v.14), which began in chapter nine (v.13).

Chapter eleven supplies us with another preview of the Second Coming. Verse fifteen records the sounding of the seventh trumpet. Again, such repeated references to the glorious return of our Lord should not surprise us, because, after all, we are studying the "Revelation of Jesus Christ."

The Second Coming is mentioned repeatedly as stated earlier, so that various occurrences may be added to this magnificent event (19:11). John was inspired by the Holy Spirit to write in this fashion to broaden our understanding and to amplify the promised blessing of the Second Coming. Such blessing is promised to the reader and the hearer (1:3).

Measuring The Temple

And there was given me a reed like unto a rod: and the angel stood, saying, Rise, and measure the temple of God, and the altar, and them that worship therein. But the court which is without the temple leave out, and measure it not; for it is given unto the Gentiles: and the holy city shall they tread under foot forty and two months. Rev. 11:1-2

Chapter ten ended with the "Mighty Angel," handing the little book to John for him to consume. Chapter eleven continues that scene. However, it begins with the Mighty Angel giving John a reed to measure the temple, the altar, and the temple worshippers. To measure a temple or an altar seems natural, but how does one measure temple worshippers?

Reed Like Unto A Rod

Although John was given a reed to measure the temple, the altar, and the worshippers, no measurements are recorded. This, along with measuring worshippers, would seem odd at first glance. The reason for this is found in the reed that is like unto a rod (v.1).

The reed is a unit of measure equal to six cubits. A cubit is about 45 centimeters (18 inches). A long-cubit, as used in Ezekiel 40, is approximately 22 inches. It is evident that the measuring of the temple is for more than just dimension and size. This is realized because the reed and the rod are interchangeable references as far as measurement is concerned (Ez. 29:6). In light of this, we must consider the rod and why this reed is likened unto it.

Obviously, the rod of which John speaks is that beyond a measurement or beyond such an instrument for measuring. The rod is also a staff, pole or stick. It was used in Old and New Testament times as a weapon (Ex. 21:20; I Sam. 14:27; Psa. 23:4) and as an instrument of punishment (II Sam. 7:14; I Cor 4:21). In addition, it was a symbol of authority such as a scepter, like that of Moses' rod (Ex. 4:20) and Aaron's rod (Num. 17:2-10). It was also used as a tool to thresh grain (Isa. 28:27).

John's reed like unto a rod refers to the "rod of the Lord's chastening" as seen in a combination of uses mentioned above. This "rod of chastening" is directed at the temple and its use. Examples of such chastening is seen in II Sam. 7:14, Psa. 2:9 and Isa. 11:4. Thus, the measurements are not given that a temple may be built, but rather for the destruction of one which already exists (Tribulation temple - discussed later). Thus, this reed like unto a rod gives reference to both measurement and chastisement.

Worshippers Found Wanting

The temple, the altar, and the worshippers will be measured in the same manner, as Belshazzar's kingdom was weighed in the balances (Dan. 5:22-31). Belshazzar, at a great feast, was polluting the holy vessels of the Lord, when the handwriting upon the wall spelled out his doom.

Belshazzar and his kingdom had been weighed in the balance and found wanting. This resulted in the defeat and takeover of the kingdom by the Medes and the Persians. Likewise, the temple, the altar, and the worshippers will come under the chastening rod of the Lord. They are measured and found wanting (lacking). This results in the taking over and the destruction of the temple.

It is obvious that these verses (11:1-2) are recorded to prove that a temple will be built at Jerusalem during the Tribulation Period. It also verifies that there will be sacrifices offered during that time (seen in the altar). The temple, or "holy place," is that of which Jesus prophesied and that of which the apostle Paul spoke (Matt. 24:15; II Thess. 2:4). It is in this temple that the Antichrist will set himself up before the world and claim that he is God (II Thess. 2:4). This contamination of the temple is the abomination of desolation revealed by Christ and the prophet Daniel (Matt. 24:15; Dan. 9:27;11:31).

At that time, the Antichrist will cause sacrifices to cease.

...and in the midst of the week he shall cause the sacrifice and the oblation to cease, and for the overspreading of abominations he shall make it desolate,... (Dan.9:27).

We know this temple is not Herod's temple, for it had been destroyed some 25 years before John's revelation. It must then refer to a future temple to be built at Jerusalem, during or just prior to the Tribulation Period.

It is not the temple of the Millennial Reign as described by Ezekiel (Ez. 4:1; 42:20), for that temple will be built at Shiloh, the place of the tabernacle's first permanent home (Ez. 48:8,21). Again, evidence reveals that

CORNERSTONE LAID 10-28-00?

John speaks of a temple that will be built for the Tribulation Period.

The building and occupancy of the temple will no doubt be short-lived. In all probability, it will be completely destroyed during the great earthquake just before or in conjunction with the sounding of the seventh trumpet (11:13,19). At that time, one tenth of the city of Jerusalem will be destroyed and some 7,000 persons killed.

Do Not Measure The Court

The temple, the altar, and the worshippers —not the court— are to be measured. John is instructed to leave the Court of the Gentiles out. It is not measured because it will already be in the possession of the Gentiles. It is their court. This designated court is considered profane by the Jews. However, everything concerning the temple pertaining to the Jew's sacrificial worship, including themselves, shall pass under the rod of chastening. They are the ones who had dismissed Jesus as the ultimate sacrifice at His First Coming. The Gentiles, in part, will be the chastening rod working on behalf of the Lord, although unknowingly. They do so in much the same manner as Nebuchadnezzar was the chastening rod against Egypt (Ez. 30:25-26).

Forty Two Months

John informs us that the temple and the holy city will be trodden down by the Gentiles for 42 months, or three and one-half years (11:2; Lu. 21:24). This refers to the last half of the Tribulation Period. This is after the Antichrist breaks his covenant with the Jews. Part of the covenant will undoubtedly be to rebuild the temple (Dan. 9:27). It is possible, as mentioned earlier, that a suspension of the mark of the beast, on behalf of the nation, will also be part of the covenant. At mid-trib, the Antichrist will break his covenant and then begin a great onslaught against the Jews (Matt. 24:15-22). As mentioned earlier, it will be another holocaust. Hitler's attack was only the birth pains for the formation of the nation (Isa. 66:8 in type). Likewise, the holocaust of the Tribulation Period will be the birth pains for the Jew's national resurrection for the coming kingdom, the kingdom of the Millennial Reign (Isa. 66:8).

The temple and the city will be given to the Gentiles for the last three and one-half years of the Tribulation Period. This "trodding down by the Gentiles" will last until the battle of Armageddon, that is, until the "times of the Gentiles" is fulfilled (Lu. 21:24).

When ye therefore shall see the abomination of desolation, spoken of by Daniel the prophet, stand in the holy place, (whoso readeth, let him understand:) Then let them which be in Judaea flee into the mountains: Let him which is on the housetop not come down to take any thing out of his house: Neither let him which is in the field return back to take his clothes. And woe unto them that are with child, and to them that give suck in those days! But pray ye that your flight be not in the winter, neither on the sabbath day: For then shall be great tribulation, such as was not since the beginning of the world to this time, no, nor ever shall be. And except those days should be shortened, there should no flesh be saved: but for the elect's sake those days shall be shortened. Matt. 24: 15-22.

Note of interest. Eight temples are mentioned in Scripture. They are:

1. The "first sanctuary" for the purpose of God to dwell among the people (Ex. 25:8).

2. The temple referred to as "Solomon's temple," the first temple of stone, built some 500 years after the Exodus. It was the dwelling for the "name" of the Lord (II Chron. 6:9; 7:1).

3. The temple called "Zerubbabel's temple," which, history tells us, was desecrated. The abominable practice of sacrificing swine was performed on its altar. It was also dedicated to Jupiter by Antiochus Epiphanes in BC 168-170.

4. The temple referred to as "Herod's temple," the one rebuilt under the jurisdiction of the Roman occupation to which Jesus came. It was destroyed in AD 70 by Titus.

5. The "spiritual temple" (I Peter 2:4-5), which neither was Herod's temple, nor made of stone. It is the spiritual temple of the Church (Born-Again Believers In Christ).

6. The "false temple" of the Tribulation Period (II Thess. 2:4; Rev. 11:2).

7. The "temple of the Millennium" (Acts 15:16; Ez. 40-43).

8. The "temple of the new Heaven and the new Earth." No temple is to be built there, but "the Lord God

Almighty and the Lamb are the temple of it" (Rev. 21:22). Eight is the number of the "new order of things."

My Two Witnesses

And I will give power unto my two witnesses, and they shall prophesy a thousand two hundred and threescore days, clothed in sackcloth. These are the two olive trees, and the two candlesticks standing before the God of the earth. Rev. 11:3-4

The identity of these two witnesses has formed some what of a controversy among students of Bible prophecy. Some contend that the two witnesses are Elijah and Enoch, while others believe them to be Elijah and Moses. However, some believe that the witnesses are not individuals, but are two covenants, two dispensations, or two denominations of witnesses.

Covenants, dispensations, or religious bodies, as we shall see, do not fit the description or purpose of the witnesses. These two witnesses are most definitely two men. They are "my two witnesses" (Christ's) and will be given power by Christ (11:3) to witness for 1260 days or three and one-half years, the last half of the Tribulation Period. They appear just prior to this last half of the Tribulation Period (Mal. 4:5). These witnesses are covered in sackcloth, a rough, bag-like garment which represents both mourning and repentance. Upon finishing their testimony, they are to be killed. Three and one-half days later they are to be resurrected. Although not specifically stated in Scripture, Elijah, Enoch, and Moses are the most likely candidates for several reasons.

First, they are referred to as the two olive trees, and

the two candlesticks which are standing before the God of the Earth.

Olive Trees & Candlesticks

The olive tree and the candlestick refer to the prophecy of Zechariah. In chapter four, Zechariah saw a vision of a golden candlestick. It had a bowl upon the top of it, seven lamps on it and seven pipes attached to the seven lamps. Upon the right and left side were two olive trees. Zechariah asked the angel of their identity (Zech. 4:11). The angel replied, These are the two anointed ones, that "stand by the Lord of the whole earth" (Zech.4:14) This is the same thing said of the two witnesses of Revelation (v.4).

The angel thus identified the olive trees and the candlesticks as two anointed ones. This implies individuality, for they are two "ones." Thus, the two olive trees and the two candlesticks represent two personages, not two systems or thoughts. They both carry the characteristics of the olive tree and the candlestick.

Olive Trees

The two witnesses are referred to as olive trees due to the fruit they bear during the time of their witness. The olive tree is a slow-growing tree which reaches a great age and bears fruit until it dies. Before dying, however, new branches sprout from its roots. Likewise, the two witnesses are to be killed. Thus, the olive tree typifies the death of the witnesses and the results of their witnessing; that is, they sprout new converts.

The olive tree fruit was harvested by beating the boughs of the tree with a stick (Deut. 24:20), or by shaking the tree (Isa. 17:6). The beating of the boughs typifies the killing of the Jews, the Tribulation holocaust. The most famous olive garden mentioned in Scripture is Gethsemane, where Christ prayed (Matt. 26:36). Gethsemane means "oil press."

The green olive fruit produced the best oil. It was used as fuel for lamps (Ex. 27:20), for anointing (Lev. 2:1), for dressing wounds (Lu.10:34), and for trade (I Kings 5:11).

Oil in Scripture is also used as a type or representative of the Holy Spirit. Thus, the two witnesses give their testimony and bear fruit under the power and authority of the Holy Spirit, the third personage of the three-fold nature of God. Verse three (chpt. 11) testifies to their God-given power.

Candlesticks

During our present age, there are seven candlesticks. These are the seven churches (1:20) and seven church ages. They are the present witnesses to and for Christ. Among those seven churches and ages, as seen in chapters two and three, are elements which typify all Christian denominations in the seven candlesticks. However during the Tribulation Period, there will be only two candlesticks (witnesses). They are not two churches, two systems of thought or two dispensations, but only two individuals. Their witness works in connection with, but is apart from, the witness of the 144,000 witnesses of chapter seven (discussed later).

Length Of Their Prophecy

The length of their prophecy is a thousand, two hundred and threescore days, that is, 1260 days. This is the same length of time that the temple will be trodden down of the Gentiles. The Gentiles will lay claim to the city 42 months, that is, three and one-half years. During the trodding down of the holy city, the two witnesses shall prophesy.

These two witnesses are very important people concerning Jewish heritage, else their message would be discarded and their appearance menial. This brings us to the personal identity of the two witnesses. It will be necessary to first look into their personal qualifications.

The Power Of The Witnesses

And if any man will hurt them, fire proceedeth out of their mouth, and devoureth their enemies: and if any man will hurt them, he must in this manner be killed. These have power to shut heaven, that it rain not in the days of their prophecy: and have power over waters to turn them to blood, and to smite the earth with all plagues, as often as they will. Rev. 11:5-6

Until these two witnesses have finished their testimony, no harm can befall them. Those who attempt to rid the Earth of these two super-witnesses will be killed by fire which proceeds from their mouth. Fire is many times used as a symbol of the power and judgment of God. This power over the life of their enemies may be literal fire or symbolic fire as that spoken by Peter to Annanias and Saphira (Acts 5:5,9,10). Peter spoke to them and they died. The power, or fire of his words, caused their deaths. Most likely this fire (v.5) refers to the fiery words of their preaching.

In addition to the spoken Word, the witnesses will possess two very notable qualities:

1. The ability to shut heaven so that it doesn't rain during the days of their testimony, as Elijah had (I Kings 17:1; Lu. 4:25; James 5:17).

2. The ability to control the waters by turning them to blood and smiting the Earth with all plagues as often as they will, as Moses had (Ex. 7:14-12:30).

Elijah

In order to fulfill Malachi (chpts. 3-4), Elijah must return and be one of the witnesses.

> Behold, I will send you Elijah the prophet before the coming of the great and dreadful day of the LORD: Mal. 4:5

Elijah did not see death that he might come back before the great and dreadful day of the Lord, that is, immediately prior to the last half of the Tribulation Period. This great and dreadful day is the Great Tribulation. Elijah did not see death for he was taken up in a whirlwind (II Kings 2:1).

Was John The Baptist Elijah?

Many say that John the Baptist was the returned Elijah. The attributes of Elijah, however, were not fulfilled in John the Baptist. Concerning John, Jesus told the multitudes that if they would receive John and his message of the kingdom, that "this is Elijah" ("Elias" - Matt. 11:14). Jesus then says, "he who hath ears to hear, let him hear."

Looking back, we know that the Jews received the message of Christ and His kingdom in their minds, but not in their hearts. They tried to make ritualistic Old

Testament Jews out of every new Christian. Neither did they receive Christ as God in the flesh. Thus, they did not receive the proper message. John was not Elijah in person, but had come in the "spirit and power" of Elijah (Lu. 1:17).

Malachi 3:1 refers to both Elijah and John due to John's message, but that verse only. The rest of Malachi concerns the mission of Elijah. The reference would have also applied to John and his message if the people had accepted it, but they didn't. Elijah must, and will, come back in his own person.

John himself said he was not Elijah:

> And they asked him, What then? Art thou Elias? And he saith, I am not. Art thou that prophet? And he answered, No. Then said they unto him, Who art thou? that we may give an answer to them that sent us. What sayest thou of thyself? He said, I am the voice of one crying in the wilderness, Make straight the way of the Lord, as said the prophet Esaias. John 1:21-23

Test By Fire

Elijah, upon Mt. Carmel, strove with the prophets of Baal through a test by fire. The Lord prevailed through him (I Kings 18:21-40). It appears that during the Tribulation Period such a test of fire will occur between Elijah and the false prophet. The false prophet will be able to do what the prophets of Baal could not do: cause fire to fall from Heaven (13:13).

The false prophet will be head of religious Babylon, the Jezebel religion. This was discussed in chapters two and three and will be reviewed again in chapter thirteen. He will rise to exceeding political and religious power during the Tribulation Period (both systems will become intermingled).

Consider Enoch

It is quite evident that Elijah will be one of the two witnesses. Now we will examine whether it is Enoch or Moses who will witness alongside him.

The first credible evidence for the other witness being Enoch is that he "walked with God and was not; for God took him" as was the case with Elijah (Gen 5:21-24; Heb. 11:5; I Kings 2:11). That is, he did not die, as Elijah did not die, but he was translated. The Bible says that it is appointed unto men once to die and after this the judgment (Heb. 9:27). Argument is that Elijah and Enoch must both return to die in order for the fulfillment of their appointed deaths. Enoch and Elijah are the only two persons recorded in Scripture who were translated and escaped death.

Also, as Elijah was a prophet of judgment, Enoch was a prophet of judgment (Jude 14). It appears that God must have had a greater purpose in mind for Enoch. It could be, however, that the testimony of Enoch's holy life and glorious exit is sufficient witness for us in that holiness is possible in Christ and that we will one day be translated. If Enoch is not to be the other witness, then he fades into history as such a witness and no more.

The enigma of Enoch is quickly laid to rest in Hebrews 11:5. Taking the verse at face value and believing that God made exception to Enoch's appointment of death, we read:

> By faith Enoch was translated that he should not see death; and was not found, because God had translated him: for before his translation he had this testimony, that he pleased God. Heb. 11:5

To read this verse at face value would mean that Enoch should not see death at all. This is possible, for all things are possible with God (Lu. 18:27).

Enoch is not a great person concerning heritage or history for the Jews, except lineage. He is though, a great testimony to the fact that one may walk with God, enjoy close communion with Him, and be separated from the world. His witness is one of progress resulting in a glorious end. No great miracles are attributed to him on behalf of the nation, the law, or prophetically, for there is only historic reference concerning him. Enoch, however, does represent the translated saints at the Rapture of the Church.

The evidence above gives credence to Moses as being the witness alongside Elijah. Let's first examine the evidence against Moses.

Evidence Against Moses

The strongest evidence against Moses as being the other witness is that no passage in Scripture refers directly to the resurrection of Moses. In addition, many believe that upon the Mount of Transfiguration (Matt. 17:3) Moses possessed a glorified body. If Moses is to be resurrected for the Tribulation Period and presently possesses a glorified body, that poses a problem. Could Moses reappear and die in a glorified body? Could Moses become mortal again?

We know a body can die, be resurrected, and die again. This is seen in Lazarus (Jn. 11:1-44), the young man in the coffin (Lu. 7:14), and the many who resurrected when Jesus arose (Matt. 27:52-53). But what about a glorified body? The answer is no. Although Elijah was seen alongside Moses on the Mount of Transfiguration, he had not died, but was translated, could he have already received his glorified body? The answer again is no. The enigma is solved in that Moses and Elijah were visualized in their spirit bodies and not their glorified bodies. In the account on the Mount of Transfiguration, it was Jesus, not Moses or Elijah who appeared glorified. This is possible because Christ is fully God and fully man.

We know that Moses died; however, no Scriptural grounds suggest that Moses, as Lazarus and others, cannot die again.

In Deuteronomy 34:5-8 we find that Moses' death was not a normal one, nor was his burial. Moses was 120 years old when he died, but he did not die due to physical impairments or impurities. His eye was not dim, nor was his natural force abated (v.7). His death was a result of the direct will of God. His burial was also unnatural: God buried him (v.6).

The devil fought for the body of Moses, evidently because the devil knew that God had another purpose for Moses. This is evident because Michael, the arch-angel, contended with the devil for the body of Moses (Jude 9). God must have taken Moses at that point for a special purpose, for if He hadn't, Michael would have to stand guard over his body continually.

Moses Chosen

The evidence for the other witness being Moses is that he had power over plagues, as seen in the Exodus account (Ex. 7:14-12:30), and that he is also seen alongside Elijah on the Mount of Transfiguration (Matt. 17:3). He is also mentioned in Malachi 4:4 concerning the law, the statutes, and judgments upon Israel. This mention is immediately followed by that of Elijah's return (Mal. 4:4). We see Moses as representing the Law and Elijah as representing the prophets. In addition, Moses fasted 40 days and 40 nights (Ex. 34:28) as did Elijah (I Kings 19:8) and Jesus (Matt. 4:2). These evidences are the foundation stones for the belief that Moses is the other witness. Moses is also an important figure in Jewish heritage and is always connected with the Law. In addition, the time-frame suggests that Moses, figuratively speaking, will be the one who once again brings the children of Israel (144,000 and respondents) to stand against Pharaoh (Antichrist and the one-world government).

With the disappearance of the Church prior to the Tribulation Period, it is not until approximately three and one-half years later that we have another appearance of Moses and Elijah. These two witnesses appear just before the wounding and supposed healing of the Antichrist and his claim to be God. Their witness will be a springboard for the urgency of the message of the 144,000 witnesses of chapter seven and the respondents (who are being killed). After all, Moses and Elijah are two very prominent figures in Israel's history. Some believe that it was Elijah and Moses at the tomb of Jesus (Lu. 24:4-7), and at the ascension of Christ (Acts 1:11); however, there is no solid basis for that belief.

Elijah And Moses Killed

And when they shall have finished their testimony, the beast that ascendeth out of the bottomless pit shall make war against them, and shall overcome them, and kill them. Rev. 11:7

Elijah and his counterpart witness, Moses, will escape the false prophet, but not the entire Jezebel system. Elijah and Moses will be killed. However, this fate does not come upon them until they have finished their testimony, that is, until near the end of the Tribulation Period, for they are to witness for three and one-half years. Their bodies will lay in the streets for three and one half days, after which, they will be resurrected (vs.11,12). Their deaths will come by the strong arm of the Jezebel system and false prophet's cohort, that is, the beast from the bottomless pit.

Beast From The Bottomless Pit

This beast is the same entity as found in chapter nine (v.11), yet, in essence, separate from the Antichrist and his government. However, this statement is not conclusive. In chapter nine we found him to be the king or angel of the bottomless pit. He was seen as *Abaddon, Apollyon*, the destroying angel who is the demonic locust king. Here we find he is the beast as well as the angel or locust king. This is due to his possession of the Antichrist (beast). Note that the separate entities of locust king, Antichrist and beast later become one and are collectively called a beast (18:8). According to the time-frame (as seen earlier), the Antichrist will become possessed by the locust king and take on his characteristics. That is, the Antichrist will take on the characteristics as those from the very abyss of Hell, Tartaros Hell, the "bottomless pit." This could only be possible if some being were to be loosed from the bottomless pit. In retrospect, we have seen in chapter nine the loosing of the locust king from the bottomless pit at the first woe. This works in conjunction with the middle of the Tribulation Period, at which time the Antichrist will take on his most beastly character and demand worship. He will set himself up as God in the temple (II Thess. 2:4).

We must remember that great demonic activity will be prevalent during the Tribulation Period. The Antichrist will, in all probability, be involved with the New-Age (old-age) movement which involves opening oneself up to the spirit world through various avenues, especially the spirit of ecumenism. The ecumenical spirit of the Antichrist will be enhanced upon being possessed by the demonic locust king, thus making him the equivalent of Satan's son. This, of course, makes him the opposite and anti-type of Christ, or Antichrist. (See chart, pg. 486)

The possessed Antichrist (beast) will support the false religious system of chapter seventeen (v.7). Thus, the one-world political system (also a beast) which is cohort with the Jezebel religion (Mother of Harlots, 18:5) will make war against the two witnesses, overcome them, and kill them. Note that they are killed near the end of the Great Tribulation.

Killed In Sodom And Egypt

And their dead bodies shall lie in the street of the great city, which spiritually is called Sodom and Egypt, where also our Lord was crucified. And they of the people and kindreds and tongues and nations shall see their dead bodies three days and an half, and shall not suffer their dead bodies to be put in graves. And they that dwell upon the earth shall rejoice over them, and make merry, and shall send gifts one to another; because these two prophets tormented them that dwelt on the earth. Rev. 11:8-10

We have seen how Moses and Elijah will be killed by the one-world political and religious system. They are evidently testifying, preaching, and greatly influencing the kingdom movement in the streets of Jerusalem. Why is Jerusalem referred to here as Sodom and Egypt?

Notice that the place where their dead bodies lay in the street is not the literal Sodom or the literal Egypt, but a spiritual Sodom and Egypt. It is the place where our Lord was crucified, which unmistakably speaks of Jerusalem. It is spiritually and prophetically called Sodom due to the resemblance of the inhabitant's character being that of Sodom in the days of Lot. This refers specifically to sodomy, unnatural sexual intercourse. The English word "sodomy" comes from Sodom (Gen. 19:5). Sodomy was prohibited by law (Deut. 23:17) and condemned by God through the writings of Paul (Rom. 1:27; I Cor. 6:9).

Jerusalem is spiritually and prophetically called Egypt because of the conduct of Israel while in Egypt (Ez. 23:3-4,8,19). It was in Egypt that Israel was first initiated as a nation into the worship of false gods. Remember the golden calf at the foot of Mt. Sinai? Jerusalem, at the time of the Tribulation Period, will be a harbor for false religion, especially for that of the false prophet and counterpart heresies. (See chapter two, "Ephesus - In the Background," concerning false gods and goddesses")

Verse eight also confirms that the two witnesses cannot be two covenants, dispensations, or denominations, for they would be completely out of character concerning the death and resurrection.

Mocked By The World

Instead of receiving a proper burial, the two witnesses' bodies are left lying in the street for three and one-half days (v.9). It is evident that a great boasting of the political system will occur. This will give rise to the promotion of the event as a holiday. The "people of the world" will see the down-trodding of the witnesses and rejoice over their death (this viewing and quick response is even now possible due to television and computer media). They will make merry and shall send gifts to one another because of the death of their tormentors. It is evident that truth will be the source of the world's torment.

Their Resurrection

And after three days and an half the Spirit of life from God entered into them, and they stood upon their feet; and great fear fell upon them which saw them. And they heard a great voice from heaven saying unto them, Come up hither. And they ascended up to heaven in a cloud; and their enemies beheld them. And the same hour was there a great earthquake, and the tenth part of the city fell, and in the earthquake were slain of men seven thousand: and the remnant were affrighted, and gave glory to the God of heaven. Rev. 11:11-13

After three and one-half days God will breathe life into these witnesses and they will stand upon their feet, striking great fear into the hearts of all who witness this great miracle. Their enemies stand in amazement as the two ascend into Heaven. Here we find the same statement which John heard at the beginning of chapter four, "Come up hither."

In that same hour is a great earthquake. One-tenth of the city of Jerusalem will fall and 7000 men will perish.

This great earthquake undoubtedly is the same earthquake that occurs with the sounding of the seventh trumpet.

Even without acknowledging the existence of God or repenting, God is glorified because His power is acknowledged. This glorification will be in much the same fashion as the atheist glorifies God. The atheist's statements of denial only build a stronger case for God's existence.

Their Message

Elijah and Moses evidently give great assurance to God's chosen people during the time of their dispersion and persecution. They are a great influence for the proclaiming and receiving of the message of the coming kingdom age, the kingdom of the Millennium Reign (20:2). To the government, they are extremists.

Elijah returns for the purpose of turning the heart of the children of their fathers (Mal. 4:5,6), that is, to teach them about the mistakes of their fathers and bring them to repentance. Moses will stand as representative of the Law, to which they cling, even today. God is not bringing Israel to Himself for their goodness, as seen earlier, but because He has given his word. It is for His name's sake (Ez. 20:44; 36:22).

> The second woe is past; and behold the third woe cometh quickly. Rev. 11:14

Woe No. 3: Seventh Trumpet

In chapter nine we witnessed the first woe at the sounding of the fifth trumpet. Chapter nine (v.13) began woe number two. Not until chapter eleven (v.15) do we find the beginning of woe number three. It is the seventh trumpet.

And the seventh angel sounded; and there were great voices in heaven, saying, The kingdoms of this world are become the kingdoms of our Lord, and of his Christ; and he shall reign for ever and ever. And the four and twenty elders, which sat before God on their seats, fell upon their faces, and worshipped God, Saying, We give thee thanks, O Lord God Almighty, which art, and wast, and art to come; because thou hast taken to thee thy great power, and hast reigned. Rev. 11:15-17

At the sounding of the seventh trumpet, there were great voices in Heaven. These voices clue us in on the events of the seventh trumpet. Seven, as we have seen, is the number of completeness. Here, once again, we have a preview of the Second Coming of Christ. The voices proclaim that the kingdoms of this world are become (as in "now have become") the kingdoms of our Lord and of His Christ. This denotes the redemption of Earth dominion back to Himself, as discussed in chapter five (of the title deed), and in chapter ten (title deed opened). This trumpet judgment also refers to the time when Christ says "no more delay." We have seen this in chapter ten (v.6). It was mentioned there that the time of that statement would be in the days of the sounding of the seventh trumpet (10:6-7). Well, here we are.

And sware by him that liveth for ever and ever, who created heaven, and the things that therein are, and the earth, and the things that therein are, and the sea, and the things which are therein, that there should be time no longer: But in the days of the voice of the seventh angel, when he shall begin to sound, the mystery of God should be finished, as he hath declared to his servants the prophets. Rev. 10:6-7

The sounding of the seventh trumpet brings the finishing of the mystery of God. Here in chapter eleven the finished acts of the Revelation of Christ begin to unfold. The next few chapters, that is, twelve through eighteen, give details of things already discussed. They also provide additional bits of information concerning the events of the Tribulation Period.

Proclamation Of Complete Messiahship

The phrase "and of his Christ" (v.15) refers to the position of Jesus. The appellation "Christ" means "the anointed, the Messiah." Thus, Jesus our Lord claims total ownership and complete Messiahship upon His return. This is also seen in that He has taken unto Himself "thy great power" (v.17).

Upon the proclamation by the voices announcing the return of Christ, the twenty-four elders fall upon their faces and worship God.

The Judgment Of Nations

And the nations were angry, and thy wrath is come, and the time of the dead, that they should be judged, and that thou shouldest give reward unto thy servants the prophets, and to the saints, and them that fear thy name, small and great; and shouldest destroy them which should destroy the earth. Rev. 11:18

At first glance one would conclude that this verse refers to the Great White Throne Judgment. However, compiled Scripture relates to us that there will be a judgment of nations immediately after the return of our Lord and prior to the setting up of the kingdom age (Millennium Kingdom).

During the Tribulation Period, there will be those nations which will help the Jews during their time of fleeing from the wrath of the Antichrist. These nations will be judged favorably. They will have the distinct privilege of going into the Millennial Reign to follow. They will enjoy the blessings of that time. However, those nations who are against the Jews and do not help them during the Tribulation will be judged unfavorably. They will be turned into Hell, as we see in Matthew 25:31-46.

General Judgment?

Some believe that Matthew 25:31-46 refers to a general judgment where both saved and lost of the church age stand before God. Those saved persons go into Heaven, whereas the lost or unsaved are cast into Hell. The saved, they say, are referred to as the sheep, and the lost as the goats. Nothing could be further from the truth.

We know that the Judgment Seat of Christ is for the saved who are taken at the "catching away" of the Church, which occurs before the Tribulation Period. Immediately after the "catching away" (Rapture), or in conjuction with it, we will pass through that judgment. We are judged at that time not to see whether we are saved or lost, but for reward or loss of reward (I Cor. 3:11-17). Only the saved will be present and stand at that judgment, given by a loving, compassionate Savior, Christ. This reveals the compassionate role of the second part of the three-fold nature of God. (Chapter nineteen of this book, "Marriage Supper Of The Lamb" and "Judgment Seat of Christ Explained." Also see author's book, "Call To Order.").

As seen earlier, the lost (the dead without Christ) shall stand before God at the Great White Throne Judgment (Rev. 20:11-15). This will be the God of judgment, the first part of the three-fold nature of God. The Great White

Throne Judgment follows the Millennial Reign (Rev. 20).
Note that the judgment of nations occurs immediately
after the Tribulation Period and before the Millennial
Reign.

Matthew 25:31-46 does not pertain to the Church
other than in figurative or spiritual interpretation concerning the acts of kindness toward others. The literal interpretation concerns the judgment of nations. Those nations
who helped "my brethren" (Jews - Matt. 25:40) are
referred to as sheep and those who do not help "my
brethren" are referred to as goats. Those sheep-nations on
the right hand of the King (the side of favor) will hear
King Jesus say "Come, ye blessed of my Father, inherit
the kingdom" (Millennial kingdom). Those goat-nations
on the left hand of the King (side of disfavor) are told,
"Depart from me, ye cursed, into everlasting fire."

It must be noted that these nations are made up of individuals. Some individuals of a particular nation may help
the Jews, while others do not. Those who help are to be
favored. However, this does not alter the distinctive nature
of this judgment. The word for nations, as used in this passage, is *"ethnos,"* meaning "race, tribe, or nation." In
chapter one, we discussed the order of events, particularly the Rapture of the Church. There we saw the outline of
major events typified in the leprous house. The judgment
of nations is pictured there in the removing of stones and
the replacing of stones (Chpt. 1 and Lev.14:33-46).

In light of the above information, let's review verse
eighteen once more (parenthesis are for explanation):

And the nations (of Trib.) were angry, and thy wrath is come, and
the time of the dead (spiritually dead races, tribes or nations), that

they should be judged (judgment of nations), and that thou shouldest give reward unto thy servants the prophets (Elijah & Moses), and to the saints (144,000), and them that fear thy name (respondents), small and great; and shouldest destroy them which should destroy the earth (antichrist systems). Rev. 11:18

Temple Opened In Heaven

And the temple of God was opened in heaven, and there was seen in his temple the ark of his testament: and there were lightnings, and voices, and thunderings, and an earthquake, and great hail. Rev. 11:19

Several mentions of this temple are found in Revelation. It is the same temple which is seen open in chapter fifteen (v.5). It is filled with the smoke of God's glory (15:8). The angels are seen coming out from this temple having the bowl or vial judgments (15:6; 16:1). There is also a great voice from this temple proclaiming, "It is done" (16:17). It is the heavenly dwelling of God, the third heaven, the one which the apostles Paul and John were caught up into (II Cor. 12:1-6; Rev. 4:1). It is the place from where John views the events of the Tribulation Period. It is the dwelling place of God in Heaven.

Ark Of God's Testament

Seen in God's temple was the ark of his testament. This ark is also referred to as the ark of the covenant. It is not the ark which the children of Israel built under Moses, but the one which was the pattern for Moses' ark. Its appearance will no doubt hold great significance for the Israelites at the appearing of Christ. They will know and realize the significance due to the ark built by their forefathers under Moses (Ex. 25:10). The appearance will bring to remembrance the particulars of that ark, including the mercy seat (Ex. 25:17-22), the two stone tablets containing the ten commandments (Ex. 25:16-21), the golden pot of manna (Ex. 16:32-34), and Aaron's rod that budded (Num. 17:1-11). These all have symbolic significance.

The mercy seat was the golden lid or covering on the ark of the covenant. It was regarded as the resting place of God (Ex. 25:17-22; I Chron. 28:11; Heb. 9:5). The ark itself marked the place where the Lord dwelled, particularly the sanctuary where the ark rested. It was also the place where the Lord communicated with Moses. (The appearance of the mercy seat, as well as the stone tablets, supplies additional evidence to Moses as being Elijah's companion.) The stone tablets are considered to be the basis of the covenant between God and His chosen people. The golden pot of manna is a testimony of God's provision. The golden pot reveals the precious care of God, even for those in rebellion. The rod of Aaron, in that it budded, reveals that they are perpetually God's people. The rod itself reveals not only His chastening, but also His staff of protection.

Power And Authority Of God

The lightnings, voices, thunderings, earthquake and hail are reference check-points. Although these five phenomena are mentioned several times throughout Revelation, only three times are all five used together or very closely related. Their first mention as such is found in chapter eight (vs. 5,7) where we find the opening of the seventh seal. The next such mention is found here (11:19) at the sounding of the seventh trumpet. The third mention is found in chapter sixteen (vs. 18,21) where the seventh vial is poured out. The vials are but details of the trumpet judgments, thus, we have a check-point marking the first steps toward the beginning of the Great Tribulation (last half) and a marker for the first steps ending the Great Tribulation.

We have seen earlier in chapter four the meaning of these lightnings. They are *"astrape:"* bright, shining lightning. This reveals the awesome power which proceeds from the throne of God. More than just flashes of light, they are powerful illuminations coming from the throne of God. The thunderings are *"bronte,"* that is, roarings. The voices heard were *"phone'"* which means "tones that disclose" (to articulate sounds whether bestial or artificial). The earthquakes and hail are self explanatory. Thus, all the representatives of Heaven sound a tribute to the power and authority of God, while the Earth responds. What an awesome time it will be for all those who know God personally. We will witness His great omnipotence and authority.

Ω

The Spiritual Forces Behind Tribulation
Chapter 12

For we wrestle not against flesh and blood, but against principalities, against powers, against the rulers of the darkness of this world, against spiritual wickedness in high places. Eph. 6:12

This chapter begins with a historical and prophetical view of the main characters of the Tribulation Period. It is an explanatory chapter concerning the struggle for ultimate control by the super powers that be. These are not the super powers of great nations, or individuals of Earth. They are the spiritual forces behind the scenes.

We know that God could speak the word and His victory be immediately accomplished; however, mankind must be considered or else the cross of Christ would be in vain. In addition, God's plan for Israel must be fulfilled according to the Scriptures. Thus, the battle will continue to rage in one form or another until the foe of Christ is cast into the pit of everlasting torment (20:10).

There Is No Middle Ground

Whether we like it or not, we are caught in the midst of the spiritual battle. It has been that way since Adam. Our position in this battle depends upon our choice as individuals. This choice determines who we follow as our ultimate leader: Christ or Satan. It doesn't matter how good our personal character may be. If we reject God's plan of escape, we are automatically on the side of Satan. There is no middle ground. The only exceptions to the rule are children under the age of accountability, those persons who are mentally impaired, and those of very remote areas where the gospel has not penetrated, that is to say, those individuals of remote areas who have the law of God in their hearts (Rom. 2:7-16).

Natives Of The Bush

Many people have stumbled over the idea that God would send people of remote areas, who have never heard the gospel of Christ, to Hell without a chance of receiving salvation. First, God would not and does not do that. We "civilized" people cannot use those who are considered natives of the bush as an excuse for a presumed flaw in the plan of God. The apostle Paul was given a revelation concerning such people. He was instructed by the Holy Spirit to write of those Jews, Christians, and non-Christians, particularly the so-called "natives of the bush." He writes concerning God's principle (law) pertaining to His respect to all persons:

> To them who by patient continuance in well doing seek for glory and honour and immortality, eternal life: But unto them that are contentious, and do not obey the truth, but obey unrighteousness, indignation and wrath, Tribulation and anguish, upon every soul of man that doeth evil, of the Jew first, and also of the Gentile; But glory, honour, and peace, to every man that worketh good, to the Jew first, and also to the Gentile: For there is no respect of persons with God. For as many as have sinned without law shall also perish without law: and as many as have sinned in the law shall be judged by the law; (For not the hearers of the law are just before

God, but the doers of the law shall be justified... Rom. 2:7-13

But Paul does not stop there. He goes on to say,

...For when the Gentiles, which have not the law, do by nature the things contained in the law, these, having not the law, are a law unto themselves: Which shew the work of the law written in their hearts, their conscience also bearing witness, and their thoughts the mean while accusing or else excusing one another;) In the day when God shall judge the secrets of men by Jesus Christ according to my gospel. Romans 2:14-16

This tells us that certain people of Paul's day in remote regions had not heard the gospel of Christ. These people, in doing those things which are right and just, because their conscience tells them what is right and just, are a law unto themselves. They will appear at the Judgment Seat of Christ for reward. There are certain peoples like that today.

Is that an excuse for us? Are we to be silent in our personal witness or refrain from sending missionaries? No. We know that many "unjust" people will respond to the message of Christ when given the opportunity. In addition, there is no excuse for people living in such a nation as the United States, a so-called Christian nation, where the gospel is published weekly, daily, hourly, and by the minute. There is a witness to be found. It would be a very remote situation for anyone living in the United States not to see or be aware of the witness of Christ. There are church buildings in practically every city, township and village in the United States, even in remote "back-woods" communities. In addition, church signs witness just about everywhere. These are all witnesses to Christ. There are also billboards, television and computer mediums. There is the medium of the newspaper and every other imaginable avenue of contact. The Spirit of witness is found in a "civilized" nation, if only one will heed. It is up to each one of us to heed the call of the witness of God when such witnesses are present. The sad mistake is that many people rely on a personal belief system foreign to Scripture (Pro. 3:5) in a civilized world.

Focal Point Of The Battle

Every battle has an objective. During this present age, the born-again believers (the Church) are the focal point of the spiritual battle. We will be such until the "catching away," the Rapture of the Church. Satan already has possession of unbelievers, so there is little or no need for him to bother them. Thus, we should be void of wonder when we see Christian congregations in conflict. We must remember that where there is great conflict, there is usually great concern.

Tribulation Focal Point

During the Tribulation Period, the children of Israel will once again be Satan's primary target. They were the focal point of the spiritual battle in Old Testament times because they were God's chosen people. Although they were God's people, they often fell into a mind-set of rejection and plunged head-long into idolatry. Their rejection climaxed when they refused God's ultimate sacrifice, Jesus (Jn. 4:22). The focal point then became the Church (born-again believers).

God, through the prophets, foretold the rejection and plight of Israel during the church age, because of their refusal of Christ as Lord (Isa. 53:1-4). He also foretold the drastic measure of chastisement, which will be necessary to bring them to Christ during the Tribulation Period (Matt. 24). It will take such a measure because God has promised to bring them back to Himself. This "bringing back" will not be due to their goodness, but for His great name's sake (Ez. 36:20-23; 39:25). Time and again Satan has struck a blow at God by cunningly drawing away Israel, the apple of God's eye (Zech. 2:8). It will be no different during the Tribulation Period. Now we'll identify and discuss the identity of the Sun-clad woman in verse one of chapter twelve.

The Sun-Clothed Woman

> And there appeared a great wonder in heaven; a woman clothed with the sun, and the moon under her feet, and upon her head a crown of twelve stars: And she being with child cried, travailing in birth, and pained to be delivered. Rev. 12:1-2

John sees a great and wondrous sight while in Heaven. A sun-clad woman is travailing in pain to give birth to a child. The woman he views is on Earth, not in Heaven. We know this because the manchild which she delivers is caught up to Heaven (v.5). He could not be caught up if he was born in Heaven. The woman also flees to the wilderness, which is on Earth (v.6). In addition, the dragon is cast to the Earth, where the woman is persecuted by him (v.13).

As with the entire book of Revelation, the identity of this woman (and her child) encompasses many ideas, doctrinal stances, and outlandish beliefs. Some conclude that the woman is the Church. However, the Church did not give birth to Christ (the manchild). On the contrary, Christ gave birth to the Church. Some say she is Mary, but the description does not fit. Too many supernatural things are said about this woman for her to be an individual. Some say the woman represents the true people of God, the ideal Zion or community of God. However, a spiritual ideal could not give birth to anything but wonder, and most assuredly, not a manchild.

It is obvious that the woman represents Israel, the very people through which Christ came in the flesh. This is also another reason for Israel being the focal point during the Tribulation Period. It was through Israel (specifically the tribe of Judah) that the Messiah was to be born. The lineage is provided in Matthew1:1-17 and Luke 3: 23-38.

It has been Satan's desire to stamp out the Jews, so they were and will be the focal point of the spiritual battle. The attacks against them in the Old Testament record the effects of this warfare against them. These attacks were their travailings and birth-pains. These labor pains occurred until the birth of Christ.

Sun & Moon

Just about every credible source, in discussing the woman as being clothed with the sun and having the moon under her feet, refers to Genesis 37:9-11. It concerns Joseph of the Old Testament.

> And he dreamed yet another dream, and told it his brethren, and said, Behold, I have dreamed a dream more; and, behold, the sun and the moon and the eleven stars made obeisance to me. And he told it to his father, and to his brethren: and his father rebuked him, and said unto him, What is this dream that thou hast dreamed? Shall I and thy mother and thy brethren indeed come to bow down ourselves to thee to the earth? And his brethren envied

him; but his father observed the saying. Gen. 37:9-11

Here Joseph gives a prophecy concerning his father Jacob (represented as the sun), his mother (as the moon), and his eleven brothers (as the eleven stars). Jacob knew it was prophetic of his whole family. This prophecy was collectively fulfilled when there was famine in the land and Joseph's family traveled to Egypt and bowed to him for help.

Odd Comparison

The verses in Genesis pertain to the identity of the patriarchal family, but do not completely explain the sun and the moon (12:1). Joseph's father, Jacob, had his name changed to Israel and his twelve sons were the progenitors of the twelve tribes. They are seen in verse one as Israel's crown of twelve stars upon the head of the woman (Israel). Until the time of King Solomon, these tribes were known collectively as either the Hebrews (children of Eber) or the children of Israel (Jacob). After the death of Solomon, they were divided into two kingdoms, the kingdom of Israel and the kingdom of Judah (Jews). However, after the Babylonian captivity, the titles Israel and Jew became synonymous.

It seems odd that Israel (the woman) is clothed with Jacob (representing itself or Israel). It's even stranger that Rachel, Jacob's wife, represented by the moon, would be placed under Israel's feet, a place of disrespect, for she had died. It becomes apparent that the prophecy of Joseph was given for identification purposes only. Thus, for Israel to be clothed with the sun and have the moon under her feet (12:1) must refer to more than Genesis 37:9-11 implies.

Clothed With The Sun

The sun not only represented Jacob for identification purposes, but also stands as a type of God (not to be confused with sun worship). Let's turn to the first mention of the sun and the moon in Scripture for clues of identification. On the fourth day of the creation week (Gen. 1:14-19), the clearing of the atmosphere reveals the greater and lesser light. This, of course, refers to the sun and moon. (For a detailed description of atmospheric clearing, see the author's book, "The Jurassic Mark.")

Here is the significance. Israel was promised time and again that as long as they walked in God's ordinances, He would pour out blessing after blessing upon them and upon others because of them. Thus, they would be clothed with His presence, protection and care. Many times Israel turned from those ordinances. Scripture relates that those wayward times were times of nakedness (II Chron. 28:19; Ez. 16:7-8; 16:20-22; also for the church II Cor. 5:2-3; Rev. 16:15).

God is seen pictured in 12:1 as clothing Israel throughout her history. He is seen doing so in her future on the condition that they accept His Messiah and live by His ordinances. Israel then, in verse one, is seen as being clothed with the protection and care of God. Their clothing during the Tribulation Period comes as a result of the witnessing of the 144,000, twelve thousand out of each of the twelve tribes. Thus, the 144,000, or the twelve tribes, are the twelve stars in Israel's crown of verse one.

For the LORD God is a sun and shield: the LORD will give grace and glory: no good thing will he withhold from them that walk uprightly. Psa 84:11

Moon Under Feet

To have something under foot is most always viewed in Scripture as having that thing or person under subjection. That is, to have conquered something or to have subdued it (II Sam. 22:10; Psa. 8:6; 18:9; Lam. 3:34; I Cor. 15:25-27; Eph. 1:22; Heb. 2:8).

No degradation is to be imposed upon Rachel being seen under the feet of Israel, for the moon here is not a direct reference to Rachel (12:1). It is a picture of the lesser light which Israel subdues while being clothed with the protection and care of God — not naked in their sins. Being clothed with God (as the greater light), she has subdued the lesser light, the false light, the light that only shines because of the greater light. Who then, is the lesser light?

The Moon

The Earth's moon, the lesser light, does not have light of itself. Its light comes from the sun's rays resting upon it. Referred to in Genesis (v.16) as the lesser light, it is the light of the night. The moon here (12:1) refers to the light of darkness. "Take heed therefore that the light which is in thee be not darkness" (Lu. 11:35). "And no marvel; for Satan himself is transformed into an angel of light" (II Cor. 11:14).

In this instance (12:1), the moon refers to Satan, the lesser light and despiser of the woman. Only in Israel's rejection of God's plan can the moon rise above her feet, in turn, bringing her under subjection. Clothed in God, it cannot happen.

Although Israel has repeatedly rejected God, they have also repeatedly returned to Him in times of despair. They are in nakedness and darkness, which speaks of spiritual blindness (Rom. 11:25). The clothing and sight of Israel will again be restored. However, it will take measures never before taken for that to happen. It will take the chastisement of the Tribulation Period.

The Great Red Dragon

> And there appeared another wonder in heaven; and behold a great red dragon, having seven heads and ten horns, and seven crowns upon his heads. Rev. 12:3

The great red dragon is unmistakably Satan, as we see clearly in verse nine. Where he is called the Dragon, the Devil, and Satan. We have just seen Satan represented by the lesser light under Israel's feet. The fact that he is here seen as the great red dragon symbolizes yet another facet of his character. A dragon is usually depicted as a huge, horrifying, fire-breathing, winged reptile, or as a Monitor Lizard called the Komodo dragon, a vicious killer. Satan is called a dragon here due to his cunning fierceness and violent character. He is red, denoting bloodshed. When associated with violence, red refers to killing and devouring (I Peter 5:8).

Satan is called by many names such as: "Beelzebub;" "Belial;" "the devil;" "our common enemy;" "evil spirit;" "the father of all lies;" "the liar;" "lying spirit;" "the murderer;" "that old serpent;" "the power of darkness," and here in verse three, the "great red dragon."

Seven Heads, Ten Horns, Seven Crowns

Satan is also identified as the spiritual force behind the one-world government and the one-world religion, as we see illustrated in the seven heads and ten horns of the beast of chapter thirteen. Note that these heads are the same as the seven heads of chapter seventeen (v.9). The horns are the same as those of chapter seventeen (v.12) and chapter thirteen (v.1). He is seen here as having seven crowns, whereas the beast of chapter thirteen reveals ten crowns. The ten crowns are ten kings (lesser rulers) through which the Antichrist receives control of the world.

The seven heads (mountains - empires -17:9) of the red dragon refers to seven world empires, through which he has attempted to control the world. They are the mountain peaks of world empires. These have been presided over by seven kings (the dragon's crowns), six of which are historical and one which is future. There are seven mountains or empires, "five are fallen [5], one is [6], and the other is not yet come [7]" (17:10). All but one of these attempts have come through world empires, which have come and gone on the scene of world history. This last one (7), the one-world government, is now in the making (this is discussed in chapters thirteen and seventeen). The number seven also refers to Satan's complete earthly dominion as "prince of the powers of the air" and the "prince of this world" (Eph. 6:12; Jn. 12:31, 14:30, 16:11). The seven heads, as seen earlier, refers to seven mountains (17:9 - kingdoms or empires). The seventh empire is the last world empire for Satan and his puppets. This empire will have control under the Antichrist when he is given his crown (6:2 - power and authority). Then, the Antichrist, as a beast, becomes an empire himself. He, himself, becomes the eighth head or eighth empire. This empire arises out of the seven (17:11).

Outline of The Dragon : No. 1

> And his tail drew the third part of the stars of heaven, and did cast them to the earth: and the dragon stood before the woman which was ready to be delivered, for to devour her child as soon as it was born. Rev. 12:4

Chapter twelve supplies us with an overview of the age-old battle Satan wages against God. It is an outline of the warfare between good and evil (not in the sense of "dualism"). Verse three has supplied us with the identity of the dragon. Verse four begins an outline of his onslaught against God and His chosen people. The first half of verse four refers to Satan's first expulsion from the Heaven where God dwells. The second half of the verse refers to his appearance thousands of years later, during the days of the Roman Empire. That was when God became flesh and dwelt among us, in the second person-age of God's three-fold nature, Christ Jesus.

Even later in this chapter, we find another appearance of Satan during the Tribulation Period. It is at the time of the revived Roman Empire. It will be approximately 2,000 years from the time of the first Roman rule. This does not discount his ever-present onslaught, during our present age, as the prince of the powers of the air (Eph. 2:2).

This chapter also presents an outline concerning the arch-enemy of God. It reveals how he has always, at least from the first point of rebellion, prompted hatred and destruction toward God. As with all outlines, this one only covers the highlights about Satan. Thus, we will briefly look into Satan's beginning, his actions against Israel and Christ, and his master attempt to once again rid the Earth of God's chosen people during the Tribulation Period.

The Dragon's Beginning

It is necessary to reveal Satan's beginning in order to explain how his tail drew the third part of the stars of Heaven. In Heaven, long before the Garden of Eden, Satan was Lucifer, an angel of the highest rank. He was the anointed cherub that covereth. This is seen in the song and/or poem which Ezekiel was instructed to lament to the king of Tyrus (28:14-19). This lamentation revealed the king's demise as that which befell Lucifer, the anointed cherub. Thus, this lamentation clearly describes Lucifer.

Thou art the anointed cherub that covereth; and I have set thee so: thou wast upon the holy mountain of God; thou hast walked up and down in the midst of the stones of fire. Thou wast perfect in thy ways from the day that thou wast created, till iniquity was found in thee. By the multitude of thy merchandise they have filled the midst of thee with violence, and thou hast sinned: therefore I will cast thee as profane out of the mountain of God: and I will destroy thee, O covering cherub, from the midst of the stones of fire. Thine heart was lifted up because of thy beauty, thou hast corrupted thy wisdom by reason of thy brightness: I will cast thee to the ground, I will lay thee before kings, that they may behold thee. Thou hast defiled thy sanctuaries by the multitude of thine iniquities, by the iniquity of thy traffic; therefore will I bring forth a fire from the midst of thee, it shall devour thee, and I will bring thee to ashes upon the earth in the sight of all them that behold thee. All they that know thee among the people shall be astonished at thee: thou shalt be a terror, and never shalt thou be any more. Ez. 28:14-19

Here we are told that Lucifer was created and anointed to protect the Earth. He was perfect in beauty and walked up and down in the Earth. He was not given dominion, as was Adam, but he was assigned to protect, guard, and oversee God's creation. This lamentation mentions that Lucifer was later in the Garden of Eden (where Adam was beguiled), and it goes on to say that Lucifer was perfect in all his ways until iniquity was found in him. His character was changed from the anointed cherub to that of a dragon because of his sinful pride. Isaiah gives us more on the fall of Lucifer:

> How art thou fallen from heaven, O Lucifer, son of the morning! how art thou cut down to the ground, which didst weaken the nations! For thou hast said in thine heart, I will ascend into heaven, I will exalt my throne above the stars of God: I will sit also upon the mount of the congregation, in the sides of the north: I will ascend above the heights of the clouds; I will be like the most High. Isaiah 14:12-14

Note: In Isaiah 14:4, Lucifer is also called the "king of Babylon." There has not yet been a king of Babylon like the one described here. This description apparently applies to a king in the "future," the coming Antichrist. In addition, the word "nations" is *"gowy"* which means "body (in the sense of massing bodies);" hence, the masses.

Lucifer became full of self pride and tried to exalt his position to that of God. This pride caused a desire within him to have dominion over all of creation. He didn't want to merely oversee or protect. He wanted to rule, to be as

God. We have seen earlier how Satan did in fact beguile Adam and Eve and receive Earth dominion (chpt. 5).

The Dragon's Tail

Lucifer was cast to the Earth, where he became the prince of the power of the air (Eph. 2:2). This reveals that he was cast to the atmospheric heaven of the Earth. Just prior to that, one-third of the angels in Heaven allied with Lucifer and were cast out with him. Revelation 12:4 also reveals that he had great influence among the angels of God. One-third of the angels followed him. "And his tail drew (as in influence) the third part of the stars of heaven and did cast them to the earth" (the origin of demons).

During the Tribulation Period, Satan and his minions will be cast out of the atmospheric heaven to the ground itself. In addition, at the sounding of trumpet number five, the first woe summoning the last half of the Tribulation Period, Satan's understudy, Abaddon, will be loosed from the bottomless pit. Then will occur the ultimate demonic incarnation and possession of a human body such as has not yet been. Satan, through Abaddon, will embody himself and work in the Antichrist. Through the Antichrist, he will once again proclaim himself to be God. This will be done in the temple. It will be a mockery of the Incarnate Christ.

The name "Lucifer" means "bright morning star." He lost that name and recognition at his rebellion. His name was changed to Satan, which means "arch-enemy, adversary." God, many times, changed names of individuals to fit their changed character. For instance, Abram ("high father") to Abraham ("father of multitudes"), Sarai ("dominative") to Sarah ("lady princess"), Jacob ("heel-catcher") to Israel ("prevail mightily"), and so on. In like manner, this "light-bearer," Lucifer, was now the "adversary," Satan.

Satan is also called the "prince of this world;" "of demons;" "of the power of the air;" "the ruler of the darkness of this world;" "the serpent;" "the spirit that works in the children of disobedience;" "the tempter;" "the god of this world;" "unclean spirit;" and "the wicked one."

Outline Of The Dragon: No. 2

The second time the dragon appears is in Bethlehem, during the time of the Roman Empire, the time of the birth of Christ (v.4).

> ...and the dragon stood before the woman which was ready to be delivered, for to devour her child as soon as it was born. Rev. 12:4 b

The second part of the outline of the dragon is the first part of the outline of the woman (Israel). He was there, ready to devour her child as soon as it was born. Satan had been working behind the scenes throughout history to wipe out the children of Israel, but he had not been successful. If he could not stamp out God's people, then he would stamp out God's Son. He tried through King Herod (Matt. 2:16). Satan evidently thought he would succeed at the crucifixion. However, the resurrection of Christ three days later proved that the cross was victory, not defeat. Jesus Christ, who died, came out alive!

Outline Of The Woman: No. 1

> And she brought forth a man child, who was to rule all nations with a rod of iron: and her child was caught up unto God, and to

his throne. Rev. 12:5

This verse works in connection with the second appearance of the dragon, Satan, in his outline. It is a portion of the first part of the outline of Israel for this chapter. The manchild is definitely identified as Christ, for He is to rule all nations with a rod of iron (during the Millennial Kingdom). This verse speaks of the birth of Christ Jesus, during the reign of the Old Roman Empire. He also ascended to Heaven after his death, burial, and resurrection, and has gone to prepare a place for us (Jn. 14:1-3).

Outline Of The Woman: No. 2

And the woman fled into the wilderness, where she hath a place prepared of God, that they should feed her there a thousand two hundred and threescore days. Rev. 12:6

This second part of the outline of the woman (Israel) refers to the middle of the Tribulation Period. This, as we saw earlier (Chpt. 7), is the time that the Antichrist breaks his covenant and begins to slaughter the children of Israel. This period lasts "one thousand, two hundred and threescore days," that is, 1260 days, again referring to the last half of the Tribulation Period. It works in conjuction with the seventieth week of Daniel's prophecy (Dan. 9:27) and the trodding down of the city for 42 months (Rev. 11:2). It is the "time" (1 yr.), "times" (2 yrs.), "and half a time" (1/2 yr.) of verse fourteen of this chapter. It is the time that Israel flees from the Antichrist. This is prophesied in Matthew 24:14-22.

Israel is to be fed during her time of refuge in the wilderness. This is seen in the phrase, "that they should feed her there." We will examine the identity of "those that feed her" later.

War In Heaven

> And there was war in heaven: Michael and his angels fought against the dragon; and the dragon fought and his angels, And prevailed not; neither was their place found any more in heaven. And the great dragon was cast out, that old serpent, called the Devil, and Satan, which deceiveth the whole world: he was cast out into the earth, and his angels were cast out with him. Rev. 12:7-9

This undoubtedly refers to the atmospheric heaven. The third Heaven, where God dwells, is a place of praise and worship, not war. After all, we have seen how Satan, first called Lucifer, was cast out of the Heaven where God dwells, into the atmospheric heaven. God would not tolerate war in His dwelling.

In the atmospheric heaven, Michael, the arch-angel, and his angelic forces are to fight against Satan and his angelic forces (four fallen angels and troops) during the Tribulation Period. (See chapter nine, "Angels" - "Demons") This war no doubt works in concert with the upheavals in the atmosphere during the sounding of trumpet judgments one through five.

Here again (v.9), we see the identity of the great dragon as the Devil, Satan, the deceiver. He and his angels (demonic angels) are cast out of the atmospheric heaven to the ground. This is the time of the demonic incarnation of the Antichrist by Satan himself through Abaddon (9:11). This casting out causes rejoicing in Heaven, but woes upon the Earth.

Woe To Earth's Inhabitants

And I heard a loud voice saying in heaven, Now is come salvation, and strength, and the kingdom of our God, and the power of his Christ: for the accuser of our brethren is cast down, which accused them before our God day and night. And they overcame him by the blood of the Lamb, and by the word of their testimony; and they loved not their lives unto the death. Therefore rejoice, ye heavens, and ye that dwell in them. Woe to the inhabiters of the earth and of the sea! for the devil is come down unto you, having great wrath, because he knoweth that he hath but a short time. And when the dragon saw that he was cast unto the earth, he persecuted the woman which brought forth the man child. Rev. 12:10-13

The casting of Satan and his minions to the ground will prompt the greatest decision for the children of Israel since Christ walked the Earth. They will either bow to the demands of the Antichrist or choose the message of the kingdom preached by Elijah, Moses, and the 144,000 witnesses. As we saw in chapter seven, multitudes will accept the message of the kingdom. Praise God! Because the kingdom message and the kingdom's Messiah is accepted, John hears a loud voice in Heaven proclaiming salvation, strength, the kingdom of God (in the hearts of the children of Israel), and the power of his Christ (v.10). There is rejoicing in Heaven because Satan is cast out. However, it means great woe to the inhabitants of the Earth, especially the Jews.

Note that verse eleven reveals the weapons used by the children of Israel to overcome the devil. They overcome by the blood of Christ, their testimony, and their loyalty to His message. Upon accepting the kingdom message, they become clothed once again with the sun (God) and have began to put the moon (Satan) under their feet.

As all of heaven rejoices, a proclamation of distress is made concerning those inhabiters of the Earth. Woe to them because the accuser of the brethren is cast down.The anger of Satan is greatly enhanced, because he then realizes his time is short.

Verse twelve states that Satan had come down. It is evident that Satan is forced to the ground by Michael and his troops, but that he does not realize his plight until he attempts to ascend. This is seen in verse thirteen, "and when the dragon saw that he was cast unto the earth." Upon discovering his situation he turns his wrath upon the woman, Israel. This wrath comes through the Antichrist, Satan's man of the hour.

The Eagle

> And to the woman were given two wings of a great eagle, that she might fly into the wilderness, into her place, where she is nourished for a time, and times, and half a time, from the face of the serpent. Rev. 12:14

Some have concluded that these two wings of a great eagle are the United States and Britain, who will help the dispersing Jews as they flee from the one-world leader and his government. This is only conjecture. Such action would prompt another world war. In addition, the greater nations are to align with the Antichrist, not war with him. The surrender of power by the United States will likely be due to the payment of collateral. The collateral, the sovereign power and control of the United States, will likely be the national debt owed to international bankers. As the payment cannot be made, these financial leaders assume power.

The eagle, symbolically used by God in the exodus from Egypt when He speedily brought Israel out of Egyptian bondage, refers to the speedy flight of Israel.

Ye have seen what I did unto the Egyptians, and how I bare you on eagles' wings, and brought you unto myself. Ex. 19:4

Two Wings

The wings in this instance illustrate the swift and safe deliverance of the children of Israel (Jews). This results from their being clothed with the sun. However, this does not mean that all Jews will escape death. We have already discussed how the Antichrist will launch a great attack against the Jews. There will be a great holocaust at that time. Millions of Jews and Gentiles alike will be slaughtered for refusal of the mark of the beast and governmental alliance.

The wings are noted as being two in number. Two, as mentioned earlier, is the number of union, division, and witnessing. As witness of Christ, Israel separates herself from the one-world system. The two wings represent both those slaughtered and those who safely flee into the wilderness. One wing represents the swift transport upward of those souls killed (to the Sea of Glass), while the other represents the swift flight into the wilderness to their city of refuge. Both aspects signify union to God.

This clarifies Paul's statement concerning the present blindness of Israel until the fulness of the Gentiles comes in. Some will be saved by death, some by physical refuge; thus, all Israel will be saved. Paul states:

For I would not, brethren, that ye should be ignorant of this mystery, lest ye should be wise in your own conceits; that blindness in part is happened to Israel, until the fulness of the Gentiles be come in. And so all Israel shall be saved: as it is written, There shall come out of Sion the Deliverer, and shall turn away ungodliness from Jacob: For this is my covenant unto them, when I shall take away their sins. Rom. 11:25-27

The Cities Of Refuge

Israel is to flee to the wilderness, where she is to be nourished for a time, times, and a half a time; that is, for three and one half years. Their fleeing is pictured for us in Numbers chapter 35, which tells of the manslayer and the avenger of blood.

The Levites had 48 cities appointed to them by the Lord (Num. 35:7). Six of those cities were appointed as cities of refuge for the manslayer, someone who indirectly caused the death of another person, ("killed him unawares" Num. 35:15). The death may have been a result of a blow in a sudden quarrel (Num. 35:22) or by an object thrown at random (Num. 35:22,23). It would often happen that the blade of an ax would fly from its handle, striking another person (Deut. 19:5). If an animal was known to be vicious, the owner was liable. Overtaking a thief at night might be lawful cause for the manslaying, but not during the day.

The cities of refuge were appointed that the manslayer might flee there in hopes of eluding the "avenger of blood." The avenger of blood was someone appointed for the vengeance of his dead friend or loved one. The manslayer was to stay in the city of refuge until he stood before the congregation in judgment. If he left the boundaries of the city, then the avenger of blood was allowed to kill him without bringing penalty upon himself (Num. 35:26-28).

The manslayer represents the Jews, the children of Israel. It was the Roman soldiers who thrust the nails in the hands and feet of Jesus, but it was the Jews who had cried "crucify him, crucify him" (Mrk. 15:9-14). They were, and we were, indirectly responsible for the death of Christ. Christ acknowledged their indirect guilt, while on the cross when He said, "Father forgive them for they know not what they do" (Lu. 23:34). The only way to escape from the avenger of blood (rep. of Satan) and his death sentence is to go to the city of refuge, a representative and type of Christ.

Petra

In the Olivet Discourse, Jesus prophesied that the Jews would once again flee for their lives. They are instructed by Jesus to flee to the mountains (Matt. 24:16). This would suggest a reference to more than just mountains in general, but particular mountains. The highest mountains in Jordan are in the Petra area. They are over 5,000 feet high and are some of the most rugged and inaccessible mountains in the world.

Petra is the ancient city of Esau, who is also called Edom (Gen. 36:8). It would seem feasible for Petra to be the city of refuge for Israel during the last half of the Tribulation Period, because Edom, the land, according to the prophet Daniel, will escape out of the hand of the Antichrist:

He shall enter also into the glorious land, and many countries shall be overthrown: but these shall escape out of his hand, even Edom, and Moab, and the chief of the children of Ammon. Dan. 11:41

Edom, Moab and Ammon form the boundaries of modern Jordan. Petra is often referred to as a "ghost town." However, a few bedouin families reside there today, providing tourists with horses and other supplies. The passage into the city is by way of a grand rock formation called the El Ciq (Siq). At the entrance to the El Ciq stand several old buildings, a hotel, a cafe, and a museum. The Ciq itself is 6,000 feet long. It is from about 30 to 12 feet wide at its broadest and narrowest points and can be easily guarded against attack if need be. The almost perpendicular cliff walls of the Ciq reach from 300 to 500 feet high. The entire Petra complex is some twenty square miles in size, including the Ciq. Petra is a natural fortress with countless cavities, passageways and corridors carved into the sandstone. It is said to have been formed by a combination of volcanic and earthquake activities. The sandstone made the perfect carving material for dwellings and elaborate temple sculpturing.

We have seen that the manslayer represents the children of Israel. Their avenger of blood will be the Antichrist (under satanic influence) and his government. Although Christ is still their refuge during this period, many will flee to this actual city in the wilderness (v.14).

The Earth Helps The Woman

And the serpent cast out of his mouth water as a flood after the woman, that he might cause her to be carried away of the flood. And the earth helped the woman, and the earth opened her mouth, and swallowed up the flood which the dragon cast out of his mouth. Rev. 12:15-16

The Antichrist will try to drown the Israelites as they flee to the wilderness of Paran, that is, the wilderness of Petra. It is quite possible that several armies will be sent out as a flood against the Israelites as they flee. However, the technology of today has supplied the means to make possible the manipulation of cloud formations and varied weather conditions. What many have thought impossible concerning weather control, is now becoming a reality. However, such methods will be unsuccessful. Attempts at weather control may well be one of the avenues to control food supplies and ultimately the people. It is also possible that the Antichrist will command that such technology be used in an attempt to completely destroy the fleeing Jews.

It is likely that the flood which will come in this dry region will be from the Med-Dead canal, an attempt to channel the water from the Mediterranean Sea to the Dead Sea. If this project is completed, the dam could be broken in an attempt to drown the Jews as they pass through the Dead Sea area. Whether this flood be by army, by canal or by weather control, the Lord will intervene through the Earth to swallow up the flood that threatens His people. This protection may occur by earthquake or volcanic action, or by whatever means the Lord supplies. Whatever the method, God's protection will abound.

One-Third Saved Alive

Not all Jews will escape to Petra. The prophet Zechariah gives the percentage of Jews which will be saved from death during this "time of Jacob's trouble."

> And it shall come to pass, that in all the land, saith the LORD, two parts therein shall be cut off and die; but the third shall be left therein. And I will bring the third part through the fire, and will

refine them as silver is refined, and will try them as gold is tried: they shall call on my name, and I will hear them: I will say, It is my people: and they shall say, The LORD is my God. Zech. 13:8,9

One-third of the Jews will make it through the Tribulation Period, with the remnant being killed. Approximately 3 1/2 million Jews reside in Israel today. Petra will not have to be evacuated except for a few bedouins who live in a few caves near the Ciq in order for 1/3 of the Jews to move in. Some of the dwellings of the city will hold approximately 3,000 people. Petra would be large enough to hold a million people in the 20 square miles of space. However, with some one million Jews escaping death, it is doubtful that a full million will flee to Petra. We must not forget the undetermined number of Jews scattered among the nations who are helped by those nations (Matt. 25:31-46). Thus, the one million approximation for those Jews fleeing into the wilderness could be altered greatly.

That They Should Feed Her

Verse six revealed that Israel would flee into the wilderness and be fed there for 3 1/2 years. Who will feed them? The water there is supplied by springs, one of which is believed to be the place where Moses struck the rock and water came forth. Also there are huge cisterns built by the Edomites and Nabateans to catch winter rain water. These resources, of course, are supplied by the hand of God.

The question asked by many is, can one million Jews survive for up to three years in the city of Petra? Note that some estimate that around two and one-half million Jews came out of Egypt. For forty years they wandered in a waterless, fruitless, and barren desert. They survived to go into the Promised Land. In AD 68, the Romans closed the gates of Jerusalem, cutting off all water and food supplies for two years. The Romans finally had to take Jerusalem by massive force. For the last 1900 years, they have been dispersed among the nations and yet have survived as a people. These people will survive because Scripture tells us they will.

God's Provision

The children of Israel will survive in Petra because of the hand of God. In respect to context, the "they shall feed them" refers to the mountains and plains of the wilderness area. The bounty of these will be opened to them by God.

The children of Israel will flee from the Antichrist because they refuse him and his terrible government. They do, however, accept the message of the true Messiah and His coming kingdom. Thus, they are "clothed with the sun," that is, the care and protection of God will be the root of their sustenance. This was the case in the wilderness wanderings when they left Egypt. Again, we refer to Zechariah concerning the Tribulation Period:

> And I will bring the third part through the fire, and will refine them as silver is refined, and will try them as gold is tried: they shall call on my name, and I will hear them: I will say, It is my people: and they shall say, The LORD is my God. Zech. 13:9

This portion of Scripture relates that one-third of the children of Israel will survive and go into the age of the Millennial Reign of Christ.

The Remnant Of The Woman

> And the dragon was wroth with the woman, and went to make

war with the remnant of her seed, which keep the commandments of God, and have the testimony of Jesus Christ. Rev. 12:17

Upon realizing that the fleeing Israelites have escaped, the anger of the Antichrist will be greatly increased. His efforts toward the destruction of the children of Israel are then turned to those Jews left behind in Jerusalem and in other nations. They are those who are keeping the commandments of God and are carrying the testimony of Jesus Christ. No doubt, as it was in the days of the Waldenses, a reward will be given to those who expose the whereabouts of the Jews. This will be a terrible time for all Jews and Gentiles alike who hold to the Messiah, Jesus, and refuse the reigning government and its head.

Ω

Identifying
The Beasts
Chapter 13

What is the most vicious and cunning creature that you can think of? Is it a lion, a bear or a Komodo dragon? What about the Velociraptor or some alien creature depicted on television? Well, there are beasts that are much worse.

This chapter concerns the beasts of Revelation 13. They are not *"zoon,"* living creatures, as the four beasts around the throne of God. Nor are they *"ktenos,"* domesticated animals, of Earth such as the cow, horse or dog found roaming hills and valleys.

The beasts of Revelation 13 are *"therion,"* "dangerous animals." They are of the most unrestrained and vicious kind. Their dangerous nature has to do with the enslavement of men, ultimately, the destiny of the human soul. They are dangerous, manipulating powers.

Many students of Scripture have become disgusted and discouraged when attempting to identify the beasts of this chapter, particularly the first beast (vs.1-11). Such guesses have ranged from Nimrod to Nero to many of today's prominent public figures. Various mathematical equations and numerical configurations have labled many such individuals as "the Antichrist." Thus, many premature and unscriptural conclusions have been made concerning the identity of the beast.

To conclude that a historical figure is the Antichrist is most often an easy-out. It is a safe haven for those who wish to claim knowledge of beast identity. The fact is that the identity of the Antichrist will not be known until his time comes. It is doubtful that even those who aid in his ascension as world leader will know his true identity as the Antichrist. Historical forerunners or types may be identified, but not the last world dictator, not yet. He will not be revealed until after the "catching away" of the Church (II Thess. 2:8). Although the search may be interesting, it is futile to attempt to name this "man of sin."

However, it is clear that the number six hundred threescore and six (666) is there for identification purposes (v.18). Thus, two questions immediately come to mind: 1. Why would the number be given, if indeed, the Antichrist cannot be identified until after the Rapture of the Church? 2. How, then, would one know for sure if he did find the true identity of the beast? After all, it is possible that a temporary leader may be placed over the coming one-world government before the real "man of sin" takes control. We will find the answers to these anomalies in the discussion of the beasts of Revelation thirteen.

Heads, Horns, And Crowns

The clues to understanding the enigma of the first beast are found in the proper interpretation of the heads, horns, and crowns represented in Revelation. John gives us the path to proper interpretation in various passages of the book. We will use John's interpretation for our basis, along with other prophetic books which deal with the same subject. Those symbols not directly identified by statement are clearly identified by context.

1. The heads. The heads are mountains (17:9). However, these mountains refer to more than just hills. The word for mountains is "*oros*" coming from the word "*oro*" which means "to rear," that is, "mountain, as lifting itself up above the plain." These heads, kept in context with 17:10-12, pinpoint not only a reference to location for the woman who sits upon the beast, but also to governments (kings and kingdoms), and are thus mountain peaks of political world history. Thus, the seven heads of the beast in this chapter also refer to seven kingdoms or empires of world history. John and other prophets provide and support this thesis, as we will see.

2. The horns. The ten horns are ten kings (17:12). These kings, of course, will reign over kingdoms. The emphasis, however, is on the leader above that of the kingdom which he represents. In general usage, the term "horn" is symbolic of "power or powers."

3. The crowns. Although crowns refer to the reward of victory, they are most often symbolic, as with horns, of power and authority. Crowns, plural, especially relating to the book of Revelation, stand for both the king and the kingdom intertwined. They refer to the position of entities as being subject to a higher authority. For example the seven crowns of the dragon, as seen in chapter twelve, refer to seven world empires through

which he has attempted to gain world dominance. Six of these empires were his crowning achievements, although not reaching the complete and desired end as the last and seventh one will. The dragon's crown, in reference to reward, is much like the hypocrites who pray in synagogues and on street corners that they may be seen of men (Matt. 6:5); the outward self-glory will be all the reward received.

These definitions serve as reference points and will aid us in determining the identity of the first beast of this chapter.

The Beast From The Sea

And I stood upon the sand of the sea, and saw a beast rise up out of the sea, having seven heads and ten horns, and upon his horns ten crowns, and upon his heads the name of blasphemy. And the beast which I saw was like unto a leopard, and his feet were as the feet of a bear, and his mouth as the mouth of a lion: and the dragon gave him his power, and his seat, and great authority. Rev. 13:1-2

John stood upon the sand of the sea and saw a great and wondrous beast. The beast rises up out of the sea. Unless specifically identified by name or context, this "sea," in Scripture, is generally the Mediterranean Sea. It is also called the Great Sea. This provides yet another point of reference.

Seven Heads And Ten Horns

This beast has seven heads and ten horns. This, as previously mentioned, is also said of the dragon of chapter 12 (v.3). This not only reveals that the Devil himself has played a great role in the formation of world empires of times past, but is the manipulating force behind the last world empire. The seven heads and ten horns will be discussed further as we proceed through beast identity. Upon the horns are ten crowns (13:1), whereas the dragon is seen with seven crowns (12:3). The ten crowns (13:1) upon the ten horns will be the crowning achievement of the Antichrist. The ten kings (horns) and their kingdoms (powers and authorities), intertwined, will be the crowns of the Antichrist, for he will bring these kings and their kingdoms under subjection. This, however, will be accomplished after the rise of the Antichrist. His ascent to power will be through the avenues provided by these kings (17:12). Their subjugation, alongside the praises of the false prophet, are the Antichrist's only earthly glory, his only crowns.

Empire Or Leader?

Is this ten-horned sea-beast the Antichrist? Or does this reference belong to something else?

Many suppose that this ten-horned sea-beast refers (vs.1-4) to the person of the Antichrist. However, it is quite obvious by Scripture that these verses speak of both the system and the Antichrist. Each entity (the man and his government) takes on the characteristics of the other.

Before sorting through the characteristics of the Antichrist and his government, we must look at the combined characteristics of the leopard, the bear, and the lion (v.2). John reveals these characteristics, as does the prophet Daniel.

> Daniel spake and said, I saw in my vision by night, and, behold, the four winds of the heaven strove upon the great sea. And four great beasts came up from the sea, diverse one from another. The

first was like a lion, and had eagle's wings: I beheld till the wings thereof were plucked, and it was lifted up from the earth, and made stand upon the feet as a man, and a man's heart was given to it. And behold another beast, a second, like to a bear, and it raised up itself on one side, and it had three ribs in the mouth of it between the teeth of it: and they said thus unto it, Arise, devour much flesh. After this I beheld, and lo another, like a leopard, which had upon the back of it four wings of a fowl; the beast had also four heads; and dominion was given to it. After this I saw in the night visions, and behold a fourth beast, dreadful and terrible, and strong exceedingly; and it had great iron teeth: it devoured and brake in pieces, and stamped the residue with the feet of it: and it was diverse from all the beasts that were before it; and it had ten horns. I considered the horns, and, behold, there came up among them another little horn, before whom there were three of the first horns plucked up by the roots: and, behold, in this horn were eyes like the eyes of man, and a mouth speaking great things. Dan. 7:2-8

Clearly, Daniel is describing five world empires and alludes to a sixth. The fourth empire has an extension which becomes the fifth empire. This extension is the unified world empire having ten kings (horns). It is the coming one-world government. This fifth empire, represented in the ten horns or kings, has yet another extension. It is the little horn (sixth empire). Before giving a detailed look into this "little horn empire," we must first determine who the first empires are.

Although the first great empire of world history did not begin with Babylon, Daniel's prophetic vision begins there and proceeds forward in time (7:2-8). These empires are described in the vision as beasts. They are:

1. The lion represents Babylon. It is also the "head of gold" of Daniel's vision of world empires (2:31-33).

The lion is king of beasts.

2. The bear represents Medo-Persia which had over-taken Babylon.

3. The leopard represents the Greek Empire, which conquered the Medo-Persian Empire.

4. The fourth beast represents the Roman Empire, which had overtaken the Greek Empire. Daniel saw this beast as dreadful, terrible, and strong exceedingly. It was during this Roman rule that God became flesh in the person of Christ Jesus in Bethlehem.

5. The fifth empire which Daniel sees is an extension of the Roman Empire. It is the end-time revival of the fourth beast and is represented by the ten horns.

Thus, Daniel's empires are: 1. Babylonian 2. Medo-Persian 3. Greek 4. Roman 5. revived or revised Roman Empire, the last world empire. John reveals to us a break between the fourth and fifth empires, whereas Daniel sees no break. This is where one needs Revelation to interpret Daniel and Daniel to interpret Revelation, as we will see.

Little Horn

The more adept students of Bible prophecy agree that the "little horn" of Daniel refers to the the Antichrist. Note that Daniel sees the ten horns appearing before the little horn appears. This reveals that the last world empire or government will be in place prior to the arrival of the Antichrist, the little horn.

Daniel's ten horns are the same as the ten horns which John sees (13:1-4). They refer to the last ten kings that will align their kingdoms to form the last one-world government. The power of this great political machine truly begins to flourish only after the Antichrist's appointment (17:12). Remember that the Antichrist must be given a crown (6:1).

Note: Three of these ten kings will be out of step with the purpose of the new government. It appears that these three kings will be removed prior to the arrival of this little horn (Antichrist), "before whom there were three of the first horns plucked up by the roots" (Dan. 7:8). The word "before" ("*qodam*") is often interpreted as "in the presence" which would mean that the government ousts three kings in the presence of the Antichrist, or the Antichrist ousts these kingdoms. This is very possible. However, "*qodam*" corresponds with the Hebrew "*qedem*" which anciently means "eastward" and or "aforetime." This would mean that before the Antichrist's appointment as ultimate leader, the established one-world government will remove three kings which lie eastward. These will not be dissolved as entities, per se, but consolidated with other kingdoms. By necessity, there will be thirteen kingdoms, three of which are dissolved in order that ten divisions of the world government may remain. Such instability and turmoil will reveal the need for a supreme leader.

Beasts In Reverse

The characteristics of Daniel's beasts are represented as a lion, a bear, a leopard and a fourth beast with ten horns. The characteristics of John's beasts are presented in reverse, that is, the sea-beast with ten horns, the leopard, the bear and the lion. They are seen in reverse order because John was looking back in time, while Daniel was looking ahead. Note that John saw all of these in reverse except the ten-horned kingdom, which was yet in his future.

John's first beast (sea-beast with ten horns) is the same as Daniel's last beast (fourth beast with ten horns). The ten-horned kingdom is the last world government (secular government). The horns, unified, rule the last world empire, which will be in place before the Second Coming of Christ. This is the one-world government over which the Antichrist will preside, but not until he is given that crown (6:1). Note again that the little horn comes from among the last ten horns (Dan. 7:8) This last governmental beast has all the characteristics of previous world powers all wrapped up in one. It will arise as swiftly as the leopard and trod down previous attempts at world dominance as the feet of the bear. It has the mouth of a lion, that is to say, the government will have an appointed spokesman who later becomes an empire of himself (Antichrist). This spokesman is fierce and truly deserves the title of "beast."

Note: remember that the personal pronouns he, him, etc., respectfully refer to both the system as a beast and an individual as a beast (both the Antichrist & his political system). Thus, portions of the characteristics given refer directly to the system, while others refer directly to the person. That is, to a large degree, these are interchangeable terms for the Antichrist and the system.

280 * Identifying The Beast

After the appearance of the Antichrist (v.5), the political beast and the Antichrist as beast are completely intertwined references. Each entity cannot exist without the other; the system cannot exist without the head and the head cannot exit without the system. The personal pronouns are used of the beast much like one would refer to a ship or car as "her" or "she."

Who Are The Seven Heads?

The heads of the beast are seven in number. Seven, as we have seen, is the number of completion. These heads represent the six major empires of the past and one that is future. Daniel began his vision of world powers at Babylon, thus revealing five empires and then the little horn. John informs us that there are seven heads. This is the same number of heads as those of the dragon (12:3). We have seen that these were seven empires through which Satan has tried to gain world domination. The seven heads are seven mountains (17:9 - kingdoms or empires). These kingdoms (mountains), of course, have seven kings (17:10). Please note that five are fallen: Egypt, Assyria, Babylon, Medo-Persia and Greece. One is; it is Rome at the time of John. "The other is not yet come" refers to the last world empire, the ten-horned empire, which will be in place prior to the rise of the "little horn" (Antichrist).

John mentions seven world empires (17:10) whereas Daniel begins at Babylon and proceeds toward the last empire. All of these empires were defeated by a succeeding power, except for the Roman Empire, which fell. Its political power shifted from the emperors to the popes.

The Old Roman Empire bordered the Mediterranean Sea. This is why John sees this sea-beast with "ten horns" rise out of the sea. This brings us to the break between the sixth and seventh empires, Rome and revived Rome, as seen by John. It is the "as it were wounded to death" aspect.

Beast Wounded Unto Death

And I saw one of his heads as it were wounded to death; and his deadly wound was healed: and all the world wondered after the beast. Rev. 13:3

The mention of these "heads" here is a direct reference to the seven heads of verse one. This is very important. The ten horns are a part of the seven heads, and indeed, make up the seventh head. Is it the sixth head ("one is" 17:10) that is wounded? John gives us the wounded aspect of one of these seven heads (empires), whereas Daniel sees no break between the fourth beast (Rome) and his horns (revived Rome). Note that Daniel begins at Babylon. Again, this is where we need Daniel to interpret Revelation and Revelation to interpret Daniel.

Antichrist Wounded?

Some say that there will be an assassination attempt upon the Antichrist (the person). He will be wounded or killed and miraculously healed or resurrected by the false prophet. If this be the case, and I believe it is, it can only be in reflection of what has happened to his system. Note, however, that this passage is not a direct reference to the person of the Antichrist. His resurrection is quite possible, for as he closely approaches death his body is possessed by Abaddon, the demonic, destroying angel from the bottomless pit (Chapter nine, "The Locust King").

We know that the Antichrist will proclaim himself as God. However, being healed by the false prophet would put more emphasis upon the powers of the false prophet as healer than upon the Antichrist as being the "god" who needs healing. In addition, the greatest miracles attributed to the false prophet are his deceptive speech and that of bringing fire down from heaven, not that he is a great healer. The Antichrist, being possessed by Abaddon and appearing to arise from the dead, will appear to arise by his own power, thus making him appear as a god. At that time, the demonic influence inside him will proclaim that he is God and demand worship.

Wounded Head, Not Wounded Horn

Although the Antichrist will appear to have risen from the dead, the above references are of the system and not directly to the Antichrist. His resurrection is but a reflection of what has happened to the one-world system. Daniel tells us that this little horn (Antichrist) comes up from among the ten horns. Note that it is one of the heads wounded, not one of the horns. The ten horns, unified, make up one of the seven heads (mountains or empires 17:9), that is to say, the last and seventh great world empire. This is where the "as it were wounded to death" aspect could not directly refer to the person of the Antichrist, for he is the eighth head (17:11). He is the little horn (Antichrist), which comes from among the ten horns, yet distinct and separate from them. Again, it must be noted that the reference to one of the heads becoming wounded points to one of the seven heads of verse one, not to one of the horns.

Eight Heads?

John makes a distinction between the horns (kings) and the heads (empires) and tells us that one of the heads is wounded, not one of the horns. It is NOT a PART or portion of the empire that is wounded, but the whole of one of the seven empires that is wounded. The horns (ten unified to make one), thus refer to the seventh world empire, the seventh head. It is not the Antichrist. He is a little horn, not a little head, which comes from among the ten horns. Not until the middle of the prophetic week does he himself become a head (an empire of himself possessed by Abaddon). It is clear that John distinguishes between the Antichrist as being set apart from the seven heads.

Observe. The Antichrist, according to Daniel, comes from among the ten horns, that is, from among the confederation of kings which make up the seventh world empire (kingdom). The Antichrist is not the seventh head, that is, the seventh world empire. In fact, when the Antichrist sets himself up as God, he becomes the eighth empire all wrapped up in one person (17:11). At that point, he will have become possessed by Abaddon, virtually becoming Satan himself. We know he is not Satan incarnated for they shall be cast into the lake of fire at separate times (20:10). The Antichrist is of the seven and is the eighth (17:11). He consummates the last world empire by claiming to be God and becomes the last world dictator. He becomes a world empire of and by himself (eighth). He and all his governmental crowns (his ten puppet-kings) shall go into perdition (17:11-13). It is one of the seven heads wounded and healed, not the eighth of which John speaks. Thus, the wounded head could not, not directly anyway, refer to the Antichrist.

The seventh head, the confederation of ten kings and kingdoms, is John's revived or revised sixth head (one is) which was wounded, and then healed (other not yet come), thus becoming the seventh. "And I saw one of his heads (one of the seven heads) as it were wounded to death: and his deadly wound was healed" (v.3). It is the revived Roman Empire restored, not the person of the Antichrist. This is only possible as a reflection of what has happened to his empire. Thus, to a degree, this is a dual reference.

It is the beast rising out of the sea, the revived Roman Empire, to which all the world will give wonder. The wonder does not come because of its healing or resurrection. This is realized because few will recognize revived Rome as a part of ancient Rome. Its wonder comes because the one-world religious leader (second beast) will cause all nations to worship this sea-beast (discussed under second beast).

More Evidence

We have heard the sarcastic question, "Do I have to draw you a picture?" Well, God has drawn us a picture through the prophet Daniel concerning world empires. He drew the picture in the form of a dream given to a Gentile king named Nebuchadnezzar, the king of Babylon. The dream God gave him greatly troubled this renowned king, who called for his soothsayers, magicians, psychics, and

so forth, to interpret the dream (Dan. 2:1-3). They could
not do it. Only a man of God could interpret the dream.

After Daniel and his prayer partners talked to God
about Nebuchadnezzar's dream, Daniel received both the
dream and its interpretation from God. The dream
revealed the unfolding of world empires pictured in a
great human-like, metallic image. This image had a head
of gold, arms of silver, belly and thighs of brass, legs of
iron, and feet of part iron and part clay (Dan. 2:31-33).
Note that each metal declines in value from top to bottom.
In addition, having feet of part iron and part clay made
this image unstable. It was both unstable and top-heavy.

Daniel began his interpretation by telling Nebuchadnezzar that he and his kingdom were the head of gold. He
went on to say that an inferior kingdom would defeat his
kingdom. Thus, the arms of silver. The arms represented
the Medo-Persian Empire (Dan. 2:39), as seen earlier.

The third kingdom from Babylon was represented by
brass, hence the Greek Empire. The fourth kingdom was
as strong as iron. It was the Roman Empire. The next
kingdom was represented by part iron and part clay. This
was the feet and ten toes of the great image. The part iron
aspect directly refers to this last kingdom as being part of
the old Roman Empire, thus Rome revived. This could
refer to a Roman treaty by which the last world government will come into existence and/or it could have to do
with papal Rome. We will see later that this is the case.

The "part clay" refers to the democratic portion represented by ten kings. It is a conglomeration of ten political
entities (ten toes), which align with and/or come into
being because of a Roman system (part iron). They repre-

sent the kingdom that in John's day had not yet come (17:9): the last one-world government. These ten toes represent the same entities as the ten horns mentioned earlier by both Daniel and John (Dan. 7:7-8; Rev. 13:1).

We know that these ten toes speak of the last world empire because of the "stone hewn out from the mountain" (Dan. 2:34-35, 44-45). This "stone" is the "rock of ages," Christ Jesus. The first coming of Christ was in the days of the Roman Empire, that is, the iron, or leg empire. His Second Coming will be during the time of the last world empire represented by the feet and toes. It will be Rome (part iron) revived or revisited. The clay aspect also represents Israel (Jer. 18:6). This is due to the covenant made with the new Rome (one-world government) and its dominant leader, the Antichrist.

Upon Christ's return (the Second Coming), He shall smite the great image in the feet and break it to pieces. The great image represents all world kingdoms. Christ will put an end to all world empires and set up His kingdom (the Millennial kingdom). His kingdom will become a great mountain and fill the whole Earth (Dan. 2:35).

Number

The reasons given thus far give evidence as to why many theologians cannot properly identify an individual as the Antichrist by using numbers. Although I believe the Antichrist is undoubtedly alive on Earth at the present time and will likely possess a matching number with his government, theologians spend precious time trying to identify a person (Antichrist) who will come on the scene after they are gone (after the Rapture of the Church).

Properly, verses one through four give us a picture of the last world empire, not of the person of the Antichrist in particular. This empire is now in the making and can be identified as a world dominating system by the number of the beast given in verse eighteen (discussed later).

The Antichrist is directly referred to in Revelation thirteen as the "mouth speaking great things and blasphemies." From that point, the beast as a system and the beast as a person become distinctly intertwined references. This is where Daniel's little horn (Antichrist) does not and cannot appear until after the one-world political beast is first in place.

Power, Seat & Authority

The dragon, Satan, is the driving force behind the New World Order, the one-world political system (v.2). It will be yet another attempt at world control, as has been attempted through past empires. This "driving force" is seen in the characteristics of the leopard (a cunning hunter), the feet of a bear (strong and forceful), and the mouth of the lion (roars greatly and devours its prey).

The seat refers to the position of reigning over the world. It is the seat of the Antichrist. Satan incarnates himself through Abaddon into the Antichrist and thus empowers him and his position. The dragon takes control through the Antichrist. Thus, the dragon gives the political beast his seat. This is another reason that the dragon is seen as having seven heads and ten horns.

The authority refers to the personal power given to the Antichrist, who will proclaim himself as the ultimate power. He will exalt himself above all that is called God, and indeed proclaim that he himself is God. This empowering will be accomplished through the forcefulness of the dragon and his evil forces.

Who Is Like This Beast?

> And they worshipped the dragon which gave power unto the beast: and they worshipped the beast, saying, Who is like unto the beast? who is able to make war with him? Rev. 13:4

Note again that the personal pronoun "him" refers to the personalized character of the "political beast" as well as the person of the Antichrist. The dragon receives worship through the recognition of the great political machine. Persons and even nations will recognize the great power and control possessed by this one-world entity. It will be a greater power than all other empires of world history combined. This last empire will not only include a portion of a known world or hemisphere, but the entire globe. This is the reason that blasphemy is revealed as being on all seven heads (v.1).

The praise and admiration given the one-world government will be blasphemous against God. It will be thought that the great Messiah has come (Antichrist) and the new age dream of a one-world utopia achieved. The first half of the Tribulation Period will be calm compared to the last half. O how the dragon deceives!

The Great Mouth

> And there was given unto him a mouth speaking great things and blasphemies; and power was given unto him to continue forty and two months. Rev. 13:5

Note: There was given unto "him" (political beast) a

mouth (beast as a person - Antichrist).

As the world wonders at the great one-world political machine and boasts of its greatness, the Antichrist as the mouth of the beast will begin to proclaim great things and blasphemies. This is where the Antichrist and the system over which he reigns are completely intertwined in reference. His beastly character is not revealed until the middle of the Tribulation Period, the time of his Satanic influence through Abaddon. His ultimate power and control over the one-world government (and the whole world) will be for 42 months, the last 3 1/2 years of the Tribulation Period. This corresponds with the sounding of the fifth trumpet, the first woe, and the loosing of Abaddon (Apollyon) from the bottomless pit.

Until that point, the world will have been operating under a democratic government. The great manipulative and influential powers of the Antichrist will have gained the support of the great political machine leading to his complete takeover. We have seen this in chapter six (vs. 1-2).

The Antichrist does not immediately assume power, nor does he assume an office which has existed through successive history, as does the false prophet. He will be given a crown (6:2). This crown represents his position as ultimate leader. Here (13:5) we see him receiving the "authority" to speak with complete world dominance.

The Antichrist is mentioned in Scripture as: The "Assyrian" (Isa.10:5-6; 30:27-33); the "king of Babylon" (Isa. 14:4); the "little horn" (Dan. 7:8; 8:9-12); the "king of fierce countenance" (Dan. 8:23); the "prince that shall come" (Dan. 9:26); the "willful king" (Dan. 11:36); the

"man of sin" and "son of perdition" (II Thess. 2:3-8); and
the "Antichrist" (I Jn. 2:18).

War Against The Saints

> And he opened his mouth in blasphemy against God, to blas-
> pheme his name, and his tabernacle, and them that dwell in heav-
> en. And it was given unto him to make war with the saints, and to
> overcome them: and power was given him over all kindreds, and
> tongues, and nations. And all that dwell upon the earth shall wor-
> ship him, whose names are not written in the book of life of the
> Lamb slain from the foundation of the world. If any man have an
> ear, let him hear. Rev. 13:6-9

Note: he (Antichrist) opened "his" mouth. This directly refers to the time when the Antichrist sets himself up in
the temple and proclaims himself to be God (II Thess.
2:4). In verse five, the pronoun "his" referred to the political beast; however, in verse six, the mouth of the beast
(one-world government, v.5), opens his mouth (Antichrist
, v.6).

The spokesman of the political beast now begins to
blaspheme against God. This is the "abomination of desolation" spoken of by Christ (Matt. 24:15). The Antichrist
will be the ruler of the most prestigious empire that the
world has ever seen, but he won't be able to handle it. The
true character of the empowering satanic influence swells
outward in blasphemy through the person of the
Antichrist. Satan and his tactics have not changed since
his expulsion from Heaven eons ago (Isa. 14:12-14).

At that point the Antichrist will demand that all individuals upon the Earth receive the mark of the beast. It
will no longer be an option for those Jews who had made
a covenant with him. Those who refuse the mark, are to be

killed. This is when covenant with the Jews will be broken and the time of their fleeing to the wilderness. Antichrist will demand that not only the Jews be completely subject to him (worship him), but that all kindreds, tongues (languages) and nations bow to his demands. All humanity will worship him, everyone except those whose names are written in the Lamb's Book of Life. They are the ones who have accepted the message of the true Messiah who was slain from the foundation of the world (Jesus).

Consider This

"Slain from the foundation of the world" refers to the redemptive plan of God. I believe that this redemptive plan was set in motion long before mankind was made from the dust of the Earth. This plan is to redeem the number of angels which followed Lucifer in the first expulsion (Jude 6). He will redeem that number through mankind. That is to say, He will redeem what was lost in Heaven by filling the void with the souls of men. It has taken some six thousand years, thus far, to fill that void. God's plan concerning Earth and man has always been that of redemption.

God wants man to choose to worship Him. This choice is not a choice like that of the angels in their first estate. They were created in a perfect environment, yet some chose to sin against God. We live in an imperfect environment with hardships and trials. We serve God out of faith and love. When we live for God in this present world, we reveal our devotion to Him. God wants us to love and worship Him by our own choosing, not as robots, machines, or beings created for that particular purpose.

Patience Of The Saints

He that leadeth into captivity shall go into captivity: he that killeth with the sword must be killed with the sword. Here is the patience and the faith of the saints. Rev. 13:10

Because of the great holocaust, imprisonment and torture during that time, the children of Israel (tribulation saints) will surely trust what God has said in His Word: "To me belongeth vengeance, and recompense; their foot shall slide in due time" (Deut. 32:35). The apostle Paul, in reference to Deuteronomy, put it another way, "...for it is written, Vengeance is mine; I will repay, saith the Lord" (Rom. 12:19). The children of Israel will know that retribution will fall upon those who kill and torture them. They will trust what God says despite what they see and experience. This is the patience of the saints.

Likewise, as the Jews of the Old Testament had "strangers among them," there will be Gentiles who will adhere to the message of the 144,000, the kingdom message, and suffer the same plight as the Jews. They, too, must exercise the same kind of patience and faith as the Jews.

The Beast From The Earth

And I beheld another beast coming up out of the earth; and he had two horns like a lamb, and he spake as a dragon. And he exerciseth all the power of the first beast before him, and causeth the earth and them which dwell therein to worship the first beast, whose deadly wound was healed. Rev. 13:11-12

This passage is not a detailed look at the first beast, as some claim, but concerns "another" beast. The first beast arises from the sea, or the area surrounding the Mediterranean Sea, whereas the second beast comes up out of the Earth. The word here for "Earth" is "*ghay*" and means, "soil, region, or the globe itself, and/or inhabitants." This beast comes from among the people and refers to a man. This man has a particular, dominant office among the people. His characteristics are religious in nature. He is the false prophet.

The question is, if the larger discussion of the first beast is directed toward the political aspect above that of its leader (Antichrist), why should the second beast be different?

As the discussion had shifted from the political system to an individual, John continues the personal aspect of this discussion in referring to the false prophet. In addition, the Antichrist and the false prophet are dealt with differently due to their respective ascensions to power.

Established Office

Let's consider the rise of the first beast in contrast to the rise of the second beast. The first beast "shall be given a crown." Thus, the Antichrist will come into power after the governmental aspect of the first beast is already in place. He will not construct the one-world political system, for it is a joint effort on the part of others. This reveals not only that the Antichrist will rise to power, but that the office will be created for him.

In contrast to the first beast, the position and power of the second beast has been established for some 1,500 years. During that time, the position or office will have remained virtually unchanged. The second beast was not given a mouth as was the first beast, but it automatically begins to speak as a dragon (13:11). He has the appearance of a lamb yet speaks like a dragon. Thus, the reference given of the second beast is directed toward its leader above that of the system over which he reigns.

The Church Of Thyatira

The false prophet's religious system has already been given much attention under the discussion of the seven churches, particularly the church of Thyatira. In chapter three, we saw a picture of this false one-world religious system. We found that Thyatira represents the papal church. Its doctrine and practice is represented by Jezebel, the seductress of idolatry. It is the false prophet or head of this system who will glorify the political system and its leader. He will seduce the world to adhere to the demands of the utopian government, thus, seducing the world to accept the system of the Antichrist.

The Antichrist will need the false prophet's assistance due to the chaotic mess of the world, earthquakes, pestilences, violent storms and famine. The false prophet will offer the world hope, the false hope of the one-world government and its leader. In turn, the false prophet will need the Antichrist and his system. This is realized because the woman (false religious system) is seen riding the beast (17:3 - discussed in chapter seventeen).

Note: The world-wide appeal and nature of the second beast will result from his ability to appear Christian, while greatly deceiving. Today several "spiritual" movements are gaining support by leaps and bounds, attracting peoples of all denominations into a spiritual brotherhood. At first these movements appear to have all the ingredients of true Christian principles. However, upon further examination, most of these successful movements have Roman Catholic roots. They exploit good works in the name of Christianity without the basis of a Christ-centered existence. Catholicism is stressed as most compatible. Beware!

In addition, these movements of the last days glorify the personage of the Holy Spirit above Christ Jesus, a tell-tale sign that something underhanded is afoot. The Holy Spirit was sent to reprove the world of sin, righteousness, and judgment (Jn.16:8), yet these movements do not reprove sin. Yes, they target certain sins, but only those universal sins common to both the Christian and the pagan. Note also that the Holy Spirit does not glorify himself (Jn. 16:13). These movements elaborate on good works, signs and wonders. They exhibit a ball-game-like spirit with spiritual wonders. Such an atmosphere easily plays upon the sincere hearts of unsuspecting Christians. A goal of unity is stressed (with Catholicism), while the fundamental basics of the Christian faith are laid aside. Beware of false unity. Any system which bases Christian unity above Jesus Christ and His principles is a system of deceit (Col. 2:8-9).

We have seen that from its very inception, the Roman Catholic system of religion has taken many avenues to assure its acceptability among the righteous. It is a subtle system of seduction, the system of Jezebel at work. Check out the underlying forces behind all movements, especially those concerning spirituality. Rely upon the Holy Spirit to convey truths to you, but beware of a "familiar spirit."

The way to try (test) the spirits is through the Word of God.

> Beloved, believe not every spirit, but try the spirits whether they are of God: because many false prophets are gone out into the world. I John 4:1

Many scholars conveniently overlook or pay little attention to the second beast (vs. 12-18), probably due to fear. The religious system, under the direction of past popes, has proved to be most heartless and vicious against those who oppose its true nature and being. It is a powerful entity, especially in our world today.

Just as the person of the Antichrist is not identifiable during the present church age, the second beast as a person is not identifiable. One cannot say that the present pope is the false prophet although he prophesies false doctrine, for popes die and are replaced. However, the "office" has remained intact for some 1,500 years. This seat, as with the seat of the Antichrist, is easily identified by number, as we will see later.

Whoever occupies the office of pope at the time of the Antichrist's appointment, especially upon his declaration as being God, shall be the false prophet of which Scripture speaks. He shall be the one that shall lead the world into the greatest deception of all time. The road for this great deception has been paved for many centuries and is broadening daily.

The Two Horns

The two horns of the second beast are not two kings, as with the other horns. They are distinguished from kings because they are horns like those of a lamb. These two lamb-like horns represent the dual nature of the false prophet, the right horn representing Christian characteristics and the left horn representing dragon-like (satanic) characteristics. Thus, the two horns represent the mixture of Christian and pagan principles as seen represented by the church at Thyatira.

Exercises Power

The false prophet will exercise all the power of the first beast. In short, he has a world system that is just as powerful as the one-world political beast. In fact, the United States, as well as other countries, have ambassadors to the Vatican. Thus, the actions by which the false prophet secures obedience to the Antichrist, are ultimately for his own good; after all, the position of pope in the teaching of Romanism is that of the "Vicar of Christ." The term "Vicar of Christ" means that the pope supposedly holds the authority to act on behalf of Christ.

The Antichrist will proclaim total authority, but there will be somewhat of a resistance against taking the mark of the beast. People will began to consider the plight of the children of Israel, hear the witness of Moses, Elijah, and the 144,000, and no doubt be concerned that the witness of the Antichrist is false. The constant threat of earthquakes, violent storms, and famine will also play a role in the unrest of the people. The one-world utopia of the Antichrist will be in danger of collapse. The false prophet will deceive the people into accepting the message of the one-world leader. His greatest and most convincing tools will be signs and wonders. The false prophet will have a great stake in moving the world to such unity. It

298 * Identifying The Beast

will give him the perfect avenue to be the pastor to the whole world.

He Doeth Great Wonders

> And he doeth great wonders, so that he maketh fire come down from heaven on the earth in the sight of men, And deceiveth them that dwell on the earth by the means of those miracles which he had power to do in the sight of the beast; saying to them that dwell on the earth, that they should make an image to the beast, which had the wound by a sword, and did live. Rev. 13:13-14

To prove that the people can trust him, the false prophet will do great wonders, including making fire come down from heaven. This is evidently a rehearsal of the duel between Elijah and the prophets of Baal. However, this time the false prophet will be able to do what the prophets of Baal could not do. He will bring fire down from Heaven. This is how he will deceive the people into accepting the Antichrist and his system. He will do these great miracles in the sight or presence of the first beast; that is, in the presence of the Antichrist and his system.

> ...saying to them that dwell on the earth, that they should make an image to the beast, which had the wound by a sword, and did live. And he had power to give life unto the image of the beast, that the image of the beast should both speak, and cause that as many as would not worship the image of the beast should be killed. Rev. 13:14b-15

The Image Of The Beast

The false prophet will also influence those of Earth to make an image to the beast. John mentions the wounded aspect again to distinguish between the beast as a man and the beast as a system. He does this in order to identify the beast to which the image is to be made. It is the beast which had the wound by a sword, and did live. What is this sword?

The Sword

As mentioned earlier, many claim that there will be an assassination attempt upon the life of the Antichrist. We have already established that this wounded entity will be the old Roman Empire wounded and healed. Only as a reflection of what has happened to his government could this be said of the Antichrist. We know that the Roman Empire fell due to internal corruption and shifted in power to the popes. How, then, was the old Roman Empire wounded by a sword?

The sword in Scripture not only refers to an instrument of war, but it also symbolizes judgment. The fall of the Roman Empire was a result of judgment upon sin. Sin always brings judgment in one form or another. This "wounded by a sword" refers to the judgment upon Rome for its corruption. As the Medes and the Persians served as the sword of judgment upon Babylon, the internal sins of Rome served as the sword of judgment against its empire status. It fell, politically, into ruin, severely wounded as an outward empire.

The People Are To Make The Image

The false prophet will have great influence. The question is, how will he persuade the people of Earth to make an image to the one-world government? Considering this on a world-wide scale, how is it even remotely possible for the people to make such an image?

This present age is the only age that could possibly fit such a description. How timely God's Word is! This image is not a statue or likeness of the person of the Antichrist unless by a visual icon. This image is a system directly linked with the one-world political system, a reflection of the governmental system. It will work hand in hand with the mark of the beast and affect all people everywhere. It is quite evident that this system is a global computer network system, which will make it possible for the people to make an image (reflection) to the beast. We must remember that this is a worldwide system, so it must be one that appeals to people everywhere.

The government is currently taking steps to regulate Internet computer networks because of verbal and visible pornography. This is a needed regulatory step because the imaginations of men are continually evil. Government monitoring would not be necessary if intentions were pure in motive.

The image to the beast will be a recognizable reflection of the one-world government, a personal link to a government-controlled computer network system. In this manner, it will be possible for people of diverse nations and languages to make an image to the beast. Such people will voluntarily adhere to the number and image of the beast because of the great communication access. It will be a connection to world communication and commodities.

The false prophet's dragon-like speech will convince the masses that the system and the personal identification that goes with it can be fully trusted. In this fashion, the false prophet will have the power to give life to the image of the beast. His power of persuasion will cause life to come to the image. In this respect, the false prophet will be more dangerous than the Antichrist. His witness will prompt the whole world to succumb to the number of the beast.

It is not at all uncommon today for computers to speak (v.15). Computers are also a tool by which every individual may be numbered. The computer will speak as witness against those who do not take the mark and will become their link to death. This is what can happen when a wonderful tool is placed into the wrong hands.

False Prophet's Witness

As seen in chapter seven, there is a difference between the mark of God and the mark of the beast. It is obvious that the false prophet will not distinguish between them. The pope's interpretive track record has never been good and will continue to be erroneous. Due to his religious nature and world-wide appeal, the false prophet will surely turn to religious materials to back up his reasoning. In all probability, he will refer to instances where God used a mark for the protection of His people. His lack of spiritual insight will deceive millions to trust the wrong mark.

God's Mark

God placed a mark upon Cain that he might easily be recognized and protected from death (Gen. 4:15). Thus, the mark was a good thing for Cain. God told Ezekiel to observe, as a man with an inkhorn went through Jerusalem and marked those who wept and cried for the abominations done by His people there. Those marked were thus protected from death (Ez. 9:4). Again, a good mark. We have seen that the 144,000 will have the mark of God in their foreheads (chpt. 7). Yet another good mark. The false prophet's misinterpretations will make the mark of the beast appear as a good thing for the people. This action, a ploy inspired by the Devil, will be portrayed as God's protective measure for the people during the time of earthquakes, violent storms, and all sorts of upheavals.

Such misuse of Scripture should not surprise us. The Devil quoted and perverted Scripture when tempting Christ in the wilderness (Matt. 4:5-6). He didn't know enough Scripture to be wise, but he knew just enough to be dangerous. This is why one must be familiar with God's Word and rely on the Holy Spirit for proper interpretation (Jn. 16:13).

The Mark Of The Beast

> And he causeth all, both small and great, rich and poor, free and bond, to receive a mark in their right hand, or in their foreheads: And that no man might buy or sell, save he that had the mark, or the name of the beast, or the number of his name. Here is wisdom. Let him that hath understanding count the number of the beast: for it is the number of a man; and his number is Six hundred threescore and six. Rev. 13:16-18

At the proper moment, everyone will be commanded to take either the mark (of beast), the name of the beast (political), or the number of the beast (Antichrist's number) in his or her right hand or forehead. The false prophet's deceptive witness will be the reason for its great success. Only those whose names are written in the Lamb's Book of Life (v.8) and others who realize the severity of the mark will escape its eternal curse. The cost for refusing the mark will be death. Those not killed will become fugitives and will be hunted continually.

Here Is Wisdom

Many believe that the number 666 will be stamped upon the hand or forehead and will be visible. However, the above verses tell us that the number will be "in" the right hand or "in" the forehead. Experimentation has been going on for some time concerning a computer microchip, being placed underneath the skin.

The computer is the only means by which every man, woman, boy and girl may be numbered and tracked. This chip may be scanned through laser technology, not only for identification, but also for encoded information. These small chips are capable of storing enough information that a book could be written within about the person in whom it is planted. Bank records, medical records, military history, family history, and all the details of each person will be readily available for the authorities to view.

It will take more than knowing about a number by which one may recognize the dreaded mark of the beast. It will take wisdom ("Here is wisdom" v.18). One must be wise to what is going on in order to realize what is and is not the mark of the beast. The hidden number will be yet another reason many will discard the witness of Moses, Elijah, and the 144,000 and receive the mark.

John relates through the inspiration of God that only those who have understanding will count the number of the beast. It is not man's number, which is six, but is the number of a man. Thus, the number of the beast (political) and the number of the man (Antichrist) are one and the same. It is six hundred threescore and six, that is, 666. It is a combination of 66, the number of idolatry, and 6, which is the number of man. It is also 600, the number of warfare (Ex.14:7), and threescore (60), the number of pride (Dan. 3:1), as displayed in Nebuchadnezzar's erection of the great image, and man (6).

Most people have heard of the number, yet are unwise to its application and use. Wisdom is the quality of knowing what to do with what you know. The manipulators and controllers of the world will have no choice but to use the number 666. It is prophesied. It will be the only number by which things will properly operate. They, knowing it is a dreaded number, shall disguise it. These manipulators will know that if the knowledge of the number can be hidden, the wisdom of resistance shall also be averted. This tactic will work. The number of the beast will be a hidden number. God has supplied the number in verse eighteen, but it is up to us to use wisdom to find and interpret it properly.

Buying And Selling

The day is coming when there will be no buying or selling except through the use of this mark. Because mortgage payments cannot be made without the mark, those who are in debt will lose all that they have unless they take the mark. In order to feed small children, many adults will lay aside any resistance. This will truly be an "hour of temptation." Only those who grow their own food and manufacture other necessities may slip through the fingers of the one-world government for a time. But they, too, will be readily sought out to surrender or be killed (20:4).

The witness of Moses, Elijah, and the 144,000 witnesses shall be of lesser concern than that of personal ease, especially since the false prophet, the great religious leader, is supporting the actions of the new government and its leader. His exposition of fire against Elijah will insure his standing as "Vicar of Christ" and make him appear authentic.

The Number Of The Beast

We have seen earlier that it is futile for the Christian to attempt to apply the number 666 to a particular man, because the Antichrist is not to be revealed until after the catching away of the Church. The proper identity of the Antichrist will be left up to Moses, Elijah and the witnesses. However, the number is given in Scripture so that we may recognize the coming one-world beast. It is a signpost to reveal to the Christian that Christ's redemption draws nigh. It should inspire us to win souls. In this section, we will reveal the use of the number and how it points to our redemption.

IMPORTANT NOTE: Use caution in how you handle the information that you are about to receive. If you go to the supermarket, bookstore, or some other merchandise outlet and set up protests and make a big scene, this book and others which are of importance to the cause of Christ might be withdrawn from bookshelves. Read the complete section, study it, and pray for wisdom in witnessing to the lost. We are to fight a spiritual warfare, not a physical one (Eph. 6:12). Only act as God directs. God hasn't lost any battles, so have faith. Faith is the opposite of worry and worry is the opposite of faith.

The Mark Is Being Used Already

Few people realize that we have been using the mark for several years. Even in our day, it is nearly impossible to escape. Although in its infant stage, the moment we pick up a can of beans, a loaf of bread, or a toothbrush at the supermarket, the mark is used. It has not yet been forced upon the people as a wearable mark. However, that day is coming.

The infant mark of the beast is found today in the Universal Product Code (UPC). The bar code found on everything from a chocolate bar to this book you are reading. This coding system is continually moving toward maturity, when humans will possess it or a comparable mark under their skin. This UPC symbol is known in Europe as the European Article Number (EAN).

These bar codes used in buying and selling are timely tools for a universal government. Few people know that these product codes contain three 6's. Each bar in the code, or the space in between, represents a number. To keep these 6's supposedly unidentifiable, three sets of bars are used as 6's. That is, three sets of bars are configured for one particular number. Certain numerals have three sets of bars ascribed to them; some have only one set. The number 6 has three sets of bars, illustrated in Figure 1 (See page 488).

Note: The bar code used in this book is for explanation purposes only and is not an actual bar code (pg. 488). Except for the number 6, the black lines are drawn in the place of numerals because they are unnecessary for our study. X's discussed shortly.

Several numbers are identified by three sets of bars, while other numbers have only two sets of bars ascribed to them. The most common bar code uses three sixes (666) taken from set no. 2 (pg. 488), while others use a variation. The 6's are the extended numbers at the bottom of the code (figure 2, pg. 488). This type of bar code is found on such items as canned goods, cereals, and breads; the list is endless. The 6's divide the UPC into two sides. There is a 6 on the left, one in the middle, and one on the right. The numbers to the left most often indicate the manufacturer and the numbers to the right are for the product (and eventually the purchaser). These particular 6's always extend a bit further at the bottom than the other numbers, the exception being the bars indicated by numbers on the outside of the bar code (marked herein with an X). They are system identification numbers.

You are probably ready to go to your kitchen pantry or clothes closet to check out the many products that are marked with this Universal Product Code.

Notice that the code is different on the bottle or can of cola. This is due to the varied use of the three sets of 6's. For example: on the canned drink, there are three sets of lines within the bar code that are longer than the others. Yes, you guessed it, they represent the number 666. There is a 6 from set no. 2, another 6 from set no. 2, and yet another 6. The last 6 is from set no. 3. Sets 2 and 3 are found in the three long lines on the right side of the Bar Code (pg. 488).

Doubtless, this little bar code, as well as the larger, will grow smaller and smaller and may eventually disappear from the naked eye, prompting the use of the microchip. Although configured differently, the chip is also encoded. Please, beware of any kind of injection for identification purposes.

Don't panic over the bar code! Just make your calling and election sure (II Peter 1:10). Be prepared to escape the hour of temptation (Rev. 3:10) through the catching away of the Church (I Thess 4:16-18). How? By becoming a part of the Church by accepting Christ Jesus as your Lord and Saviour. (Romans Road to Salvation: Rom. 3:10; 3:23; 5:12; 6:23; 5:8; 10: 9-10)

Signature Of The One-World Government

The UPC and EAN are specific indicators of a one-world buying and selling system, and are definitely associated with the number of the beast. Although it does not call out the name of the beast, it is the signature of the beast, a universal signature. The bar code as well as the similarly encoded credit card magnetic strip, are avenues used by government manipulators for world control. (For possibilities, read "Observation," pg. 311)

Signature Of The False Prophet's Office

The false prophet will readily adhere to the Antichrist's system because it aligns with his own religious system and office, even by number. The church of Thyatira has provided the evidence to determine from whence the false prophet will arise: the office of the highest leader in the Roman Church, the pope. However, the pope who is in office at the appointment of the Antichrist will likely be the false prophet. As with the Antichrist, his identity cannot be determined by number as yet, but his office or position can be.

V =	5	F =	0	D =	500	112
I =	1	I =	1	E =	0	53
C =	100	L =	50	I =	1	+ 501
A =	0	E =	0	=	501	= 666
R =	0	I =	1			
I =	1	I =	1			
V =	5	=	53			
S =	0					
=	112					

On the papal bonnet are the words "VICARIVS FILEII DEI," which can be identified with the number of the beast by the use of Roman numerals. Originally, only six Roman letters were used as numerals: I=1; V=5; X=10; L=50; C=100 and D =500. Later M was added for 1,000.

Doctrinal ties with the historic pagan Rome and the number of the beast clearly establish the office of the pope will be that of the false prophet, who will oversee the one-world religion.

Number Note

We have seen in the discussion of Biblical mathematics that numbers carry great significance throughout Scripture. It is interesting to note the numerical ties concerning the number 666. Not only is the number 666 a whole number, but dividing it into two sides gives us the numbers 66 and 6. 66 is the number of idolatry, while 6 is the number of man. Nebuchadnezzar's image was three-score (60) cubits high and six (6) cubits wide. This connects the number 66 with idolatry. As we know, to worship anything other than God, as with the one-world system, is idolatry. The number of man is six (6), for he was created on the sixth day, his days to work are six, and so on. Thus, the number 666 refers to man's idolatry.

The number 666 as a whole stands for the number of the beast as seen in verse eighteen, which begins with "Here is wisdom." The next time the word "wisdom" is used, is in chapter seventeen, verse nine. There, several numbers are used to describe the end-time political system. There are, in verse nine, seven heads, seven mountains, one woman. In verse ten there are seven kings: five fallen, one that is, and one coming.

There is the beast that is the eighth and is of the seven in verse eleven. Verse twelve gives ten horns, ten kings and one hour. Verse thirteen reveals one mind.

These numbers added together total 66, the number of idolatry. In verse fourteen we find that there is war.

> These shall make war with the Lamb, and the Lamb shall overcome them: for he is Lord of lords, and King of kings: and they that are with him are called, and chosen, and faithful. Rev. 17:14

The number of "war" is six hundred (600). This is seen in the chosen chariots of Egypt (Ex. 14) and when Israel, under Shamgar, slew six hundred Philistines (Judg. 3:31). Six hundred Benjamites escaped during war (Judg. 20:46-47). Goliath's spear, a weapon of war, weighed six hundred shekels of iron (I Sam. 17:7).

In chapter thirteen, verse fourteen, we see that the beast will make war with the Lamb. Adding the number of war, 600, to the idolatry of the political system (66), one comes up with 666. The number six hundred, threescore and six (666), as well as all numerals, have great significance. These signature marks within the very words and numbers of Scripture prove God's divine inspiration.

Observation

In 1957 under a Roman treaty, six nations came together to form what has been known, since 1994, as the European Union (EU). They were Belgium, France, Germany, Italy, Luxembourg, and the Netherlands. In 1973, three more nations were accepted into the EU: Denmark, Ireland, and Britain. Greece became the tenth member nation in 1981. Then in 1986, these unified nations expanded to include Portugal and Spain. In 1995, three more nations joined the Union: Austria, Sweden, and Finland. To date, fifteen nations comprise the European Union, which continues to engulf the world bit by bit. This organization could well be the one-world government of which the Bible speaks. It presently exceeds 360 million in population and the European Article Number is there in which to buy and sell. It is evident that Europe will be the leader in the scheme of a one-world controlling system. Its divisions into smaller nations has proved insignificant as being the ten-horned unit within itself, as member nations now exceed thirteen. Several nations are waiting on the sidelines to join. However, it is not unlikely that, upon gaining world membership, the nations of the world, under European leadership, will be divided into several groups (10 or 13?).

According to the prophet Daniel, the end-time government will be separated into thirteen divisions of power. These power blocs will doubtless have thirteen kings or leaders, one per division. Quite possibly, three of these kings (horns) will not be able to operate under the guidelines of the overall union and will be removed. Their particular power bloc will be absorbed, leaving ten. Daniel says that these three kings and kingdoms will be plucked up by the roots (Dan. 7:8).

It is evident that Europe will be in the lead. It is in that part of the world that rebellion against God first began on Earth. In addition, the European Union came into being under a Roman treaty (part iron) and is democratic in nature (part clay). The European Union is indeed an entity to watch.

Ω

Pictures
Of
Victory
Chapter 14

There are times in our lives when we wonder what else can happen to turn simple bumps into huge impassable mountains along life's road. Troubles just seem to pile up. It is during those times that we need relief. We need to know that everything will turn out all right. No matter how confident we may be, we sometimes need assurance that a brighter day is coming. This chapter seems to offer that assurance. Found in the midst of the book of Revelation is a series of road signs telling us to stop and take account, as if to say, "don't lose the vision of victory in the midst of these terrible things"!

No doubt John needed a picture of hope, as we often do, and was given this foreview of victories. At the very onset of the chapter, assurance begins to stream forth to the reader. This assurance is seen in seven divisions of the chapter. Given within each division is a summation and end result of a particular aspect of the Tribulation Period. Thus, each division ushers in hope for the time of "Jacob's trouble."

Assurance Number One

> And I looked, and, lo, a Lamb stood on the mount Sion, and with
> him an hundred forty and four thousand, having his Father's name
> written in their foreheads. And I heard a voice from heaven, as the
> voice of many waters, and as the voice of a great thunder: and I
> heard the voice of harpers harping with their harps: And they sung
> as it were a new song before the throne, and before the four beasts,
> and the elders: and no man could learn that song but the hundred
> and forty and four thousand, which were redeemed from the earth.
> These are they which were not defiled with women; for they are
> virgins. These are they which follow the Lamb whithersoever he
> goeth. These were redeemed from among men, being the first-
> fruits unto God and to the Lamb. And in their mouth was found no
> guile: for they are without fault before the throne of God. Rev.
> 14:1-5

Note where Christ the Lamb is standing. He is standing on the Mount Sion, another name for Jerusalem.
However, this is the heavenly Jerusalem. Standing with
Him are the 144,000 witnesses. This is a picture of their
victory over the trials of the Tribulation Period. Here John
hears voices proclaiming the victory. The first voice he
hears is the voice of God. The overwhelming sound is
both soothing and thundering, as the sound of many
waters. We have seen in chapter ten that thunder in
Scripture is often a sound of confirmation proclaiming
God's powerful and overwhelming presence.

In addition, John hears the sound of harpers. Who are
they? The answer is found in chapter 15:2.

> And I saw as it were a sea of glass mingled with fire: and them
> that had gotten the victory over the beast, and over his image, and
> over his mark, and over the number of his name, stand on the sea
> of glass, having the harps of God. Rev. 15:2

In chapter five, we found that the four beasts and the 24 elders all have harps. However, the harpers in the discussion at hand are those redeemed out of the Tribulation Period who had gotten victory over the beast, his image, and his mark. "These are they" (7:14) who had accepted the message of the 144,000 witnesses. They had been killed for the cause of Christ. This is part of the aspect discussed in chapter twelve that all of Israel shall be saved (subtitle "Two Wings"). — some by death, some by escape. These harpers are the respondents to the message, who were killed and are not the 144,000 themselves, for the 144,000 are protected from death by the seal of God in their forehead.

In addition, the respondents sang a brand new song. No man could learn the song except for the 144,000. Thus, the 144,000 will hear a song that only they can understand (learn - "manthano,"). It will be a song to which only they and the singers can relate, a song of victory for those redeemed from the Tribulation Period.

A great portion of this song is found in chapter fifteen, verses 3-4:

> And they sing the song of Moses the servant of God, and the song of the Lamb, saying, Great and marvellous are thy works, Lord God Almighty; just and true are thy ways, thou King of saints. Who shall not fear thee, O Lord, and glorify thy name? for thou only art holy: for all nations shall come and worship before thee; for thy judgments are made manifest. Rev. 15:3-4.

The "song of Moses" is one of victory over the enemy. Found in Exodus 15:1-19, it concerns the crossing of the Red Sea and the death of Pharaoh and his army there. It proclaims God's power, glory, and holiness in delivering the children of Israel out of Pharoah's hand.

Harps Of God

The harpers will play the most noble of instruments, the harps of God. Mentioned more than any other musical instrument in the Bible (over 60 times in variation), the harp is obviously a special instrument to God.

Styles of harps in Scripture include the psaltery or lyre (I Kings 10:12), believed to be a smaller version of the harp, the viol (Isa. 5:12), and the lute, which was even smaller than the psaltery and had only three strings.

David used the harp to play for King Saul during the time of his "distressing spirit" (I Sam. 16:16,23). This harp is often referred to as the lyre and was considered to be the most noble of musical instruments. It was used both for sacred and secular purposes (II Chr. 29:25; Isa. 23:16). It could be plucked with a pick or with the fingers. The harp was often made of silver or ivory.

Shadrach, Meshach, and Abednego were to bow and worship the great image of Nebuchadnezzar when the harps and other instruments were sounded. This included the sackbut (Dan. 3:5). Some believe the sackbut to be the seven-stringed harp used in Babylon. Each version of the harp, such as the ten-stringed lyre, was distinct by name, size, and sound, such as the ten-stringed lyre or the three-stringed lute.

Each version of harp will be represented at the victorious occasion for those redeemed out of the Tribulation Period.

Firstfruits To God And The Lamb

The character of these 144,000 witnesses has already

been discussed, however, they are also referred to here as the firstfruits to God and the Lamb. This reflects that they are the first Jews to be saved during the Tribulation Period. This first assurance is thus a picture of the 144,000 and of the respondents to their message. This assurance also reflects the eternal standing of the 144,000 and the respondents. They can sing the song of deliverance out of the hand of a most terrible Pharaoh, the Antichrist and his evil system.

Assurance Number Two

And I saw another angel fly in the midst of heaven, having the everlasting gospel to preach unto them that dwell on the earth, and to every nation, and kindred, and tongue, and people, Saying with a loud voice, Fear God, and give glory to him; for the hour of his judgment is come: and worship him that made heaven, and earth, and the sea, and the fountains of waters. Rev. 14:6-7

Here we have the assurance that the everlasting gospel will be preached to the entire Earth. This will not be the message of the kingdom, or that of grace. Rather, this message, delivered by an angel, will include a rebuttal for those who have trusted in theories of evolution and like absurdities. The message will be to "fear God," for He is the one who created all things, Heaven, Earth, sea, waters beneath the Earth, everything, and to give glory to Him, for He alone is worthy. That is the everlasting gospel.

In addition, the angel will proclaim that God's hour of judgment is come. It is a time that His power over the elements, indeed over all creation, is being revealed. Fall and worship the Creator!

This passage points to the ending of the Tribulation Period and that God will be victorious over all. It is the "good news" to Israel that the end of their troubles is near.

Assurance Number Three

And there followed another angel, saying, Babylon is fallen, is fallen, that great city, because she made all nations drink of the wine of the wrath of her fornication. Rev. 14:8

Here we have a picture of victory over the one-world religious system. The fornication of this system gives direct reference to the end-time church of Thyatira. It is the papal system and its leader, the false prophet. (The plight of this religious system will be discussed in detail in chapter eighteen.)

This passage calls out, as if to say, "Come out from among them, and be ye separate" and "come out of her, my people, that ye be not partakers of her sins, and that ye receive not of her plagues." (II Cor. 6:17; Rev. 18:4).

Assurance Number Four

And the third angel followed them, saying with a loud voice, If any man worship the beast and his image, and receive his mark in his forehead, or in his hand, The same shall drink of the wine of the wrath of God, which is poured out without mixture into the cup of his indignation; and he shall be tormented with fire and brimstone in the presence of the holy angels, and in the presence of the Lamb: And the smoke of their torment ascendeth up for ever and ever: and they have no rest day nor night, who worship the beast and his image, and whosoever receiveth the mark of his name. Here is the patience of the saints: here are they that keep the commandments of God, and the faith of Jesus. Rev. 14:9-12

Here we find that judgment will fall upon the disobedient. It is an assurance to tribulation saints, indeed all saints, that justice will be executed. During the Tribulation, it will appear that those who have taken the mark of the beast are the fortunate ones. They are not hunted by the government and slaughtered, but are aided by the government during Tribulation calamities and appear to live with less hardships. The bad guy, so to speak, will seem to be the good guy and vise versa. Thus, a great assurance is needed, a motivation for the patience of the saints. This, they are given. Those who accept the message, who live the message, and who hold the faith of Christ Jesus may rest assured that justice will ultimately reign.

This also relates that the taking of the mark of the beast is a serious matter. Those who take the mark will receive the wrath of God and be tormented with fire and brimstone forever. The elements of fire and brimstone refer to the casting of those souls into Hades, and eventually, into Gehenna Hell, the Everlasting Hell.

Assurance Number Five

And I heard a voice from heaven saying unto me, Write, Blessed are the dead which die in the Lord from henceforth: Yea, saith the Spirit, that they may rest from their labours; and their works do follow them. Rev. 14:13

Assurance number five tells of the faithful; those who die in the Lord. Refusing the mark of the beast shall take the greatest of faith, even faith unto death. Here we find a comforting statement from the Holy Spirit relating rest and peace to the faithful. They will rest from their struggles and receive rewards for their faithfulness.

Assurance Number Six

And I looked, and behold a white cloud, and upon the cloud one sat like unto the Son of man, having on his head a golden crown, and in his hand a sharp sickle. And another angel came out of the temple, crying with a loud voice to him that sat on the cloud, Thrust in thy sickle, and reap: for the time is come for thee to reap; for the harvest of the earth is ripe. And he that sat on the cloud thrust in his sickle on the earth; and the earth was reaped. Rev. 14:14-16

The reaper here can be none other than Jesus Christ himself. He was the "Sower" and shall be the "Reaper." He wears a golden crown and holds a sharp sickle. The crown signifies more than just kingship. It is a "golden crown" which signifies the holiness of the Lord, as pictured in Exodus 39:30. This crown was made during the work of the tabernacle, as commanded by the Lord. Engraved upon it were the words, "Holiness to the Lord."

The sharp sickle mentioned along with this golden crown is a small hand tool used for cutting stalks of grain during harvest. In John's day, the grain was held in one hand and cut off near the ground with the sickle. The combined mention of crown and sickle denotes a righteous and holy judgment.

This particular judgment gives us yet another preview of the Second Coming of Christ. It is also connected with the Battle of Armageddon, as seen in verse 20. As we know, the Battle of Armageddon will be finished by Christ. Thus, this judgment refers to the time when Christ returns to judge in righteousness (Holiness - 19:11) and to make war (at Armageddon).

Verses fourteen through sixteen do not refer to the Rapture of the Church, as some believe, for that occurred before the Tribulation Period. Neither is it a reaping of those martyred saints of the Tribulation Period, mentioned in the previous verses. It is a judgment and reaping of the Gentile nations as depicted in Joel 3:9-14:

> Proclaim ye this among the Gentiles; Prepare war, wake up the mighty men, let all the men of war draw near; let them come up: Beat your plowshares into swords, and your pruninghooks into spears: let the weak say, I am strong. Assemble yourselves, and come, all ye heathen, and gather yourselves together round about: thither cause thy mighty ones to come down, O LORD. Let the heathen be wakened, and come up to the valley of Jehoshaphat: for there will I sit to judge all the heathen round about. Put ye in the sickle, for the harvest is ripe: come, get you down; for the press is full, the vats overflow; for their wickedness is great. Multitudes, multitudes in the valley of decision: for the day of the LORD is near in the valley of decision. Joel 3:9-14

Those nations which help the Jews during the time of the Tribulation Period will receive reward (going into the Millennial Reign), while those who do not will be cast into Hell. Note, however, that this reaping will be done by Christ, a reaping of the favored sheep nations (see Matthew 25:31-46).

John, as well as the reader, is assured here that those who help the Jews during the Tribulation will receive the reward of being reaped by Christ. Upon judging the nations, Christ, will use the sickle to harvest. Thus, as with the use of the sickle in John's day, the hand of Christ will be upon the harvest (sheep nations). They will be the privileged nations that will go into the Millennial Reign of Christ. The goat nations (disfavored nations) will be told to depart and will thus be harvested by an angel, as seen in the verses which are shortly to follow.

The reaping by Christ will occur simultaneously with the next reaping initiated by an angel. The "time is come for thee to reap" reveals that a great delay has ended. This reaping, as that of the angel, is connected with the battle of Armageddon. It is at the valley of decision, the valley of Megiddo, a valley of judgment.

Valley Of Megiddo

Armageddon comes from the words *"har"* meaning mountain and *"megiddown"* meaning "rendezvous", hence, the "Mountain of Megiddo" or "Mount of Rendezvous." When the armies of the world meet in the great valley of decision, it will be the summit of rendezvous, the ultimate gathering of nations. This is the place where the Battle of Armageddon will be fought at the end of the Tribulation Period. Scholars disagree about the exact location of this place, but it is most likely the valley between Mount Carmel and the city of Jezreel. Armageddon is the Greek word for this area, which was the scene of many ancient battles. It is here where the cup of the wine of the fierceness of God's wrath will be poured out (Rev. 16:19). At that time, Satan will be bound for 1,000 years, marking the beginning of the Millennial Reign of Christ on Earth. The sheep nations (chosen nations by Christ) will enter into this Eden-like paradise.

Assurance Number Seven

And another angel came out of the temple which is in heaven, he also having a sharp sickle. And another angel came out from the altar, which had power over fire; and cried with a loud cry to him that had the sharp sickle, saying, Thrust in thy sharp sickle, and gather the clusters of the vine of the earth; for her grapes are fully ripe. And the angel thrust in his sickle into the earth, and gathered the vine of the earth, and cast it into the great winepress of the wrath of God. And the winepress was trodden without the city, and blood came out of the winepress, even unto the horse bridles, by the space of a thousand and six hundred furlongs. Rev. 14:17-20)

Another angel now appears on the scene. This one comes out of the temple in Heaven. He, like Christ, has a sharp sickle. The angel does not have to judge the nations, for the nations left behind by Christ are the doomed.

In connection with his reaping is yet another angel who has power over fire. The fire will be to burn the chaff of the vine. Who is this vine of the Earth that is to be gathered with the clusters?

Israel was a "vine" which was brought forth out of Egypt (Psa. 80:8). However, when God inspected them for "good fruit," He found "wild grapes" (Isa. 5:1-2). Thus, Israel is not the reference here. Jesus is also referred to as a "vine" (John 15:5). However, Jesus is not the vine of the Earth in the above reference, for the vine is to be cast into the winepress of the wrath of God.

The vine of the Earth here refers to the Antichrist. The clusters represent all those who follow him and his system. Notice that the vine and the grapes are cast into the great winepress of the wrath of God. So great will be the slaughter that blood will stream for 200 miles (1600 furlongs). This is in reference to the Battle of Armageddon and will be discussed further in chapter nineteen.

The above passages assure us that there is to be a harvest of the ungodly nations of the world. They are those nations which will arise against the very witness of God during the Tribulation Period. They are the goat nations and shall be turned into Hell.

The wicked shall be turned into hell, and all the nations that forget God. Psa. 9:17

With the ending of assurances of chapter fourteen
comes the return to the reality of the Tribulation Period in
chapter fifteen. The needed assurances, however, provide
a better outlook over the terrible calamities of the coming
"Day of the Lord." The greatest assurance in our present
time is to know the Lord Jesus personally and rest in the
"blessed hope" which that privilege affords.

Ω

Introducing
The
Last Seven Plagues
Chapter 15

And I saw another sign in heaven, great and marvellous, seven angels having the seven last plagues; for in them is filled up the wrath of God. Rev. 15:1

Here we leave the assurances of the previous chapter and resume our study of the events of "Jacob's trouble." It seems that John was also reassured as he is immediately introduced to the last seven plagues. This chapter covers John's introduction to those plagues and concerns the receiving of the seven vials containing the last seven plagues. These plagues fill up the wrath of God; that is, they bring God's wrath to the end of the Tribulation Period. The plagues are covered in detail in chapter sixteen; this chapter only introduces them.

The seven last plagues are mentioned at the onset of the chapter, but are put on hold for a time, as John once again views the Sea of Glass.

The Sea Of Glass

And I saw as it were a sea of glass mingled with fire: and them that had gotten the victory over the beast, and over his image, and over his mark, and over the number of his name, stand on the sea of glass, having the harps of God. And they sing the song of Moses the servant of God, and the song of the Lamb, saying,

Great and marvellous are thy works, Lord God Almighty; just and true are thy ways, thou King of saints. Who shall not fear thee, O Lord, and glorify thy name? for thou only art holy: for all nations shall come and worship before thee; for thy judgments are made manifest. Rev. 15:2-4

We saw in chapter 4:6 that the Sea of Glass is where the souls of those who die in the Lord during this present age are taken to await the Rapture of the Church. We also saw that paradise was within the Earth until the resurrection of Christ, when it was emptied and the Old Testament saints, those who died in the Lord, were taken to this Sea of Glass. This was when Christ led captivity captive (Eph. 4:8). (See chapter four "Sea Of Glass.")

At the Rapture of the Church, prior to the Tribulation Period, this sea will be emptied for the uniting of those souls with their new bodies at the resurrection (I Thess. 4:16-17). Afterward, the Sea of Glass will be used for the keeping of the souls of those martyred during the Tribulation Period. We must keep in mind that during our present dispensation, those who die in the Lord are taken to this Sea of Glass, a tranquil sea of rest.

However, the Scriptures above refer to a time after the emptying, re-filling and re-emptying of the Sea of Glass. We know this because those slaughtered during the Tribulation Period are seen standing upon the Sea of Glass. The redeemed are seen once again in chapter fifteen because the vial judgments will have been poured out on their behalf. These vial judgments, which consummate the Tribulation Period, will be their earthly vindication.

Mingled with Fire

The Sea of Glass mentioned in chapter four was clear

as crystal; however, this mention of the Sea of Glass reveals it as being mingled with fire. Why? People of the Old Testament times placed great emphasis on fire, not only for heating their homes, cooking, and forging tools and weapons, but also as a symbol of God's presence, power and judgment. Israel was warned against worshipping fire, as did the Medes, Persians and Cannanites, for it was an abomination to God (Ez. 16:20,21; 2 Chr. 28:3).

God did, however, instruct Israel to keep a fire burning continuously on the altars of sacrifice (Lev. 6:13). The consumption of offerings by fire assured the people that God had accepted their sacrifices (Judg. 6:21; 1 Kings 18:38). The Sea of Glass being mingled with fire reveals that the sacrifice unto death during the Tribulation Period will be an acceptable sacrifice to God.

Temple, Tabernacle, Testimony

> And after that I looked, and, behold, the temple of the tabernacle of the testimony in heaven was opened: And the seven angels came out of the temple, having the seven plagues, clothed in pure and white linen, and having their breasts girded with golden girdles. Rev. 15:5-6

After seeing the scene concerning the Sea of Glass, John looked and beheld the temple of the tabernacle of the testimony in Heaven. Just what are the temple, the tabernacle, and the testimony?

Temple

The temple in Heaven is mentioned twelve times in Revelation. Each reference indicates that it is not merely a spiritual aberration; it is a literal temple in which God sits upon a throne. It is seen in verse five as opened, indicating that the heavens must be opened or rolled back in order to view the Heaven where God dwells, the third Heaven into which the apostle Paul was caught up (II Cor. 12:1-7).

There is not any reason to believe that this temple is not a literal temple. This heavenly temple is the one after which both the tabernacle of Moses and the temple of Solomon were patterned (Ex. 25:9,40; Num. 8:4; I Chron. 28:11-19; Heb. 8:5; 9:23).

Tabernacle

Two Hebrew words (*"ohel* and *Mish-kawn"*) and three Greek words (*"Skene, Skenonia* and *Skenopegia"*), for "tabernacle," all denote a temporary dwelling. The phrase "temple of the tabernacle" places the emphasis on the temple, for the tabernacle was built after the pattern of the heavenly temple. All earthly temples are actually tabernacles, temporary dwellings. Their true nature should reflect the heavenly temple. The tabernacle is mentioned here to express that fact. In addition, the "temple of the tabernacle" refers to the inner sanctuary of the Old Testament tabernacle, the Holy of Holies or Most Holy Place. This brings attention to the fact that the judgment of God will come from the Most Holy Place, from God's own presence and power.

Testimony

The testimony is none other than that of the temple and dwelling of God. It will be an open testimony expressing the awesome power, authority and holiness of God to the world. This testimony will come at the hand of the seven angels who come out of the temple having the seven last plagues (v.6).

These angels are clothed in pure and white linen, symbolizing the holiness of Heaven. They represent God's holiness, His righteousness, and His justice. They also wear golden belts, the symbol of royalty, authority and power. They are sent out from the holiness of God to execute righteous judgment upon the world.

Seven Golden Vials

And one of the four beasts gave unto the seven angels seven golden vials full of the wrath of God, who liveth for ever and ever. And the temple was filled with smoke from the glory of God, and from his power; and no man was able to enter into the temple, till the seven plagues of the seven angels were fulfilled. Rev. 15:7-8

The seven angels are given seven golden vials full of the wrath of God. These vials are bowls with no lids, denoting that these judgments will be poured and nothing will be able to stop them. They are to complete the plagues of the Tribulation Period. They will be poured out quickly and efficiently upon the world. We are not told which of the four beasts will hand these vials to the angels; however, it will likely be the beast with the face of a lion, the king of beasts. This beast represents the untamed beast, and the unleashing and untamed effects of the pouring of the vial judgments.

Smoke

The temple is seen here as being filled with smoke. When Moses finished the tabernacle and when Solomon had finished the temple, there was a cloud, the "Shekinah Glory," but no smoke. Smoke means "judgment." The temple is seen opened and full of smoke to reveal the glory and power of God and for judgment. It is the judgment that will be poured out from seven vials. Smoke is found in connection with judgment ten times in Revelation (8:4; 9:2,3,17,18; 14:11; 15:8; 18:9,18; 19:3). The smoke, hence the vial judgments, are seen as coming from the glory and power of God.

No man will be able to enter the temple during the pouring out of the seven plagues, not until the plagues are fulfilled. This speaks of the entrance into the temple where God's throne is, not that no one will enter the Sea of Glass. This is realized due to the fact that many will be killed during the last half of the Tribulation Period, including the two witnesses. Such martyrs will enter into their rest.

Ω

The Last Seven Plagues
Chapter 16

A plague is an epidemic disease of high mortality, a pestilence, a widespread affliction or calamity. This chapter deals with the diseases or plagues that will befall men, sea creatures, water sources, the sun, the river Euphrates, the air, and the Antichrist and his kingdom during the Tribulation Period.

As we saw in chapter fifteen, these plagues are the last seven calamities which will hit the Earth during the Tribulation. The word "last," as used in chapter fifteen, is *"eschatos,"* which has to do with those things in a series which are in continuous connection.

These plagues not only succeed one another and are closely related, but are also closely connected with each of the seven trumpets. This assertion is disputed by some and embraced by others. However, as we progress through our study of the vials, we will see that these vials are indeed the "spreading effects" of the trumpet judgments.

These vials, poured out and governed by angels, do not occur simultaneously with the trumpets, but they begin their working, individually, after each trumpet is blown. For example, the first trumpet sounds and shortly thereafter vial number one is poured out and its effects begin their progression.

We also see the connection through the fact that both the trumpet and vial judgments are part of the seventh seal. In addition, between the trumpet judgments of chapters eight through eleven and the vial judgments of this chapter, there are interval chapters. These interval chapters are given for explanation. The events of these "parentheses" or interval chapters are not altogether in chronological order. They merely add more information and explanation to the events of the Tribulation Period. Take the interval chapters out and the trumpets and vials overlap as the chronological order of events progress. The fact that the interval chapters are given for more detail and explanation adds credence to the trumpet judgments and the vial judgments being connected.

Note, however, that the trumpets and the vials are different in execution. The vials are "poured" whereas the trumpets are "sounded." This "pouring" signifies the spreading effect, as that of a plague. For example, the "pouring" of water results in the spreading of liquid across a given area. Likewise, the vials are the spreading effects of the trumpet judgments.

Remember the term "repetition and expansion?" The seven plagues relate once again to one of those times that John reviews and retraces events previously covered. Only this time, the emphasis is on the effects rather than the cause. For a clearer understanding we will briefly review the trumpet judgments as we study the vial judgments. The page number of each may be readily found in the chapter outlines in the back of this book.

Vial Judgment No. 1

And I heard a great voice out of the temple saying to the seven angels, Go your ways, and pour out the vials of the wrath of God upon the earth. And the first went, and poured out his vial upon the earth; and there fell a noisome and grievous sore upon the men which had the mark of the beast, and upon them which worshipped his image. Rev. 16:1-2

Seven angels will sound the trumpets and seven different angels will pour out the vials. John hears a great voice from within the temple commanding the seven angels to "go your ways." The phrase "go your ways" refers to the widespread effect of the wrath of God, which will be poured out. The spreading effect of trumpet number one begins. It is vial number one. Note, again, that these plagues relate to the effects and not to the cause. (See chart, pg. 487)

At the command to "go your ways," the first angel will pour out his vial upon the Earth. This vial contains noisome ("*kakos*"- "injurious") and grievous ("*poneros*" - "evil") sores. These sores are "*helkos*" "ulcers." They are ulcerous sores, open either to the surface of the body or to a natural cavity and accompanied by the disintegration of tissue and the formation of pus. They are often referred to as boils.

These sores will affect all those who have taken the mark of the beast and worshipped the image. That is an important note. We saw in chapter thirteen how the microchip will play a major role in incorporating the mark of the beast. Quite possibly, vial number one will unleash tormentous and hurtful sores resulting from the implanting the microchip underneath the surface of the skin. Thus, this plague of boils will be a world-wide disease.

It would thus be safe to say that the hail and fire, mingled with blood of trumpet number one will not only bring havoc to the atmosphere and the Earth, but will greatly affect those who have taken the mark of the beast. In all probability, it will be due, in some fashion, to the chemical compounds of the microchip. The inhalation of the smoke from the burning trees and grass (trumpet one) will undoubtedly ignite a reaction in the bodies of those with the implanted microchip. A great plague of boils will be the result. Remember that it is a "pouring" or spreading judgment which will come upon those who have taken the mark of the beast.

Vial number one repeats the sixth Egyptian plague (Ex. 9:8-12). That plague was a literal plague, so there should be no doubt that the plagues of the Tribulation Period will be literal plagues as well.

Vial Judgment No. 2

And the second angel poured out his vial upon the sea; and it became as the blood of a dead man; and every living soul died in the sea. Rev. 16:3

In studying trumpet number two, we find that 1/3 of the sea was turned to blood, 1/3 of the creatures of the sea died, and 1/3 of the ships were destroyed. Here, in vial number two, we find that every living soul in the sea died. It is a spreading plague, a reaction to and an effect of a previous judgment (the sounding of trumpet number two). Here the ships are not mentioned because trumpet number two was a volcanic blast upon the waters of the sea, whereas vial number two is a spreading plague due to that trumpet. The ships are not mentioned, but those who operate them are mentioned.

The spreading effect wipes out all life. Both man and beast alike are killed. Note that Scripture relates that every soul in the sea dies. The word "soul" in 16:3 is "*psuche*" and refers to the "breath or life-spirit" and is used of both man and beast (Rom. 13:1; 1 Thess. 5:3). It is evident, then, that all life in the sea dies. We must remember that 1/3 of the ships operated by men were destroyed at the sounding of trumpet number two. Here, the vial spreads to include the remainder of human life. Those who operate the ships and other sailing vessels, as well as sea life, die.

Vial Judgment No. 3

And the third angel poured out his vial upon the rivers and fountains of waters; and they became blood. And I heard the angel of the waters say, Thou art righteous, O Lord, which art, and wast, and shalt be, because thou hast judged thus. For they have shed the blood of saints and prophets, and thou hast given them blood to drink; for they are worthy. And I heard another out of the altar say, Even so, Lord God Almighty, true and righteous are thy judgments. Rev. 16:4-7

Our study of trumpet number three revealed that 1/3 of the rivers will be polluted by a meteoric mass which will hit the Earth. The fountains of water beneath the Earth's surface shall also be affected, and 1/3 of the world's waterways will become polluted, killing many of Earth's inhabitants. Here, the effects of the trumpet judgment are seen as far-reaching; they spread to all waters. Again, we see the "pouring" effect.

Vial number three is a plague given for those who tormented the saints of God. At this point during the Tribulation Period, all waterways will become uncontrollably polluted. Water is a necessary commodity and affects everyone. Efforts to clean the polluted waters will be futile. All rivers and fountains of waters will be turned to death.

Angel Of The Waters

Here we meet the angel of the waters. As mentioned earlier, angels play a vital role in overseeing all of God's creation. Imagine how long this angel labored to keep the waters pure. Here they become polluted. However, the angel is not possessive. How often do we become selfish with those things which the Lord has entrusted to us, thinking we know what is best above God's judgment? We do not see such selfishness in this angel. The waters which have been overseen by him are graciously and willfully released to the Lord. The angel then proclaims that the righteousness of the Lord is justified in His giving blood to drink for those who had shed innocent blood. This is further verified by yet another angel who speaks from the altar.

Vial number three repeats the first Egyptian plague (Ex. 7:19-24).

Vial Judgment No. 4

And the fourth angel poured out his vial upon the sun; and power was given unto him to scorch men with fire. And men were scorched with great heat, and blasphemed the name of God, which hath power over these plagues: and they repented not to give him glory. Rev. 16:8-9

Trumpet number four revealed that 1/3 of the sun, moon, and stars were darkened. Here the rays of the sun once again hit the Earth. This Scripture reveals that the darkness of trumpet number four is but temporary. The dissipation of the darkness brings scorching heat.

We find that men will, once again, run from repentance and cling to the act of resisting God. It is apparent that these men are now aware that God is doing the punishing and they willfully reject any notion of repentance. They show this in their blasphemous acts toward God. This also indicates that they will be given a choice, but will continue to harden their hearts. They are well aware of God's judgments because of the witnessing of Moses, Elijah and the 144,000. The very fact that this vial will be "poured out" would fulfill its prophecy, thus, repentance to God would, evidently, shorten this vial judgment. However, the shortening of this judgment does not occur because men will not repent.

Vial Judgment No. 5

> And the fifth angel poured out his vial upon the seat of the beast; and his kingdom was full of darkness; and they gnawed their tongues for pain, And blasphemed the God of heaven because of their pains and their sores, and repented not of their deeds. Rev. 16: 10-11

Trumpet number five (woe no. 1) revealed the descent of the powerful star-angel having the authority of binding and loosing (9:1-2). He opens the bottomless pit from whence arises smoke full of tormenting locusts. These demonic creatures torture those men who do not have the seal of God in their foreheads. This is the time that men will seek death and not be able to find it. We also found in that discussion that trumpet number five marks the middle of the Tribulation Period. At that time the Antichrist will be possessed by Abaddon (chapter nine, "The Locust King"), will break the covenant with the Jews (Dan. 9:27), set himself up in the temple as God (II Thess 2:4), and demand total worship.

The fifth vial is poured upon the seat of the beast and all those of his kingdom. This "pouring" causes the spreading of demonic spirits throughout the kingdom. Those who hold governing positions, from top to bottom, are affected. They will gnaw their tongues because of the pain. The spreading of the tormenting locusts (9:3), along with the pollution of the waters of vial number four, reaches to the very fabric of the one-world kingdom. Instead of repenting to God, they prepare for war against God. This is seen in the discussion of the next vial.

Vial number five repeats the ninth Egyptian plague (Ex. 10:21-23).

Vial Judgment No. 6

And the sixth angel poured out his vial upon the great river Euphrates; and the water thereof was dried up, that the way of the kings of the east might be prepared. And I saw three unclean spirits like frogs come out of the mouth of the dragon, and out of the mouth of the beast, and out of the mouth of the false prophet. For they are the spirits of devils, working miracles, which go forth unto the kings of the earth and of the whole world, to gather them to the battle of that great day of God Almighty. Behold, I come as a thief. Blessed is he that watcheth, and keepeth his garments, lest he walk naked, and they see his shame. And he gathered them together into a place called in the Hebrew tongue Armageddon. Rev. 16:12-16

The sixth vial is poured out for the drying up of the Euphrates River, the most important and longest river of western Asia. Nearly 1800 miles long and from 300 to 1200 yards wide, its depth ranges from 10 to 30 feet. It would appear to be a great feat to dry up such a river. Dams, irrigation projects, lakes, canals, and the like, can be built today to alter huge lakes and rivers. However, such measures will not be needed to dry up the Euphrates River. To be "dried up" is "xeraino" to desiccate; to shrivel, to pine or wither away. The river shall cease.

We must not forget that great natural disasters will occur during the Tribulation Period. Many upheavals affecting large areas of the world will occur from the seals and trumpets and connected events.

The pouring of vial number six is doubtless an effect of trumpet number six (woe number 2). In the discussion of trumpet number six, we found the release of the four angels which were bound in the Euphrates River. These four angels are evil spirits which in times past have overseen four major attacks and enslavements of the historic city of Babylon. They are very powerful, very evil spirits who are to command a supernatural army of 200 million, as seen in 9:16-19. We have seen that their battle is not with the men of Earth, but it is a spiritual battle in the heavens. However, this literal battle shall greatly effect the Earth and its inhabitants.

We know by example that the expulsion of evil spirits causes havoc upon the victims when they are cast out. In the case at hand, the victim is the Euphrates River. In Mark 1:23-27, there was a man in the synagogue with an unclean spirit. This unclean spirit consisted of multiple demonic beings congregated in this man's very being. When Jesus cast out this multi-faceted spirit, the flesh of the man was torn. Doubtless, the Euphrates River will be "torn" and terribly disrupted when the four powerful and evil angels are cast out of the Euphrates. Thus, vial number six, one of the effects of trumpet number six, will complete the disruption of the Euphrates River, causing it to be completely drained and dried. This too, will make way for the kings of the east to approach Armageddon.

Kings Of The East

The drying up of the Euphrates will be accomplished so that the kings of the east may have clear passage to the west. It is evident that all the nations east of Palestine will march, in one form or another, toward Israel. These nations will desire to preserve the land of Palestine, while annihilating the remnant of the Jews. In order to preserve a land, foot soldiers are needed, another reason for the drying of the river. The move toward Israel is also another measure of preparation for the battle of Armageddon. It is a preparation for the supper of the great God that will be given to the fowls of the air (19:17-18). Armageddon is one of the greatest gatherings for battle in the history of the world. Thus, we refer to the spirits which are responsible for this gathering.

Spirits Like Frogs

John saw three unclean spirits like frogs come out of the mouth of the dragon, and out of the mouth of the beast, and out of the mouth of the false prophet. Many wars have been set forth in deception for the personal gain of elite manipulators. The Battle of Armageddon will be no different. This battle is the result of the corrupt leadership of Earth while fulfilling the Scriptures. The march will be set in motion by the Antichrist (beast), Satan (dragon), and the false prophet (one-world religious leader), the sources of the three unclean spirits. The march will be the ultimate attempt to rid the Earth of its troubles by annihilating those considered to be God's people. At this point, the one-world government will have already set up the image in Jerusalem. However, there will be continued opposition. Thus, these beastly leaders will send out a proclamation to invade and overwhelm the land of Palestine. The going forth of their proclamation appears to John as frogs leaping from king to king, kingdom to kingdom, throughout the world. It is the combined influence of Satan, the Antichrist (possessed by Abaddon), and the false prophet. This onslaught will result in the death of millions. These spirits of devils appeared to John to be "like" frogs.

Immediate Warning

Verse fifteen gives a glimpse of the Second Coming of Christ in the form of a warning. "Behold, I come as a thief. Blessed is he that watcheth, and keepeth his garments, lest he walk naked, and they see his shame." Note that Jesus is coming back for the believers of the Tribulation Period also, not only for those of us in this dispensation. The gathering of nations in the Valley of Megiddo (v.16) will be a sign to the believers of the Tribulation Period to hold fast to their profession, even in the midst of extensive peril (Matt. 25:13; Luke 12:37; Rev. 16:15).

Vial Judgment No. 7

> And the seventh angel poured out his vial into the air; and there
> came a great voice out of the temple of heaven, from the throne,
> saying, It is done. And there were voices, and thunders, and light-
> nings; and there was a great earthquake, such as was not since
> men were upon the earth, so mighty an earthquake, and so great.
> And the great city was divided into three parts, and the cities of
> the nations fell: and great Babylon came in remembrance before
> God, to give unto her the cup of the wine of the fierceness of his
> wrath. And every island fled away, and the mountains were not
> found. And there fell upon men a great hail out of heaven, every
> stone about the weight of a talent: and men blasphemed God
> because of the plague of the hail; for the plague thereof was
> exceeding great. Rev. 16:17-21

The pouring of the seventh vial affects the atmosphere
of Earth. A great voice, the voice of God, pierces the
atmosphere from the throne in Heaven proclaiming the
finishing acts of "Jacob's trouble." The voice proclaims,
"It is done."

Trumpet number seven and vial number seven occur
more closely together than the other trumpets and vials.
The reason is that they both finish the mystery of God
(10:6-7). The vial is a more detailed view of the finishing
acts of the Tribulation Period. The "finishing of the mystery of God" is stated under the discussion of the seventh
trumpet and revealed in the seventh vial as, "It is done."

In trumpet number seven (woe number three), we saw
that great voices are heard in Heaven and that the temple
of God is opened up. Here, there are voices, thunders,
lightnings, great hail, and also a mighty earthquake. The
voices will proclaim that the kingdoms of this world have
become the kingdoms of the Lord (11:15). This, as seen

earlier, denotes the redemption of Earth dominion back to Christ by His own will and action (See chapters 5 and 10). At the proclamation of "no more delay" (10:6-7), the finishing of the mystery of God begins. Thus, vial number seven and its events finish trumpet number seven.

Great Earthquake

There will be an earthquake greater than anything that has ever occurred on Earth before (vs.19-20). It will be so great that entire cities will fold — not just one or two cities, but every city of every nation which has rejected God. Only those nations considered "sheep nations" will escape such destruction. Every island will disappear and every mountain will be flattened. That, friend, is a great earthquake! The Earth's crust will be as a wave of water which ripples across a stormy sea, bringing unprecedented destruction.

This earthquake will affect the one-world system as nothing else has. Referred to here as Babylon, it will be as Babylon (v.19), brought up for remembrance before God and targeted for destruction. It will greatly affect all cities of the ten-division global network. Note that the governmental and religious systems, during the Tribulation Period, will become virtually one and the same. Their mixing and destruction is discussed in the following two chapters.

This great quaking of the Earth will occur when Christ Jesus sets His feet upon the Mount of Olives, as foretold in Zechariah 14:3-5. This is when the Mount of Olives will split in two and a great valley will appear. The armies marching toward their doom for the Battle of

Armageddon will occur just prior to this great earthquake.

> Then shall the LORD go forth, and fight against those nations, as when he fought in the day of battle. And his feet shall stand in that day upon the mount of Olives, which is before Jerusalem on the east, and the mount of Olives shall cleave in the midst thereof toward the east and toward the west, and there shall be a very great valley; and half of the mountain shall remove toward the north, and half of it toward the south. And ye shall flee to the valley of the mountains; for the valley of the mountains shall reach unto Azal: yea, ye shall flee, like as ye fled from before the earthquake in the days of Uzziah king of Judah: and the LORD my God shall come, and all the saints with thee. Zech. 14:3-5

The great earthquake will also divide the city of Jerusalem into three parts. Note that the Mount of Olives is split into two parts, whereas the city of Jerusalem is divided into three. The city will be divided into three parts because it will have been polluted by the Antichrist and the false prophet, which are both led by Satan. This is an ungodly trinity of Satan (anti-God), the beast (anti-Christ), and the false prophet (anti-Spirit). The number three, as we have seen, is a holy number. Thus, these "three parts" depict God's holy judgment, holy authority, and holy power brought upon the city polluted by an unholy trinity. Note again that this great earthquake will occur when "the LORD my God shall come, and all the saints with thee." This time-frame is also realized due to the existence of mountains upon Christ's return, whereas the earthquake mentioned above flattens every mountain. Thus, this dividing of the city cannot occur until the return of Christ.

Great Hail

As we saw earlier, men will be aware that these judgments are from God, but they will continue to reject any notion of repentance. Even after the raining of great hail, these men will cleave to rejecting God.

This hail is great indeed. It is about the weight of a talent. A talent is a weight of measure ranging from 100 to 125 pounds. Imagine the destruction caused by such large hail. This will undoubtedly cause the death of many. There will be few places to hide from this plague, as cities and mountains will have been flattened by the great earthquake. It is the wrath of the winepress of God unleashed. The "Law" required that the "blasphemer" should be stoned to death (Lev. 24:16). These huge stones from heaven, at the end of the Tribulation Period, will be a fulfilling of that law.

Vial number seven repeats the seventh Egyptian plague (Ex. 9:13-35).

Ω

Mystery
Babylon The Great
Chapter 17

False religions have done more to doom people's souls than anything else on Earth. While promising life, they give death. They offer salvation while hoarding souls for damnation.

The apostle Paul tells us that the deceivers themselves are deceived and will wax worse and worse (II Tim 3:13). That is certainly the case today. This chapter concerns the fall and doom of the ultimate false religion, the one to which all religions will ultimately bond. It is Mystery Babylon, ruled by the false prophet.

An Angel Talks To John

And there came one of the seven angels which had the seven vials, and talked with me, saying unto me, Come hither; I will shew unto thee the judgment of the great whore that sitteth upon many waters: With whom the kings of the earth have committed fornication, and the inhabitants of the earth have been made drunk with the wine of her fornication. Rev. 17:1-2

One of the seven angels who had the seven vials tells John of Babylon's fall. It is not stated which of the seven angels it was who talked with him.

At first, one might think that all seven vials had been poured when the angel talked with John. The past tense of the sentence would make it appear so. However, it is evident that it was one of the first angels of the seven. That is to say, not all the vials had been poured when this angel talked with John. We know this because the angel shows and explains to John the judgment of the great whore. This beforehand explanation from the angel is revealed in his first words, "Come hither, I will shew thee." That statement denotes that the fall of the whore, although close at hand in the vision, is yet future. If all the vials had already been poured out, having finished the mystery of God, then John would have witnessed the fall and would need no special vision from the angel.

The Great Whore

We must note that chapter seventeen is yet another parenthesis chapter of Revelation. Its primary focus is to show the judgment of the great whore. This is the first time that such a term (whore) has been used to explain any entity in Revelation. Who, then, is this great whore?

The answer is obvious. She is the one of whom John spoke in the letters sent to the seven churches. This whore is the seductive system of religion represented by the Thyatira church of chapter two. She represents that form of religion which descended from the tower of Babel and was expanded to appear compatible with Christianity by Attalus III and Constantine (chapter two, "Pergamos Historical"). She is Jezebel, the papal system which was to be cast into a bed in order that the kings of the Earth should commit fornication with her (2:20-22).

This great whore is seen as sitting upon many waters. These "waters" are explained in verse fifteen.

And he saith unto me, The waters which thou sawest, where the whore sitteth, are peoples, and multitudes, and nations, and tongues. Rev. 17:15

Verses one and two of this chapter supply proof that the kings of the Earth will indeed commit fornication with the religious system of Rome. This is happening, even today.

Not only will the kings of the Earth, but also the inhabitants will commit fornication with her (v.2, peoples, multitudes, nations, tongues). They are those people who have been, and who will be, seduced by her. They are the followers drunk on the wine of Rome's fornication and the inhabitants who have been carried away as if drunk by her world-wide religious appeal and seductive nature. Thus, it is the people of Earth who give the great whore her seat of authority (where the whore sitteth).

The whore's seat of authority will make her attractive to the beast and his cohorts. The great reverence given this whore by the multitudes of all peoples of the world, will earn her respect from the beast on which she rides. That beast, the political one-world system, of course, will be operated by the Antichrist and the ten kings. As we will see later, that attractiveness will have political motives only.

Mystery, Babylon, The Great Whore

So he carried me away in the spirit into the wilderness: and I saw a woman sit upon a scarlet coloured beast, full of names of blasphemy, having seven heads and ten horns. And the woman was arrayed in purple and scarlet colour, and decked with gold and precious stones and pearls, having a golden cup in her hand full of abominations and filthiness of her fornication: And upon her forehead was a name written, MYSTERY, BABYLON THE GREAT, THE MOTHER OF HARLOTS AND ABOMINATIONS OF THE EARTH. Rev. 17:3-5

Here we find that John is once again "in the spirit." This phrase, in conjuction with the "come hither," marks the third major vision of Revelation and reflects the future aspect of the vision.

Scarlet Colored Beast

We saw earlier this woman sitting upon many waters, but here she is sitting upon a scarlet colored beast. This is not a contradiction. Whereas the people, multitudes, nations and tongues support the great whore, they do not instigate where she will go. They merely supply the saddle of her seat of authority. They supply the seat by giving her allegiance and following her pernicious ways. The whore will go where she desires, due to the beast upon which she rides.

The beast has the color of scarlet —"scarlet" is "*kokkinos*" or crimson, a deep purplish-red. Its appearance is deceiving in that it appears purplish, but is truly red. Purple was the most precious of ancient dyes. It took a total of 250,000 mollusks to make one ounce of purple dye. This accounted partly for its great price. It was highly valued within the nation of Israel. This purplish attire represents the attractive and seductive lure of this wealthy beast. Purple was also the color of royal robes (Judg. 8:26), as well as the garments of the wealthy (Prov. 31:22). In New Testament times, purple dye was an important item of trade (Acts 16:14; Rev. 18:12). This beast, however, is actually red. We saw in chapter twelve that the color red, as that ascribed to the dragon, Satan, denotes bloodshed. So the reality of the scarlet-colored beast is that its nature is truly satanic, ungodly and corrupt.

Seven Heads, Ten Horns

The beast on which the woman rides has seven heads and ten horns. We saw in chapter thirteen that this beast is none other than the one-world government led by the Antichrist, also called a beast. We also saw that the one-world government and the one-world religion will bind together with one purpose: to govern the world. The above verses reveal that the religious system will be the weaker of the two. However, each system will need the other in order to achieve global power. Once that power is fully achieved, the weaker system will become dispensable (discussed later).

The Woman Decked In Purple

The woman, also decked with purple and scarlet, is the epitome of wealth and corruption. The wealth of the religious system is very appealing to the beast upon which she rides. However, she too, is a deceiver. Note that these colors are the colors of the Catholic clergy, cappa magna, a long, hooded cloak of purple wool for bishops and scarlet watered silk for cardinals. This woman (Romanism) aligns perfectly with her counterpart beast upon which she rides. In fact, the religion she offers is the worship of the Antichrist (beast) and the world government. She holds a golden cup in her hand, but offers pious gifts such as filthy doctrine and fornication. It is the doctrine of devils and the offering of the yoke of bondage. Paul has given warnings of such evil (1 Tim. 4:1; 11 Cor. 6:14).

Today thousands of men, women, boys and girls are literally starving to death and overlooked by wealthy religions. Imagine the greater needs during the Tribulation Period after great catastrophes have hit the Earth.

Mystery Babylon

And upon her forehead was a name written, MYSTERY, BABYLON THE GREAT, THE MOTHER OF HARLOTS AND ABOMINATIONS OF THE EARTH. Rev. 17:5

The woman accomplishes what has only been sought after in times past. She brings under one canopy the different religions of the world. She is called "Mystery" because she descends from the mystery religions of Babylon. This makes her attractive and compatible with differing religions. She is "Babylon the Great" because Babylon is where her roots lie and from whence came her devilish doctrines. We saw in chapter two the roots of Roman Catholicism and how that particular system of religion descended from ancient Babylon through the worship of Nimrod and particularly Semiramis (chapter two, subtitle, "What is Paganism?").

As seen earlier, the head of the religious systems of the end-times will without a doubt spring from the Vatican, the seat of Roman Catholicism and the ultimate false prophet, the pope. There will be, and are now, many tentacles reaching from the Vatican which are uniting various religious denominations across the world.

It is true that the Church of Jesus Christ (born-again believers) should be united and become as one in Christian principle. Christ prayed for such unity (Jn. 17:11). However, the coming together of many differing denominations and religions of the world means that the true principles of Christ must be sacrificed, thus, no complete truth. This is why the whore is called the MOTHER OF HARLOTS AND ABOMINATIONS OF THE EARTH. She seduces all religions to unite with a common bond foreign to the Bible and Christian principles.

Son Of The Harlot

Note that the only way various religions and denominations may adhere to one another is to be spiritually weakened to the truth through blind leadership. Tragically, this is occurring in many mainline Protestant churches today. This spiritual weakening is happening through the counterpart religion of Romanism. As Roman Catholicism continues the religion of Semiramis, the Masonic Lodge continues the religion of Nimrod (See chapter two, "Gods & Goddesses." See also the author's book, "The Masonic-Christian Conflict Explained").

Masonic Connection

The Masonic system will indeed play an important role in the formation of the one-world political and religious systems of the Antichrist. Indeed, the Antichrist will be an instrumental figure in Freemasonry (Masonic Lodge). This is only logical because the Masonic Lodge is the only world-wide organization holding to the worship of Nimrod, the son-husband of Semiramis. Nimrod, the leading figure of idolatry between the flood of Noah and the time of Abraham, is often referred to in classical history as "the husband of the mother." Nimrod was worshipped under the names of Moloch, Merodach, Osiris, and a host of other names. He is the sun-god, Baal, worshipped as the Sun as well as the "all-seeing eye" found in Masonic Lodges (*"Morals & Dogma"* pgs. 476,477).

The teachings of Freemasonry run completely parallel with the new idea and "new age" utopian dream. Note the following new age philosophy:

"According to the Wisdom teachings, the Masonic Movement is one of the three main channels through which the preparation for the new age is going on." ... It is a far more occult organization than can be realized, and is intended to be the training school for the coming advanced occultists" (excerpt from letter sent to Omega Publishing 5/19/87).

The universal and ecumenical teaching of the Lodge is one of its great boasts. The principles of Christ are sacrificed in order that religious unity may exist.

"Masonry, around whose altars the Christian, the Hebrew, the Moslem, the Brahmin, the followers of Confucious and Zoroaster, can assemble as brethren and unite in prayer to the one God who is above all the Baalim, must needs to leave it to each of its initiates to look for the foundation of his faith and hope to the written scriptures of his own religion." Taken from *"Morals & Dogma"* written by Albert Pike, 33 degree Freemason and occultist, page 226.

Thus, Freemasonry recognizes no particular redeemer, yet places emphasis on God, "who is above all the Baalim." Such universality places Christ Jesus in the category of all the Baalim! "Baalim" principally and simply refers to "false gods" or "idols." The sad truth is that many governing positions of the Church are held by members of the Masonic Lodge. This is sad indeed, especially since a recent vote by the largest Protestant denomination in the world accepted Freemasonry as a compatible system of belief. This is a clear manifestation of the spiritual blindness and falling away of the present age (II Thess. 2:3). This blunder is a true sign of the times. Since that time, many religious movements have come upon the ecumenical scene. These movements are bolting unsuspecting Christians toward unscriptural unity.

The Drunken Woman

And I saw the woman drunken with the blood of the saints, and with the blood of the martyrs of Jesus: and when I saw her, I wondered with great admiration. Rev. 17:6

This verse brings home the reality of the evil character of Romanism. Although many good people are deceived into her clutches, her history of evil cannot be overlooked.

The true nature of Romanism's character is here openly revealed. Not only will she be drunken (*"methuo"* - "to drink [consume] to intoxication") with the slaughter of those saints during the Tribulation Period, but also with the slaughter of those throughout her history, such as the Waldenses and many other dissenters of Rome (Chapter 2, "The Beast Revealed"). Romanism's counterpart, Freemasonry, also clings to a bloody history (See the author's book *"The Masonic-Christian Conflict Explained"*).

John viewed the woman with great admiration. Not that he admired her conquests with respect, but with great wonder (admiration, *"thauma"* (Gk) - "wonder"). Seeing the great number of martyrs, John marveled at the sight.

The Woman & The Beast Explained

> And the angel said unto me, Wherefore didst thou marvel? I will tell thee the mystery of the woman, and of the beast that carrieth her, which hath the seven heads and ten horns. The beast that thou sawest was, and is not; and shall ascend out of the bottomless pit, and go into perdition: and they that dwell on the earth shall wonder, whose names were not written in the book of life from the foundation of the world, when they behold the beast that was, and is not, and yet is. Rev. 17:7-8

John marvelled at the sight of the great whore. The Greek word for "marvel" is *"thaumazo,"* "to wonder." John's wonder prompted the angel to reveal more about the whore and the beast upon which she rides. It is a mystery, something not readily revealed, something that needs more explanation. Thus, the angel begins to further explain the mystery of the woman and the beast. We must keep in mind that the overall intent of this chapter is to reveal the judgment of the great whore (v.1). The woman, as we have seen, represents Romanism, the papal system of religion. However, the above verses emphasize the beast upon which she sits. Note that it is the beast that "was, and is not; and shall ascend out of the bottomless pit." This beast thus symbolizes the kingdom, the Antichrist, and the satanic forces behind this kingdom.

1. The aspect of the beast that "was" - This, for John, was a prediction of the fall of Rome as a great, political empire. However, the time-frame which concerns this chapter places it in history (was). Yet it will revive as a world political power.

2. The aspect of the beast that "is not" - This refers to the Antichrist, who, in John's day, had not yet come, but who would appear in the last days. He takes on his beastly character when possessed by the beast from the pit.

3. The aspect, "shall ascend out of the bottomless pit" reveals the ascension of Abaddon who shall take possession of the Antichrist. He is a spirit being from the very depths of Hell, that is, Tartaros Hell, the bottomless pit.

These three characteristics reveal the complete one-world make-up.

1. "The kingdom," the one-world government comprised of the ten kings and kingdoms.

2. The Antichrist, who becomes head of this one-world kingdom.

3. The governing angel, Abaddon, who is under Satan's command, and virtually Satan's son, who ascends from the bottomless pit and controls the Antichrist. He is a satanic force against God, a destroying angel.

The combination of these characters and characteristics causes the people of Earth to wonder at the beast. This great wonder will undoubtedly peak at the assassination attempt upon the Antichrist. It will be at his possession and presumed resurrection (wounded unto death) by the beast from the bottomless pit. Those who wonder at the beast are those whose names are not written in the Book of Life from the foundation of the world. The above reference concerns those non-Christians who adhere to the one-world system and its leader, the Antichrist.

The Mind Of Wisdom

> And here is the mind which hath wisdom. The seven heads are seven mountains, on which the woman sitteth. And there are seven kings: five are fallen, and one is, and the other is not yet come; and when he cometh, he must continue a short space. Rev. 17:9-10

This pinpoints the location of the woman for the seat of the papacy, the Vatican. Rome is often referred to as the city of seven hills. The *"Catholic Encyclopedia"* states, "It is within the city of Rome, called the city of seven hills, that the entire area of Vatican State proper is now confined." We saw in chapter thirteen that this reference applies not only to location, but also to governmental entities (seven heads are seven mountains). This dual reference addresses the combining of the one-world religion and the one-world government. Here the reference plainly points to the whore and her seat, whereas chapter thirteen's seven mountains refer to governments.

The Antichrist

> And the beast that was, and is not, even he is the eighth, and is of the seven, and goeth into perdition. And the ten horns which thou sawest are ten kings, which have received no kingdom as yet; but receive power as kings one hour with the beast. These have one mind, and shall give their power and strength unto the beast. Rev. 17:11-13

Again we see the three-fold aspect of the beast. The

beast that "was" and "is not" refers to the government as a beast and the Antichrist as a beast. As we saw in chapter thirteen, Daniel speaks of a little horn which springs up from among the ten horns. That is, the ten horns or kings make up the one world government through which the Antichrist arises. Remember, he is "given a crown" as seen in chapter six. Upon reaching the middle of the Tribulation Period, Daniel's seventieth week, the Antichrist breaks the covenant with the Jews and begins a great slaughter against the people. They are those who will accept the witness of the 144,000, of Elijah and of Moses. The total rule given to the Antichrist, at that time, makes him a government within a government, the ultimate ruler. He, himself, becomes the eighth world government all wrapped up in one man. He is the Abaddon-possessed man of sin, the Antichrist. He will be cast into perdition, that is, eternal damnation.

One Mind

At the time of the division of the world into thirteen groups of nations, the Antichrist will make his way through the ranks to the ultimate position of world dominance. The appointed rulers of the thirteen-become-ten groups of nations will gain control by appointing this leader (given a crown). The ten kings shall have "one mind" and give all their power and strength to the Antichrist. Thus, they will receive power (as kings) "one hour" alongside the beast (Antichrist). This "hour" is the same hour spoken of as the "hour of temptation" mentioned earlier and is same hour to which born-again believers are promised escape (See "Hour Of Temptation" chapter three).

Making War With The Lamb

> These shall make war with the Lamb, and the Lamb shall over-
> come them: for he is Lord of lords, and King of kings: and they
> that are with him are called, and chosen, and faithful. Rev. 17:14

Here we see that the Antichrist and the ten kings will make war against the Lamb. This refers to the Battle of Armageddon ("these shall"). We saw in chapter sixteen how three unclean spirits will issue from Satan (dragon), the Antichrist (possessed by Abaddon) and the false prophet (religious leader) to cause the armies of the world to march toward Armageddon, the valley of decision.

This is a picture of great victory, a preview of the Second Coming of Jesus Christ. This time He is not coming as a babe in a manger, but as Lord of lords, and King of kings. Here, we get a glimpse of those who will return with him. They are the bride, the Church, those who are to be "caught out" (I Thess 4:13-18) prior to the Tribulation Period.

They are those who will escape the "hour of tempta-tion," the born-again believers of our present age (Zech 14:5; Col. 3:4; I Thess. 3:13; Jude 14). They are the called, the chosen, and the faithful.

The Judgment Of The Whore

> And he saith unto me, The waters which thou sawest, where the
> whore sitteth, are peoples, and multitudes, and nations, and
> tongues. And the ten horns which thou sawest upon the beast,
> these shall hate the whore, and shall make her desolate and naked,
> and shall eat her flesh, and burn her with fire. Rev. 17:15-16

Verse fifteen, as discussed earlier, reveals the seat of authority given to the religious system by the nations of the world. They revere the whore, making her attractive to the Antichrist and his purpose. He cannot gain the trust of the people of the world without this religious whore. Note, however, that the motives of the Antichrist are purely political.

Here John gives us a picture of the true nature of the ten kings (ten horns). They are those who have given their power and strength willfully to the Antichrist. They and their appointed leader (Antichrist) will have only used the religious beast as a catapult for world dominance. Outwardly, they have embraced the whore. Inwardly they hate her. We saw earlier that the Antichrist and his government will need the assistance of the one world religion. We also saw that the false prophet has particular aims at world dominance also, for he, the pope, claims to be the "vicar of Christ." The alliance and motivation between the two systems is purely political.

Because of their hatred for the religious system, the ten kings, and of course, the Antichrist, will make her desolate ("to lay waste and come to nought"), and naked ("nude, stripped of all protection") and will eat her flesh (they will take the spoils and riches of the apostate church) and burn her with fire (do away with the remnants of religion, for there is a new religion). The false prophet himself, however, is not destroyed as of yet. We find no evidence of his demise by the government. It is possible that he, after seeing the brutality of the government and the failure of his personal plan, completely aligns with the intent of the Antichrist. After all, the Antichrist, at this time, is the "new religion" and "new messiah." The reasoning will undoubtedly be that there is no longer a need for religion because the world redeemer (Antichrist) has come.

The Will Of God

> For God hath put in their hearts to fulfil his will, and to agree, and give their kingdom unto the beast, until the words of God shall be fulfilled. Rev. 17:17

The judgment of the whore comes about because of the will of God. It is not His will that any should perish but that all should come to repentance (II Peter 3:9). However, as we have seen time and again, men and women who cling to the one-world government shall not repent. In addition, those who cling to the false religion will also perish because of non-repentance. Due to His will for judgment to befall the false religious systems of the world, God causes the ten kings to agree and give their kingdoms to the beast until the words of God be fulfilled. These are the very words we are studying.

> Daniel answered and said, Blessed be the name of God for ever and ever: for wisdom and might are his: And he changeth the times and the seasons: he removeth kings, and setteth up kings: he giveth wisdom unto the wise, and knowledge to them that know understanding: He revealeth the deep and secret things: he knoweth what is in the darkness, and the light dwelleth with him. Daniel 2:20-22

That Great City

> And the woman which thou sawest is that great city, which reigneth over the kings of the earth. Rev. 17:18

The great city mentioned here can be none other than Vatican City. Again, we see the arrow of guilt pointing to Romanism. The ten kings hate the religious system for she appears to carry more influence with the Antichrist than they do. We discussed in previous chapters how kings and nobles alike feared the popes after they assumed power from the Roman emperors. This same fear drives the ten kings to destroy the religious system.

Kings Of The Earth

Note that there is a great difference between the "ten kings" and the "kings of the earth." The ten kings are those who shall rule the world alongside the Antichrist. They are the kings of ten divisions of the world. They will hate the whore (religious system), whereas the kings of the earth lament over her destruction (18:9). The "ten kings" will bring destruction to the whore by fire (17:16), and the "kings of the earth" who will suffer due to her burning (18:9). The kings of the earth are those political leaders, merchants, mighty men and rulers who have become rich from the wares of the whore and lived deliciously with her (18:8, 11-19).

Ω

The
Collapse
Of
Babylon
Chapter 18

Will the literal city of Babylon be rebuilt? That is the question on the lips of many Bible scholars.

Many scholars connect chapter eighteen with the literal rebuilding of the city of Babylon. Many Scriptures allude to that scenario. The ancient city of Babylon may indeed be rebuilt during the Tribulation Period. However, this is not clear from the book of Revelation because chapter eighteen does not concern that literal city.

We must keep in mind that there will be yet another great assault against the righteousness of God. It will be a time when the men of Earth will allow Satan to persuade their hearts once again. That time will be long after the Tribulation Period is over and has become history. It will be near the end of the Millennial Reign of Christ, a time after the binding of Satan for a thousand years. Afterward, according to Scripture, Satan will be loosed for a short season to deceive the nations (20:3). It is quite possible that at that time the Scriptures will be fulfilled concerning a literal city of Babylon (Isa. 13:19-20, Jer. 50:41, 51:26, 51:43). There must be a literal Babylon at some point for such prophecy to be fulfilled. After all, Babylon was where the first incorporated assault by man against God occurred (Tower of Babel). It will doubtless be the last place for such an assault. It would only seem proper to end organized rebellion at the very place it began on Earth. This will be discussed in chapter twenty.

It is very clear that chapter eighteen speaks of the same harlot as chapter seventeen. She is also called Babylon and her city, as we saw in the previous chapter, is Vatican City. Comparing chapter seventeen with chapter eighteen, we find that she is called Babylon the Great (17:5; 18:2). It is she who commits fornication with the kings of the earth (17:2; 18:3). She is the great and mighty city (17:18; 18:10). She is dressed in fine linen, purple, and scarlet (17:4; 18:16). This whore is to be burned with fire (17:16; 18:9). In addition, as chapter seventeen ends speaking of the whore (religious Babylon), chapter nineteen begins with the words, "After these things" which refers to the coming explanation of chapter eighteen and goes on to confirm that the judgment was that belonging to the whore of chapter seventeen.

The Babylon of chapter eighteen is thus the one-world religious system. Whereas chapter seventeen reveals the judgment of the great whore, and also those who execute the judgment, chapter eighteen gives the details of the judgment. Thus, it "explains the judgment." That explanation also reveals the outsiders who will be affected by her judgment.

Babylon The Great Is Fallen

And after these things I saw another angel come down from heaven, having great power; and the earth was lightened with his glory. And he cried mightily with a strong voice, saying, Babylon the great is fallen, is fallen, and is become the habitation of devils, and the hold of every foul spirit, and a cage of every unclean and hateful bird. For all nations have drunk of the wine of the wrath of her fornication, and the kings of the earth have committed fornication with her, and the merchants of the earth are waxed rich through the abundance of her delicacies. Rev. 18:1-3

The "after these things" does not merit a change of subject here, but rather a change of focus. In chapter seventeen, it was one of the first angels having a vial who talked with John (17:1). Here, John sees yet another angel coming down from Heaven. This one is, in all probability, the same angel as seen in chapter fourteen (v.8). There, we were assured that justice would be served upon religious Babylon. It is here in chapter eighteen that this judgment is given and explained.

The judgment falls upon religious Babylon due to her fornication, false doctrine, and deceptive practices. During the Tribulation Period, she becomes the very embodiment of evil. During that time, every foul and devilish doctrine will be under her care and protection. She fully becomes the habitation of devils, the hold of every foul spirit. She is a cage for every unclean and hateful bird. Whether it's Buddhism, Hinduism, Freemasonry, Mormonism, or any other devilish doctrine, this whore of Babylon will embrace and care for it as her own. We are only seeing the tip of the iceberg concerning such spiritual fornication in our present age. Nations, government leaders, and the world's merchants will be corrupted by her and her wares.

A Voice Of Warning

And I heard another voice from heaven, saying, Come out of her, my people, that ye be not partakers of her sins, and that ye receive not of her plagues. For her sins have reached unto heaven, and God hath remembered her iniquities. Reward her even as she rewarded you, and double unto her double according to her works: in the cup which she hath filled fill to her double. How much she hath glorified herself, and lived deliciously, so much torment and sorrow give her: for she saith in her heart, I sit a queen, and am no widow, and shall see no sorrow. Rev. 18:4-7

Here John seems to receive a message that relates to the church world of his day as well as to that of our day: "Come out of her, my people." This voice is undoubtedly the voice of the Lord himself.

We saw in chapter two that there are people of our day who are a part of Romanism, yet are unaware of the inner workings and evil of the system. We have seen that they will not receive the same plight as those who are aware and are willfully blind (chapter two, "Thyatira Spiritual"). However, all people, by creation, are God's. Thus, a general plea is sent to the people of God, "Come out from among them," as both John and the apostle Paul state (II Cor. 6:17,18).

The Boasting Whore

We see in verse seven that the one-world religious system glorifies herself and boasts of being a queen. In her heart she boasts of being "no widow" because she has bound herself with the kings and merchants of the Earth and with nations and kingdoms. However, her reward of sin will be doubled upon her in like manner as she rewarded others. Peering down through her history and even into the Tribulation Period, there are those greatly persecuted by this mother of harlots. We discussed in chapters two and three the persecution of the Paulicians, Waldenses and others, who suffered at her hand. During the Tribulation Period, the number of those persecuted will only increase. Millions will be turned to the Antichrist and the mark of the beast at the urging of this great whore. To the extent that this great religion has lived luxuriously, she will be tormented.

The One-Hour Judgment

Therefore shall her plagues come in one day, death, and mourning, and famine; and she shall be utterly burned with fire: for strong is the Lord God who judgeth her. And the kings of the earth, who have committed fornication and lived deliciously with her, shall bewail her, and lament for her, when they shall see the smoke of her burning, Standing afar off for the fear of her torment, saying, Alas, alas that great city Babylon, that mighty city! for in one hour is thy judgment come. And the merchants of the earth shall weep and mourn over her; for no man buyeth their merchandise any more:Rev. 18:8-11

We discussed in chapter seventeen that the ten kings hate the whore and will make her desolate and burn her with fire. Their fury will be poured out toward her in one day. Such an onslaught against this massive religion and her cohorts will have to be carefully planned and swiftly executed. We also discussed that the kings of the Earth are a different reference than the ten kings. Those kings of the Earth and merchants who have gained wealth from the wares of the papal system will weep and mourn because of the destruction of this great religious entity. They will be filled with fear because of the apparently unstable future they now foresee, due to her destruction.

The wealth of the Vatican will be consumed in a day by the one-world political machine. There will be death, mourning, and famine. Note that such plagues come in a day. This is either a twenty-four hour day or a short period. Her judgment comes in an hour. This, too, could mean one of two things:

1. That the planned demise of the religious system comes about due to a decision made during a one-hour session of the allied kings.

2. That this hour is the same as the "hour of temptation" and the "hour" that the ten kings rule with the Antichrist, that is, the whole Tribulation Period, seven years. Either interpretation would work.

The Reason For Mourning

The merchandise of gold, and silver, and precious stones, and of pearls, and fine linen, and purple, and silk, and scarlet, and all thyine wood, and all manner vessels of ivory, and all manner vessels of most precious wood, and of brass, and iron, and marble, And cinnamon, and odours, and ointments, and frankincense, and wine, and oil, and fine flour, and wheat, and beasts, and sheep, and horses, and chariots, and slaves, and souls of men. And the fruits that thy soul lusted after are departed from thee, and all things which were dainty and goodly are departed from thee, and thou shalt find them no more at all. The merchants of these things, which were made rich by her, shall stand afar off for the fear of her torment, weeping and wailing, And saying, Alas, alas, that great city, that was clothed in fine linen, and purple, and scarlet, and decked with gold, and precious stones, and pearls! For in one hour so great riches is come to nought. And every shipmaster, and all the company in ships, and sailors, and as many as trade by sea, stood afar off, And cried when they saw the smoke of her burning, saying, What city is like unto this great city! And they cast dust on their heads, and cried, weeping and wailing, saying, Alas, alas, that great city, wherein were made rich all that had ships in the sea by reason of her costliness! for in one hour is she made desolate. Rev. 18:12-19

Thirty kinds of merchandise are mentioned in the above Scriptures. Imagine all the businessmen and commercial people affected, all the factories, plantations and farms. Think of all those who are responsible for transporting all those goods, all the laborers and their families.

Rejoicing In Heaven

Rejoice over her, thou heaven, and ye holy apostles and prophets; for God hath avenged you on her. And a mighty angel took up a stone like a great millstone, and cast it into the sea, saying, Thus with violence shall that great city Babylon be thrown down, and shall be found no more at all. And the voice of harpers, and musicians, and of pipers, and trumpeters, shall be heard no more at all in thee; and no craftsman, of whatsoever craft he be, shall be found any more in thee; and the sound of a millstone shall be heard no more at all in thee; And the light of a candle shall shine no more at all in thee; and the voice of the bridegroom and of the bride shall be heard no more at all in thee: for thy merchants were the great men of the earth; for by thy sorceries were all nations deceived. And in her was found the blood of prophets, and of saints, and of all that were slain upon the earth. Rev. 18:20-24

Heaven shall rejoice over the fall of the greatest, largest and oldest organized religious system in the world. It is that same system of religion descended from Babel, the worship of Nimrod and Semiramis, culminated in Roman Catholicism. It is the same system of religion promoted by Jezebel of the Old Testament who caused all of Israel to sin through idolatry. Note that it was Jezebel, the instigator of the day, who killed the prophets of God. It was the same system of religion that prompted the killing the apostles at the time of Nero. It is the same system of religion which will kill Elijah and Moses during the Tribulation Period (11:7). Little wonder why Heaven will rejoice at the destruction of Babylon. Thus, the apostles and the prophets, indeed all those who have been martyred because of false religion, shall be avenged by Babylon's destruction.

The Mighty And Complete Fall

One cannot help but notice the complete fall and destruction which will come upon religious Babylon. This is readily noticed in the phrase, "no more at all." This most positive phrase is found six times in four verses (14, 21, 22, 23). The very nature of it echoes a complete and total fall. The fall of Babylon is great. The example given to John also portrays a destructive end to Babylon. John sees a mighty angel take up a great millstone and cast it into the sea (v.21). This was an object lesson for John, and for us as well. The angel says, "Thus with violence shall that great city Babylon be thrown down, and shall be found no more at all." It was not just any stone, but a millstone, a circular stone used for crushing and grinding grain. This is a picture of a violent destruction which will be as swift as that of casting a great stone into the sea. The impact upon the whole world will be as that of violent waves rushing away from a great stone. The waves ripple in every direction. It splashes, disturbs and ripples the waters. Babylon, like the millstone, will disappear quickly. It shall completely and wholly sink and will exist no more at all (religious Babylon).

There will be no more music, no commerce, no light, "no more at all." There will be no witness of the bridegroom or the bride. The bridegroom is calling today to "come out from among them" as stated by Paul, and as stated by John earlier, "come out of her my people." There are those today, like Luther of old, part of the "bride of Christ," who are trying to change the whore from within. That witness will cease and be "no more at all" forever. What a sad testimony for millions caught up in religion. The witness of Christ, having been there, departs forever.

By Thy Sorceries

The merchants will weep and wail over the demise of Babylon, for by the sorceries of Babylon were all nations deceived. This word "sorceries" is *"pharmakeia"* which means medication and, by extension, "magic, sorcery and witchcraft." It is common knowledge that the practice of witchcraft also descends from the Babylon of old, as does Romanism. The above reference pinpoints the drunkenness of those who follow religious Babylon. They will be "drunk with the wine of the wrath of her fornication" as if medicated by her (v.3).

Ω

The Revelation Of Jesus Christ
Chapter 19

In chapter 19, we have a picture of the glorious Second Coming of Jesus Christ.

Christ is not coming again as a lowly babe in a manger, but as Sovereign King and Sovereign Lord. He will come as a consuming fire and a fierce conqueror. Upon His vesture and upon His thigh shall be written, KING OF KINGS AND LORD OF LORDS. This wipes away any doubt as to who will execute judgment upon the ungodly.

However, John views events in Heaven which occur prior to that wondrous Second Coming.

The Alleluia's Of Heaven

And after these things I heard a great voice of much people in heaven, saying, Alleluia; Salvation, and glory, and honour, and power, unto the Lord our God: For true and righteous are his judgments: for he hath judged the great whore, which did corrupt the earth with her fornication, and hath avenged the blood of his servants at her hand. And again they said, Alleluia. And her smoke rose up for ever and ever. And the four and twenty elders and the four beasts fell down and worshipped God that sat on the throne, saying, Amen; Alleluia. And a voice came out of the throne, saying, Praise our God, all ye his servants, and ye that fear him, both small and great. And I heard as it were the voice of a great multitude, and as the voice of many waters, and as the voice of mighty thunderings, saying, Alleluia: for the Lord God omnipotent reigneth. Rev. 19:1-6

Here we have a scene in Heaven of praise and adoration for the works of God. This is the rejoicing of Heaven that was proclaimed in chapter 18:20, for God "hath judged the great whore, which did corrupt the earth with her fornication and hath avenged the blood of his servants at her hand. And again they said, Alleluia." Alleluia means "praise ye *Jah* (or *JE*)." "*Jah*" or "*Je*" is an abbreviated form of the name Jehovah. It is the name of God speaking that Jesus came as the great I AM. "*Je*" is connected with "SUS," of JeSUS, which is *Oshea, Hosea* or *Houshaia*, and means "help." This reveals Jesus as "Jehovah helps." Jesus came "to seek and to save that which was lost" (Lu. 19:10). Indeed, Jesus has helped those who could not help themselves.

The praise of "alleluia" is proclaimed four times in the verses above. The number four, as we discussed earlier, is the number of the world. It will be an "alleluia" of salvation (v.1), of victory (vs. 2-3), of worship (v.4), and of God's omnipotent reign over the entire world (vs. 5-6). It is a time of great praise and worship. The Lord God omnipotent, the infinite in power, the Almighty reigneth!

The Marriage Supper Of The Lamb

Let us be glad and rejoice, and give honour to him: for the marriage of the Lamb is come, and his wife hath made herself ready. And to her was granted that she should be arrayed in fine linen,

clean and white: for the fine linen is the righteousness of saints.
Rev. 19:7-8

The preceding chapters have dealt primarily with
events upon Earth, whereas verses 1-16 of this chapter
deal with events occurring in Heaven. Here we peer into
the events pertaining to the Raptured Church of chapter
four. These events occur in Heaven, while the events of
the Tribulation Period are unfolding upon the Earth.

John was viewing the glory of the Raptured Church,
yet did not record an important event which will occur.
The Raptured Church (born-again believers of the present
age) will pass through the Judgment Seat of Christ. It is
evident that the Holy Spirit intended that John not men
tion this judgment when viewing the events in Heaven.
This is due to the blessing of Revelation (1:3; 22:7). One
of the great blessings is that one may gain the knowledge
of rightly dividing the Word and be given the ability to
find astounding truths, while diligently comparing
Scripture. Thus, the apostle Paul, as well as others, were
given the facts of the Judgment Seat of Christ, which are
not recorded here.

Thus, immediately after (or in conjunction with) the
Rapture of the Church and before the Marriage Supper of
the Lamb is the Judgment Seat of Christ. This event
occurs that we may receive reward or loss of reward (I
Cor. 3:11-17). We know that the Judgment Seat occurs at
the Rapture ("catching away") and before the Marriage
Supper due to the "witness of Luke" (Lu. 21:36) and due
to the "preparation of the wife" who is to be attired in fine
linen (vs.7-8).

Luke, quoting Christ, reveals a pre-tribulation "catching away," and a believer judgment as being before the Marriage Supper:

> Watch ye therefore, and pray always, that ye may be accounted worthy to escape all these things that shall come to pass (Tribulation Period), and to stand before the Son of man (Judgment Seat). Luke 21:36 (my emphasis and parenthetics)

The Wife Hath Made Herself Ready

Yet another proof that the Judgment Seat occurs before the Marriage Supper is that the wife is able to make herself ready. This is seen in verse seven. How does the wife make "herself" ready?

Who Is The Wife?

In this present age, the Church (born-again believers) is referred to as "the Bride of Christ."

> For I am jealous over you with godly jealousy: for I have espoused you to one husband, that I may present you as a chaste virgin to Christ. But I fear, lest by any means, as the serpent beguiled Eve through his subtilty, so your minds should be corrupted from the simplicity that is in Christ. II Cor. 11:2-3

In the Old Testament, Israel, which will eventually be forgiven and restored, is found to be the adulterous wife of Jehovah God. We know that Israel is not the wife as seen in 19:7, for they, those not having been saved by grace in the present age, will be on Earth during the Tribulation Period. The events in the above verses (19:7-8) occur in Heaven before the Second Coming of Christ and before the Battle of Armageddon. Thus, the wife can be none other than the bride become the wife. That is, the wife is made up of the Raptured Church. The bride becomes the wife (in an eternal bond) at the Rapture. It is only natural that the bride becomes the wife. The Millennial Reign, as we will see, is likened to a honeymoon for the bridegroom and the bride, for we (the bride) are to be joint heirs with Him (Rom. 8:17) and shall rule and reign with Him (II Tim. 2:12).

Christ will present to Himself the bride at the Rapture of the Church (Eph. 5:27). The bride will be tried by fire for the Judgment Seat ("type" found in II Kings 2:11 concerning Elijah and the "chariot of fire"). Thus, the bride, then the wife, being purified, is thus able to make "herself" ready. Until the Judgment Seat of Christ, she is not yet ready to be arrayed in fine linen. Why? This fine linen is the "righteousness of saints" (v.8). However, the Bible tells us that our righteousness is as "filthy rags" (Isa. 64:6). What then?

Fire purifies. Thus, the bride (become the wife) will have been purified (at the catching away) and is thus able to be arrayed in fine linen. After such cleansing, she may be granted "that she should be arrayed" (v.8). Again, she is thus able to "make herself ready."

Judgment Seat of Christ Explained

But why dost thou judge thy brother? or why dost thou set at nought thy brother? for we shall all stand before the judgment seat of Christ. Rom. 14:10

For we must all appear before the judgment seat of Christ; that every one may receive the things done in his body, according to that he hath done, whether it be good or bad. II Cor. 5:10

The apostle Paul was warning the Christians in Rome that neither they, nor we, should pass judgment upon others. To judge others is a condemned judgment. John 7:24

tells us to "judge not according to appearance," or, in other words, do not make firm statements pertaining to things that only appear to be such and such. This kind of judgment is to form an opinion without facts or firm foundations. Nor can we judge persons to Heaven or Hell. That judgment belongs to the Lord (Jn. 5:22).

Paul tells us that we are to judge ourselves (I Cor. 11:31). Thus, we avoid the chastening of the Lord (See author's book *"The Bridal Feast"*). However, we do find that judgment must begin at the house of God. I Peter 4:17 concerns the discerning of spirits; the ability to discern between good and evil. It is a commanded judgment. This judgment, concerning ourselves, is made easy, due to the lists found in Scripture (Rom. 1:29-32; I Cor. 5:9-13; Gal. 5:19-20; Eph. 5:3-5).

However, the subject at hand concerns our being judged at the Judgment Seat of Christ. This brings yet another misconception to light mentioned in chapter eleven, the belief in a "general judgment."

General Judgment

Paul clearly states in both Romans and Corinthians that we will appear before the Judgment Seat of Christ. As discussed in chapter 11, the Judgment Seat of Christ and the Great White Throne Judgment are two separate events. The Judgment Seat of Christ is for born-again believers only. It is for reward or loss of reward (I Cor. 3:15). This is NOT to determine who is saved or lost.

Many believe in a general judgment, where the saved and the lost stand together and are judged at the same time. There is no basis in Scripture for such a general judgment in which the just and the unjust stand together before Christ.

The misconception revolves around Matthew 25:31-46. This Scripture is taken completely out of context when used to substantiate a general judgment. We have seen that Matthew 25:31-46 refers to the judgment of nations. We find in Revelation (20:4-6) a one-thousand year gap between the Judgment Seat of Christ and the Great White Throne Judgment. This is in addition to the seven-year Tribulation Period. Note that Revelation 20:4-6 states, "and they lived and reigned with Christ a thousand years," which refers to the saints of the Tribulation Period. Then, these verses go on to state, "But the rest of the dead lived not again until the thousand years were finished."

What of the Church, the bride? Those "saved" individuals who die during the present age are referred to as the dead IN Christ (I Thess 4:16). They, at this point, will have already been resurrected at the Rapture (prior to the Tribulation Period), and like the Tribulation saints, shall reign with Christ (I Thess. 4:16-18). This reign with Christ occurs during the Millennial Reign. Not until after the Millennial Reign of Christ will the Great White Throne Judgment occur. This is when the DEAD are to be judged (20:2-4), NOT the "dead IN Christ."

Concerning the Judgment Seat, Luke 14:14 reveals a resurrection of the just only. The apostle Paul calls it a better resurrection (Heb. 11:5). It certainly would not be a "better" resurrection for unsaved persons, if resurrected and judged at the same time as the saved persons.

Judgment Seat Explained

The Judgment Seat (*"bema"* Gk) is discussed in I Corinthians 3:11-15. As we have seen, this judgment refers to "believers only," for the Epistle was written to the Church and the saints (I Corinthians 1:2).

> For other foundation can no man lay than that is laid, which is Jesus Christ. Now if any man build upon this foundation gold, silver, precious stones, wood, hay, stubble; Every man's work shall be made manifest: for the day shall declare it, because it shall be revealed by fire; and the fire shall try every man's work of what sort it is. If any man's work abide which he hath built thereupon, he shall receive a reward. If any man's work shall be burned, he shall suffer loss: but he himself shall be saved; yet so as by fire. I Cor. 3:11-15

The above passages affirm that this judgment is for "believers only," because of the foundation built upon, Jesus Christ. We have seen (II Cor. 5:10) that we must be judged "that every one may receive the things done in his body, according to that he hath done, whether it be good or bad." The word "good" (II Cor. 5:10) comes from the Greek word *"agathos,"* which means "benefit or will." The word "bad" comes from *"kakos,"* meaning "worthless (intrinsically such; properly refers to effects). The word "things" of II Corinthians 5:10 are the two "sorts" of I Corinthians 3:13, that is, the things beneficial and the things worthless. These categories are broken down into the beneficial and worthless "sorts" as: the good - gold, silver and precious stones; and the bad - wood, hay, stubble.

As Jesus related to people through common terms of the day, gold, silver, wood and hay, and so on, are common references for the recognition of things precious and things worthless, in accordance to our being judged at the Judgment Seat of Christ.

Sort Number One

Sort number one consists of three things which are good or beneficial. They are gold, silver, and precious stones.

Gold

Gold comes from the Greek word *"chursos"* which reflects the utility of the metal. Gold is a soft, yellow, corrosion-resistant metallic element capable of being shaped or formed into jewelry or other decorations. It is also used as an international monetary standard. Gold can be used as a plated coating on a wide variety of electrical and mechanical components.

Man esteems gold as one of the most precious and attainable of metals. It is apparently used as an expression, in relation to our work as Christians, as being most precious to Christ. It represents tenderheartedness (soft), a colorful manner (bright in color), and most importantly is a characteristic of being non-adherent to the world (corrosion-resistant). This refers to someone who sets a Christian standard, not only for those around him, but for anyone. Such a person can be formed into many uses pertaining to godliness, always holding the same value despite the situation.

Silver

Silver comes from the Greek word *"argos,"* which means "shining." It is a lustrous white, ductile, malleable, metallic element used for jewelry, coinage, photography, dentistry and so on. Silver is not changed by moisture, dryness, alkalis, or vegetable acids. However, sulfur or air that contains sulfur will cause it to tarnish. As gold is most precious and sets the standard, silver, even though lesser in value, is nonetheless of tremendous value. Silver represents "shining," or the personality of the Christian. This personality is pure (lustrous white) no matter what the situation (ductile). Silver also represents our exchange to the world (coinage), unchanged by the changing atmosphere (not changed by moisture, dryness, and so on). A continuous bad atmosphere can tarnish (dull or discolor) such a personality, but its value remains steady.

Precious Stones

Precious stones, or "gems," are cut or polished to use in jewelry. They are costly stones, such as diamonds or rubies. Their value is determined by their hardness, color, brilliance, rarity and demand. Gems are very often imitated by costume jewelry, which has no apparent value other than appearance. Most imitation gems are made from a soft glass called "paste" or "strass," a very clear and brilliant powdered rock crystal, which can be easily scratched.

Precious stones represent those persons who are precious to Christ determined by their appearance through true, firm character. Christ gave His life to change these rough, hard, uncut stones into something beautiful. These are costly stones, formed and polished to brilliance, and often imitated. The imitations, however, when rubbed the wrong way are easily scratched. Have you ever seen similar characteristics? The true stone, holds its luster and character.

Sort Number Two

Sort number two also found in I Cor. 3:12 also consists of three things. These, however, are bad ("*kakos*," "worthless"): wood, hay, and stubble.

We all like to think of ourselves as having only good qualities, but is that always the case? Probably not, if we are honest with ourselves. Are the bad qualities only worthless, or are they of unrighteousness? Sort number two will only reveal worthlessness. Unlike gold and silver, wood, hay and stubble cannot be melted into something beautiful. These things, when burned, form only ashes. They are dissimilar to precious stones due to their hardness and color, and they deteriorate through time unless great care is administered. What then are their characteristics and why would these three corruptible substances represent bad work?

Wood

The Greek word for "wood" is "*xulon*," meaning "timber (as fuel or material), by implying, a stick, club, or tree, or other wooden articles or substances." Wood is a tough, fibrous-supporting and water-conducting substance lying beneath the bark of trees and shrubs, used for various purposes such as building, sculpting, and so on. Wood will rot, change color, twist, shrink and swell, depending on how much moisture it loses or absorbs. Manufacturers obtain several useful chemicals and by-products from wood. For example, cellulose is used in making explosives, fabrics, paints, paper, and many other products. The extracts of certain woods provide oils, pitch, turpentine, and tar.

Wood represents the born-again person who is very useful in many ways, but who holds no lasting value within himself. This type of person must be protected and cared for to have any lasting qualities. Without such care, these persons absorb things of the world (moisture) causing swelling, twisting, change of "color," shrinkage, and eventual rot. Their very substance is of no lasting value as gold, silver, or precious stones, but is corruptible if not cared for continually.

Note that each individual may hold characteristics as those of gold, as well as some characteristics of wood. It would be rare indeed to find an individual having nothing but characteristics represented by gold only. Thus, an individual may carry certain characteristics of each division of the two "sorts" according to their individual situations and circumstances. It is not for us to categorize others, but only to strive to obtain those things which are beneficial to ourselves, as well as to the cause of Christ.

Hay

The Greek word for "hay" is *"chortos,"* meaning "court or garden." Hay is used to feed horses and cattle and like beasts, and is made of dried stems and leaves of plants. Hay must be cared for because if it contains too much moisture, it will spoil. Hay will sweat (heat) after it is stored in a barn, sometimes creating so much heat that it sets itself on fire. For this reason, farmers take great care to dry their hay adequately before they store it.

As "hay" stands for "court or garden," and must be constantly nurtured and tended, it represents those persons who have only the value of being fed upon and are among those who demand constant spiritual care by someone else. Such dependent persons are usually mis-used by clever, corrupt minds and are easily hurt. The per-son who truly cares for these persons receives pleasure and reward for their labor. Nonetheless, labor is required. Hay persons will burn themselves out if stored with too much moisture; which is why constant care is required.

Stubble

The Greek word for "stubble" is "*kalame,*" meaning a stalk of grain. Stubble refers to short, stiff stalks as of grain left behind on a field after harvesting.

Stubble thus represents those persons who were once full of life and were bearing fruit only to dry up. These persons, retaining the stand as at first, are still around fill-ing their spaces, yet they no longer produce fruit. They serve only as a similar supporting structure for windbreak, support, and soil enrichment.

Such things are good within themselves, however, they are "worthless" as far as reward is concerned. Thus, such deadness is but loss.

As previously stated, it is not for us to categorize oth-ers, but only to strive to obtain those things which are ben-eficial to ourselves as well as to the cause of Christ. We may see the hay in others and overlook the gold or vise versa. Thanks be to God, that He has a clear record of us all.

Judgment Fire

Every man's work shall be made manifest: for the day shall declare it, because it shall be revealed by fire; and the fire shall try every man's work of what sort it is. I Cor. 3:13

Our judgment will be by fire. Is this literal, figurative, or symbolic fire?

The word "fire" is found 83 times in 79 verses in the New Testament. It is translated from six Greek words which differ slightly in meaning. These are: *"phos"* meaning "shine" or "lumination" (Mr. 14:54; Luke 22:54); *"anthrakia,"* meaning "fire of coals" (Jn. 18:18, 21:9); *"pura"* meaning "a fire" (Acts 28:3, coming from *"pur"*); *"phlogizol"* meaning "to ignite" (James 3:6, second and third mention); *"purinos"* meaning "flaming" (Rev. 9:17); and *"pur,"* meaning "fire," that is, as ignited materials such as wood or gas or vapor which flames and causes heat.

The bulk of translated words for "fire" in the New Testament is *"pur,"* a literal burning flame of fire. It must be noted that the intensity of flames of fire may range in degree. For instance, under natural conditions, the red flame is not as hot as the blue flame. The hottest known flame is completely black. This would align with the terms given concerning Hell. The fire of Hell is "pur." Jesus referred to Hell as "outer darkness" (Matt. 8:12; 22:13; 25:30). He also connects Hell and individuals who go there with a flame of fire (Lu. 16:24), indicating a personal flame of fire for lost individuals.

The fire of the Judgment Seat is also *"pur,"* a literal burning flame of fire. However, we are not to worry. This fiery judgment will be instantaneous. Because our change is said to be in a "moment, in a twinkling of an eye" (I Cor. 15:52), or about eleven one-hundredths of a second. That's fast!

The Revelation Of Jesus Christ * 389

Behold, I shew you a mystery; We shall not all sleep, but we shall all be changed, In a moment, in the twinkling of an eye, at the last trump: for the trumpet shall sound, and the dead shall be raised incorruptible, and we shall be changed. For this corruptible must put on incorruption, and this mortal must put on immortality. So when this corruptible shall have put on incorruption, and this mortal shall have put on immortality, then shall be brought to pass the saying that is written, Death is swallowed up in victory. I Cor. 15:51-54

We are thus purified instantaneously. To be caught out in a moment, in a twinkling of an eye, an instant, would mean that our bodies shall pass into the presence of God through the atmosphere (for we are raised upward) so quickly that they will burn with fervent heat as does a meteor, only faster. This purification process will reveal works which appear at the Judgment Seat of Christ. Good works remain while worthless works (not evil works) will be burned. The burning away of bad (worthless) works constitutes the loss of rewards, which would otherwise be reward. Remember, that those who are "caught away" are the saved only.

Note: The last trump refers here to the last trump of God. Jesus returns with a shout, with the voice of the archangel, and with the trump of God. Note that the trump of God is separate from the trumpet judgments of the Tribulation Period. They are sounded by angels, not by God (Jesus). The last trump refers to the "catching away" of the saints at the Rapture of the Church (I Thess. 4:16-17).

The Wife Ready

We saw in verse seven how the wife "hath made herself ready." After the purification of the Raptured Church and the Judgment Seat of Christ for reward or loss of reward, the bride become the wife is ready to be arrayed in fine linen. She is thus dressed for her appearance upon Earth with the Bridegroom, Jesus Christ. We saw earlier that those "caught out Christians" will be with Christ at the Second Coming (Zech. 14:5; Col. 3:4; I Thess. 3:13; Jude 14), thus escaping the "hour of temptation" (3:10). The wife will be purified at the Rapture for the Judgment Seat and is thus able to be arrayed in fine linen. We are thus granted to dress for the occasion of the Second Coming.

Blessed Are They

> And he saith unto me, Write, Blessed are they which are called unto the marriage supper of the Lamb. And he saith unto me, These are the true sayings of God. And I fell at his feet to worship him. And he said unto me, See thou do it not: I am thy fellowservant, and of thy brethren that have the testimony of Jesus: worship God: for the testimony of Jesus is the spirit of prophecy. Rev. 19:9-10

John is given yet another immediate message of hope for those of the church age (Pentecost to Rapture). In short, blessed are those who accept Christ and are "caught out" to be a part of the Marriage Supper. John surely realized that he too would be in that number, for he immediately falls down to worship.

John is so taken by his foreview of the glory of the Church being with Christ, that he worships. However, he worships wrongly. He begins to worship the angel. Many today pray to angels or esteem them more highly than they do God. The angel quickly corrects John, "See thou do it not," he proclaims! "Worship God!" All the majestic creatures of God, even the angels in Heaven, are to be appreciated, but they are not to be worshipped. The angel proclaims that he is a servant like we are. He carries the testimony of Jesus, as we should. The testimony of Jesus is the spirit of prophecy (19:10). It is the testimony that the things to come are true. We can only believe the prophecies because of Christ's testimony. Jesus said:

> I have yet many things to say unto you, but ye cannot bear them now. Howbeit when he, the Spirit of truth, is come, he will guide you into all truth: for he shall not speak of himself; but whatsoever he shall hear, that shall he speak: and he will shew you things to come. Jn. 16:12-13

Marriage Supper Explained

The Marriage Supper of the Lamb will be the most glorious and blessed celebration in all of history. In most wedding celebrations, the emphasis of honor is placed upon the bride. However, this is not the case with the Marriage Supper of the Lamb. Because not one being could be present without the sacrifice and resurrection of the Lamb. Without Him there would not be a Marriage Supper. The Marriage Supper honors God. The angel had told John not to worship anyone or anything except God and it is revealed at the Marriage Supper. (Jesus accepted worship because He is God.)

We should be preparing for that event now, in this present age. Many are too busy to think of the coming glory and the things that God has prepared for us. Sometimes we get caught up in the everyday tasks that drag us down and make us weary and tired. Sometimes we dread the next day. If we would keep our eyes and hearts upon the testimony of Jesus and look forward to meeting Him in the air, the trip would go more smoothly. If we could but grasp the idea that we are to prepare ourselves as the bride of Christ for His return as the Bridegroom, our hopelessness would return to hope. Oh, how mundane and insignificant our problems would become if only we would exercise faith instead of worry. Let's not get too busy for Christ. Take a little time and read Matthew 22: 1-14 or Luke 14:16-24, and consider ourselves, lest we be too busy to prepare for the Marriage Supper.

The Revelation Of Jesus Christ

And I saw heaven opened, and behold a white horse; and he that sat upon him was called Faithful and True, and in righteousness he doth judge and make war. His eyes were as a flame of fire, and on his head were many crowns; and he had a name written, that no man knew, but he himself. And he was clothed with a vesture dipped in blood: and his name is called The Word of God. And the armies which were in heaven followed him upon white horses, clothed in fine linen, white and clean. And out of his mouth goeth a sharp sword, that with it he should smite the nations: and he shall rule them with a rod of iron: and he treadeth the winepress of the fierceness and wrath of Almighty God. And he hath on his vesture and on his thigh a name written, KING OF KINGS, AND LORD OF LORDS. Rev. 19:11-16

The Second Coming of Christ will be the most glorious and wondrous event that the world has ever witnessed. Thus far in our study, we have seen several passages that preview this event. Let's review those passages for a better understanding of the overall picture of the Second Coming.

At the Second Coming of Christ, we know that:

* "every eye shall see him" (1:7). That covers all those in Hades, those unsaved persons surviving the Tribulation Period and those who pierced Him. We, too, shall witness this wondrous event as we will be with Him.

*Jesus will stand with one foot upon the sea and one foot upon the Earth as the kinsmen redeemer (10:2,5,6). He is the one who comes to redeem the Earth back to Himself. He has with Him the title deed to the Earth (5:6-7). It is opened to validate His claim (10:2). He will take to Himself His great power, authority, and His complete and total Messiahship (11:17-18).

*Jesus is the reaper with a golden crown and a sharp sickle who reaps the "sheep" nations of the Earth (14:14).

*He is the Almighty (1:8; 4:8) who comes to judge and make war (19:11).

*There will be thunders (10:4; 16:18) and an earthquake (16:18) as His Mighty voice proclaims "there should be time no longer," that is, "no more delay" in redeeming the Earth, "It is done" (10:6-7; 16:17). The great earthquake will divide the great city, Jerusalem, into three parts and every island and every mountain will flatten and disappear (16:20). The Second Coming of Christ will be awesome! Also we have:

The Armies Of Heaven

Jesus will return on a white horse with all the armies of Heaven. They (we), too, will be riding upon white horses (v.14). The white horse is not only a symbol of peace, but also a sign of victory. In ancient times, Roman generals entered conquered cities upon white horses to celebrate victory.

We, the Church, the bride who has become the wife, shall be a part of that great army (Zech. 14:5; Col. 3:4; I Thess. 3:13; Jude 14).

"And Enoch also, the seventh from Adam, prophesied of these, saying, Behold, the Lord cometh with ten thousands of his saints, To execute judgment upon all, and to convince all that are ungodly among them of all their ungodly deeds which they have ungodly committed, and of all their hard speeches which ungodly sinners have spoken against him" (Jude 14-15).

The armies of Heaven will not only include the wife, but will also be made up of holy and innumerable angels.

When the Son of man shall come in his glory, and all the holy angels with him, then shall he sit upon the throne of his glory: And before him shall be gathered all nations: and he shall separate them one from another, as a shepherd divideth his sheep from the goats: Matt. 25:31-32

And to you who are troubled rest with us, when the Lord Jesus shall be revealed from heaven with his mighty angels, In flaming fire taking vengeance on them that know not God, and that obey not the gospel of our Lord Jesus Christ: II Thess. 1:7-8

This army will be the greatest ever assembled. What a wondrous event for the believer! We'll be there with all the mighty angels of Heaven, but not to fight. The battle is not ours, or the angel's, but Christ's. This we will see in the next few paragraphs of discussion.

Righteous Judge

Christ is called Faithful and True (v.11). We can depend upon a righteous judgment against all the evil of the world. The conquest and judgment will be true as opposed to false. Jesus will judge all nations with perfect justice. This is a result of His true and faithful witness. He will judge and make war.

Jesus Shall Be A Fierce Conqueror

The Lamb will become the Lion. Jesus will execute judgment with the utmost fierceness. Note that His eyes will be as a flame of fire, piercing, penetrating and consuming (v.12). Not only does Christ wear a "golden crown," signifying His great holiness (14:14), but He wears many crowns, denoting His rule and authority over all kings and kingdoms of the world. He has a name written that no man knows, only He himself. It is futile to guess this name.

Jesus is also clothed in a vesture dipped in blood (v.13). This is not the redemptive blood of the cross, but the blood of His enemies, as seen in Isaiah 63:1-6:

> Who is this that cometh from Edom, with dyed garments from Bozrah? this that is glorious in his apparel, travelling in the greatness of his strength? I that speak in righteousness, mighty to save. Wherefore art thou red in thine apparel, and thy garments like him that treadeth in the winefat? I have trodden the winepress alone; and of the people there was none with me: for I will tread them in mine anger, and trample them in my fury; and their blood shall be sprinkled upon my garments, and I will stain all my raiment. For the day of vengeance is in mine heart, and the year of my redeemed is come. Isa. 63:1-4

Note that Jesus will conquer alone. There is none to help because vengeance belongs to Him alone (Rom. 12:19). All the armies of Heaven are present to be witness to the faithful and true judgment and testimony of Jesus. The seven thunders will sound out a confirmation exclaiming God's powerful and overwhelming presence (10:4).

Christ accomplishes victory through His name, the Word of God, for out of His mouth proceeds a sharp sword with which He smites the armies gathered at Armageddon. He will take up the rod of iron. He uses these instruments with the fierceness and wrath of Almighty God. It shall be a terrible and bloody event.

The Supper Of The Great God

And I saw an angel standing in the sun; and he cried with a loud voice, saying to all the fowls that fly in the midst of heaven, Come and gather yourselves together unto the supper of the great God; That ye may eat the flesh of kings, and the flesh of captains, and the flesh of mighty men, and the flesh of horses, and of them that sit on them, and the flesh of all men, both free and bond, both small and great. Rev. 19:17-18

We know that Jesus is to judge the angry nations (11:18). However, there is another judgment of nations just prior to the sheep and goat judgment of nations. It is a judgment of wrath poured out upon the armies of the nations at Armageddon. The nations, by necessity, must then be gathered together (16:16). It is Jesus who allows the spirits of devils to work in bringing the kings and nations to the Battle of Armageddon (16:13-16). Jesus, the reaper with a sharp sickle and a golden crown, will reap the sheep nations with righteous judgment just after

Armageddon (14:14) and just prior to the Millennial Reign.

The battle of Armageddon will be the meeting of the allied armies of the Antichrist and their confrontation with Christ. There is no evidence that the kings of the Earth, or the beast, or the false prophet launches an attack. The armies of the world are only seen gathering for the battle. Due to the overwhelming fierceness of Christ, even if the armies of the world attack, the battle is seemingly over before it begins.

Therefore, an angel stands in the sun (v.17), thus commanding attention, and cries with a loud voice to all flying fowls, "Come and gather yourselves together unto the supper of the great God."

Note that this great supper is not the Marriage Supper of the Lamb. The Marriage Supper consists of a feast, joy and fellowship in Heaven. Here the Lamb takes on the characteristics of the Lion. This judgment is not a compassionate gesture on the part of the Lamb, but a fierce judgment through the attributes of the second personage of the three-fold nature of God, Jesus as fierce conqueror. It will be a feast for fowls.

There will be so much bloodshed that there will be 200 miles of blood (1600 furlongs; 14:18-20). This slaughter will be from all the allied armies of the Antichrist that will cover the whole of "the valley of decision." Isaiah speaks of this time and says that the land will be "soaked with blood" (Isa. 34:1-8).

Thus, the fowls are summoned to eat the flesh of kings, of captains, of mighty men, of horses and their riders, and of men from all walks of life.

Antichrist's And False Prophet's Doom

And I saw the beast, and the kings of the earth, and their armies, gathered together to make war against him that sat on the horse, and against his army. And the beast was taken, and with him the false prophet that wrought miracles before him, with which he deceived them that had received the mark of the beast, and them that worshipped his image. These both were cast alive into a lake of fire burning with brimstone. And the remnant were slain with the sword of him that sat upon the horse, which sword proceeded out of his mouth: and all the fowls were filled with their flesh. Rev. 19:19-21

John once again rehearses the coming together of the armies of the world for the great battle against God and the armies of Heaven. They gather in the Valley of Megiddo, the valley of decision, located in the heart of Palestine. This is the location of many great battles of the Old Testament.

The Antichrist, driven by the power of the satanic forces within him, and his cohorts, evidently expect a great war, but are ignorant of the outcome. This is Satan's attempt to overthrow the Lord, for he knows his time is short (12:12). It will be the "time" when the "harvest of the earth is ripe." The kings of the Earth, who bewailed the fall of the whore, apparently blame God for her destruction and are eager to align with the Antichrist and make war. These kings, also part of the make-up of the Antichrist's kingdom, were among those who blasphemed God when torment came upon them (16:10, "Vial No. 5").

Cast Alive

Note that the Antichrist (beast) and the false prophet will be cast alive into a lake of fire burning with brimstone. They are the first occupants of Gehenna Hell, the everlasting stage of Hell. This is the same lake of fire that Satan will be cast into one thousand years later. Note that they are still there when Satan is cast into this lake of fire (20:10). There is no greater proof than this of the eternal state of Hell. They are still burning after one thousand years.

We found in chapter nine that Gehenna Hell, is presently unoccupied, and will remain so, until the Beast and the false prophet are cast there immediately following the Battle of Armageddon.

Brimstone

Brimstone is a bright yellow, highly combustible, odorous mineral usually found near active volcanoes. The Hebrew and Greek words from which the word brimstone comes denote a divine fire (Gen. 19:24; Ezek. 38:22; Luke 17:29). Brimstone is often associated with fire (Rev. 9:17-18; 20:10; 21:8) and was considered an agent of God's judgment (Gen. 19:24). His breath is likened unto it (Isa. 30:33). In the New Testament, brimstone is used to explain God's wrath and punishment of those who die without Christ (Rev. 9:17-18; 14:10; 20:10). Another word for brimstone is sulfur, a very odorous substance.

The Remnant Slain

Although the beast and the false prophet will be cast into the lake of fire and brimstone, the remnant will be slain with the sword of the Lord's mouth. Their dead bodies will be consumed by the fowls. It is the ending of the Tribulation Period and the end of the one-world government under the Antichrist. In one battle, the great world empire will be thrown down and left for nought.

The souls of the slain will descend into Hades, as all those who have died before them not having accepted God's grace and salvation. They will be resurrected 1,000 years later to be judged at the Great White Throne (discussed in chapter twenty) and later cast into Gehenna Hell (20:14-15).

Ω

The Binding,
The Millennial Reign,
And The
Great White Throne
Judgment
Chapter 20

Did you ever wonder what the world would be like without the presence of evil? This chapter will preview such a time.

A day is coming when Christ Jesus will set up His Kingdom and establish righteousness upon the Earth. This time comes after His Second Coming and after the judgment of nations, as discussed in chapter nineteen. We know that Christ has already set up a spiritual kingdom in the present church age. However, there will be a literal reign of Christ upon this Earth, a time when He will sit upon the throne of David. It is prophesied and will be fulfilled (Dan. 2:35; Psa. 2:9; Lu. 1:32-33; II Tim. 2:12; Rev. 2:27; 12:5; 19:15).

This particular reign of Christ is most often referred to as the Millennial Reign. The word "millennium" comes from two Latin words, *"Mille"* (1,000) and *"Annum"* (year). During the 1,000 year period called the Millennial Reign we will begin our reign with Christ as joint heirs. It

402 * Binding, Millennial, Great White Throne

is not to be confused with the kingdom teaching of today's cult of Jehovah's Witnesses.

Note that Christ did not teach the disciples to pray for the Millennial Reign, but for "thy kingdom come" (Matt. 6:10). The term "millennium" or "Millennial Reign" has overshadowed the term "kingdom," due to the mention of the length of this period and as a means to keep down confusion between the spiritual and literal kingdoms of Christ. The expression "thousand years" is mentioned six times in chapter twenty. Thus, the "Millennial Reign" or "the kingdom" have often become interchangeable terms.

We saw in chapter nineteen the demise of the Antichrist and the false prophet. However, for Christ to reign in peace for one thousand years, Satan must be dealt with also. Thus, chapter twenty begins with,

The Binding Of Satan

> And I saw an angel come down from heaven, having the key of the bottomless pit and a great chain in his hand. And he laid hold on the dragon, that old serpent, which is the Devil, and Satan, and bound him a thousand years, And cast him into the bottomless pit, and shut him up, and set a seal upon him, that he should deceive the nations no more, till the thousand years should be fulfilled: and after that he must be loosed a little season. Rev. 20:1-3

John sees an angel come down from Heaven with the key to the bottomless pit. This is the angel who has great rank, authority and power. He is the star-angel of chapter nine, verse one. His angelic job is that of loosing and binding, opening and closing (See chapter 9).

This angel has a great chain in his hand and lays hold on Satan and binds him in the bottomless pit. This chain is for the binding of a spirit being. Thus, it is not necessarily a chain of iron, but an instrument for binding or restraining. Also in chapter nine, we saw that the bottomless pit is the lowest abyss of Hell, Tartaros Hell. Satan is to be sealed and shut up in Tartaros Hell for 1,000 years. He is bound in this bottomless pit so that he should deceive the nations no more. That is to say, he won't be released until the 1,000 year period is fulfilled. At the end of the 1,000 year period, he will be loosed for a short season. This will be discussed beginning with verse seven.

The binding of Satan proves that God can stop the evil work of Satan at any time. However, when the prescribed time comes for this "chaining up," God empowers one single angel for the job. No armies of Heaven are needed, not even God himself has to do it. Note, however, that Satan is not cast into the lake of fire (eternal Hell) at the same time as the Antichrist and the false prophet. He is to be cast there 1,000 years later. He is bound for 1,000 years because God has further use for him at the end of the Millennial Age. (discussed under, "Satan Loosed")

Tribulation Saints

And I saw thrones, and they sat upon them, and judgment was given unto them: and I saw the souls of them that were beheaded for the witness of Jesus, and for the word of God, and which had not worshipped the beast, neither his image, neither had received his mark upon their foreheads, or in their hands; and they lived and reigned with Christ a thousand years. But the rest of the dead lived not again until the thousand years were finished. This is the first resurrection. Rev. 20:4-5

We know that the Raptured Church will rule with Christ as the wife during the Millennial Reign. Likewise, those who are killed for the witness of Jesus, during the

Tribulation Period, will live and reign with Christ. Then will come the fulfillment of 3:21 concerning those who stand for Christ out of the apostate church age, after the Rapture of the true Church. They are those saved out of the fully blossomed Laodicean church age (discussed in chapter three). They are those who will give their lives, literally, for the cause of Christ, during the Tribulation Period.

Their Resurrection

The resurrection of the Tribulation saints will undoubtedly occur at or just before the Second Coming of Christ. We know this because of the cry for vengeance of those from under the altar of seal number five. "How long, O Lord, holy and true, dost thou not judge and avenge our blood on them that dwell on the earth?" The reply was "that they should rest yet for a little season, until their fellow-servants also and their brethren, that they should be killed as they were, should be fulfilled" (See 6:10-11).

In addition, we saw that the terrible slaughter of the Jews and the strangers among them will begin on a massive scale when the Antichrist sets himself up in the temple and claims to be God (II Thess. 2:4). This beastly nature of the Antichrist will last 42 months, or three and one-half years. That time frame covers the last half of the Tribulation Period.

Also, the children of Israel are to flee the Antichrist and stay hidden for 1,260 days, or three and one-half years. There would be no need for them to hide for that length of time without cause. Thus, there will be a slaughter of God's people until the time of the Second Coming of Christ. With these evidences, the resurrection of those killed for the cause of Christ evidently occurs in conjuction with the resurrection of Elijah and Moses immediately prior to the Second Coming. Note that there will be those who make it alive through the Tribulation Period and will pass into the Millennial period in their physical bodies. Thus, there will be those of us in our glorified bodies (raptured saints and Tribulation saints) and those on Earth in physical bodies coexisting during the Millennial Reign of Christ.

First Resurrection

Speaking of those martyred saints, John writes, "This is the first resurrection." Does this mean that there have been no resurrections before this? Absolutely not. This is the first resurrection of the dead, who die for the cause of Christ during the Tribulation Period. Note that the above passages speak of the Tribulation saints only (vs.4-5).

If this "first resurrection" meant the very first or the only resurrection, then all of us have missed it. The first resurrection from the dead recorded in Scripture is that of the Zarephath widow's son, whom Elijah raised from the dead (I Kings 17:20-24). However, the above mention of the "first resurrection" refers to "those that belong to Christ" and to the end of the Tribulation Period.

They That Are Christ's

Note that I Corinthians 15:23, concerning the resurrection, states, "But every man in his own order: Christ is the firstfruits; afterward they that are Christ's at his coming" (See I Cor.15:20-28). Thus, this is the resurrection of "they that belong to Christ" (Tribulation saints), just as we "belong to Christ." We must keep in mind also that the Second Coming is in two distinct stages, the Rapture of the Church (when we meet Him in the air, Lu. 21:36; II Thess. 4:16-18) and the Second Coming (when we, the Church, return with Him, Zech. 14:5; Col. 3:4; I Thess. 3:13; Jude 14). At His Second Coming, the Tribulation saints will also receive of the first resurrection. Their resurrection evidently occurs simultaneously with that of Moses and Elijah, just previous to, yet a part of, the Second Coming. It is the first resurrection of the Tribulation Period of those "that belong to Christ." Obviously they are to be set apart as a separate company of the first resurrection. They are those having experienced the Tribulation Period, whereas the Church (born-again believers of the present age) is to be kept from that terrible time (3:10). It is their "own order."

Blessed And Holy

Blessed and holy is he that hath part in the first resurrection: on such the second death hath no power, but they shall be priests of God and of Christ, and shall reign with him a thousand years. Rev. 20:6

This is yet another immediate message to those of the church age, as well as for those who will pass into the Tribulation. Remember that these verses, in particular, refer to those of the Tribulation Period. They are the Tribulation saints, as discussed earlier, who respond to the message given by the 144,000 concerning the coming kingdom. They are those killed during that time for the testimony of Jesus (7:13-14) and who will serve in the

Lord's temple (7:15), during the Millennial Reign and on the new Earth.

This company of believers is not the bride, nor does it make up the bride, and thus cannot become the wife. These believers, however, are those who will make up the ruling and reigning body of Christ, during the Millennial Reign and upon the new Earth.

The Millennial Or Kingdom Reign

This "kingdom reign" is called that because Christ will set up a divine government on Earth over the nations of the world. It is "thy kingdom come" (Matt. 6:10).

Note the following Scriptures which pertain to the kingdom:

*It is the "one-thousand year" reign of Christ (Rev. 20:1-10).

*It is the dispensation of the fulness of times (Eph. 1:10); the day of the Lord (Isa. 2:12; 13:6,9; 34:8; Ezek. 30:3; Amos 5:18; Joel 2:1; Zeph. 1:7,8,18; 2:2,3; Zech 14:1-21; Mal. 4; I Thess. 5:2; II Thess. 2:1-8; II Peter 3:10).

*It is "that day" (Isa. 2:11; 4:1-6; 19:21 24:21; 26:1; Ezek. 39:22; 48:35; Hos. 2:18; Joel 3:18; Zech. 12:8-11; 13:1; 14:1-9; Mal. 3:17); the "world (age) to come" (Matt. 12:32; Mark 10:30; Luke 20:35; Eph. 1:21; 2:7; 3:21; Heb. 6:5).

*It is the "kingdom of Christ and God" (Eph. 5:5; Matt. 20:21; Luke 1:32-35; 19:12-15; 22:29,30; 23:42; II Tim. 4:1; Jn. 18:28-37; I Cor. 15:24-28; Dan. 7:13,14).

*It is the "kingdom of God" (Mark 14:25; Lu. 19:11; 22:14-18).

*It is the "kingdom of heaven" (Matt. 3:2; 4:17; 5:3,10,19,20; 7:21; 8:11; 10:7; 13:43; 18:1-4; Lu.19:12-15).

*It is the "regeneration" (Matt. 19:28; Eph. 1:10).

*It is the "times of restitution (restoration) of all things" (Acts 3:20,21); the "consolation of Israel" (Lu. 2:25); the "redemption of Jerusalem" (Lu. 2:38).

Why Have A Millennial Reign?

One must wonder why we have a Millennial Reign or kingdom at all. Why not just wipe out everything and begin the new heaven and new Earth?

The most dominant reason is that Scripture must be fulfilled. God's promises to man in His Word must be fulfilled. Note also that God created the Earth and set up the Earth for man to have dominion upon it. God gave man dominion and man lost it to Satan. At the return of Christ, as seen in chapters five and ten, the Earth must be redeemed back to Himself. He must then rule the Earth and bring the righteousness to it that was intended. As seen in previous chapters, the Second Coming is also for the redemption of the Earth. The kingdom is necessary because Christ is to rule on the throne of David, an earthly throne (Lu. 1:32), thus fulfilling Scripture.

Some facts cannot be overlooked concerning the Millennial Reign and Christ's rule during that period. Note again some interesting Scriptures:

*Christ is coming back to rule and reign over the Earth (Isa. 2:4; 9:7; 55:4; Psa. 22:28; 67:4).

*Christ Jesus will rule and judge the ends of the Earth (I Sam. 2:10; Psa. 72:8; Zech. 9:10).

*Nations will see His glory during the Millennial Reign (Isa. 66:18).

*All things of the world will be subject to Christ (Heb. 2:5-8).

*The kingdoms of the world will become the kingdom of Christ (Rev. 11:15), and shall fill the whole Earth (Dan. 2:35).

*The kings of the Earth will bring gifts to Him and serve Him (Psa. 72:10-11).

*The people will serve and obey Christ (Gen. 49:10; Dan. 7:14) and shall fear Him (Isa. 25:3).

*Christ will bring peace and security during the Millennial Reign (Isa. 2:4; 9:7; Zech. 8:5; Mic. 4:3).

What a wonderful time for those who will go into that time of peace. It will be a secure place with all the pleasures of the kingdom at our fingertips. There will be no evil actions of nation against nation (Zeph. 3:13-15). Even the animals will be at peace (Hos. 2:18). The wolf shall lay down with the lamb. The cow and the bear will feed together. The child shall place his hand in the den of a venomous snake and not be harmed.

The wolf also shall dwell with the lamb, and the leopard shall lie down with the kid; and the calf and the young lion and the fatling together; and a little child shall lead them. And the cow and the bear shall feed; their young ones shall lie down together: and the lion shall eat straw like the ox. And the sucking child shall play on the hole of the asp, and the weaned child shall put his hand on the cockatrice' den. They shall not hurt nor destroy in all my holy mountain: for the earth shall be full of the knowledge of the LORD, as the waters cover the sea. Isa. 11:6-9

The Millennial Reign is the period that even the animals have travailed for (Rom. 8:19-22). There will be peace even among both wild and tame animals. What a beautiful thing to witness! Note also that there will be:

*no sickness (Ex. 23:25-26; Isa. 35:5-6).

*fruitfulness among man and beasts, no barrenness or miscarriages (Ex. 23:26; Deut. 28:4,11).

*plenty for everyone to eat (Amos 9:13-14; Deut. 28:5-6, 8, 12; Joel 3:18).

*long life (Ex. 23:26; Isa. 25:8; 65:20; Zech. 8:4).

*praise and joy (Isa. 25:8; 35:10; 51:11); all shame and guilt will be removed (Zeph. 3:11; Joel 2:26-27).

*the establishment of Israel as a nation forever (Jer. 31:35-37); even the Gentiles among them will receive an inheritance (Ezk. 47:22-23).

*a government of righteousness (Psa. 67:4; Isa. 16:5). Praise God for His divine government!

We saw earlier in our study how ungodly religions and ungodly worship have permeated nearly every aspect of life. This is true, especially during the Tribulation Period. However, during the kingdom reign, there will be only true worship (Psa. 22:27; 86:9; 102:15, 21-22; 138:4-5; Jer. 4:2; Zech. 8:23).

To be with Christ as "joint heirs" and to rule and reign with Him has to be one of the most joyous and wondrous things imaginable for the Church and those martyred for Christ during the Tribulation Period. In addition, it will be a wondrous place to live for those who will go into that time in their physical bodies (those surviving the Tribulation Period and judgment of nations).

Satan Loosed

And when the thousand years are expired, Satan shall be loosed out of his prison, And shall go out to deceive the nations which are in the four quarters of the earth, Gog and Magog, to gather them together to battle: the number of whom is as the sand of the sea. And they went up on the breadth of the earth, and compassed the camp of the saints about, and the beloved city: and fire came down from God out of heaven, and devoured them. Rev. 20:7-9

We saw in verse three that Satan must be loosed for a short season. He will once again begin to deceive the nations. Thus, after the 1,000 year reign of Christ with its peace and security, something happens. Great unrest and insecurity begins to flow. The unrest and insecurity, however, does not come from the throne of David in Jerusalem where Christ reigns, but from those persuaded by the wiles of the Devil after he is loosed.

As with all the previous dispensations of man from Adam and into the Tribulation Period, those who live during the Millennial Reign will be given a choice. Remember that there are those born and raised to maturity during the reign of Christ who have known nothing at all but the authority and rule of Christ. They too, must be given a choice. Satan is loosed that they may choose of their own volition to serve Christ or rebel against His authority.

The attempt to overthrow Christ will once again be made. This is seen in the fact that nations from the four quarters of the Earth gather to battle against the camp of the saints and against Jerusalem. These nations are called Gog and Magog. This then, could not mean the Gog and Magog of Ezekiel 38-39, which, Bible scholars agree refers to Russia and its leader, but rather to the anti-christ sentiment of the people (Magog) and their leaders (Gog). Gog is a symbolic name for "antichrist," while Magog means "anti-Christian party." Again, this could not mean Russia, as does Ezekiel 38-39, for these nations come from all over the world.

The Instigating Force

Not only will Satan instigate against the rule and reign of Christ, but a hot-spot of the world will also get the ball rolling, so to speak. It is the same spirit of false unity that began shortly after the flood of Noah's day in ancient Babylon. Babylon of old began the revolt against the righteousness of God after the flood. It was there, in the land of Shinar, that the tower of Babel was erected. It will be the new rebuilt Babylon that instigates the movement of Satan against the righteousness of God after the 1,000-year reign of Christ. It is obvious that it will be erected and populated during Christ's reign.

It was at Babel where the first great organized attempt to overthrow the rule of the Lord began and at Babel where the last such attempt will undoubtedly spring. Some believe that Babylon will be rebuilt just before or during the Tribulation Period. This may be the case, but I am persuaded that it will be rebuilt during the Millennial Reign.

Reasoning

The new world, during the Millennium, will be centered around Jerusalem. Our Lord will rule from Jerusalem with a rod of iron (Isa. 4:5-6; Jer. 3:12; 31:38-39; Joel 3:17; Zech 8:3). It will be the seat of government. At the beginning of the kingdom reign and just after the Tribulation Period, Jerusalem will have been trodden down by the Gentiles, until the "times of the Gentiles be fulfilled" (Lu. 21:24). Thus, Jerusalem will be rebuilt during the Millennial Reign. The prophet Ezekiel describes the restored land and city (Ezek. 48:1-35).

Also the camp of the saints will be compassed about. What is the camp of the saints? Undoubtedly, it is the "holy oblation" (Ezek. 48:10, 20-21), a tract of land divided into three sections for the Levites and priests and for the Millennial temple. A full description of the temple or sanctuary is given in Ezekiel 40:1- 44:31. Many nations will be gathered to the Jerusalem area during the Millennial Reign (Jer. 3:17). Jerusalem, the beloved city and the camp of the saints will be compassed about by the nations in revolt against Christ, after the loosing of Satan.

Scripture relates that the stones of Babylon were not to be used for building purposes (Jer. 51:26). This is not the case today. After the Millennium, however, the Earth will be purified by fire and will make it possible that the stones may never be found anymore.

The Arabs or shepherds will never dwell in Babylon again (Isa. 13:20). This may be totally fulfilled after the Earth's purification by fire (II Peter 3:7). Babylon is to be destroyed and totally desolate and all sinners destroyed out of it "forever" (Isa. 13:9, 19-22; Jer. 50:3, 23,39,40; 51:26, 29,37, 43). The "sinners destroyed out of it forever" most definitely refers to a post-millennial destruction. None of these Scriptures have been completely fulfilled. They will be fulfilled at the end of the Millennial Reign of Christ. At that time, all the nations from the four quarters of the Earth which align with the satanic scheme will be devoured by fire, which comes down from God out of Heaven. Thus, Babylon will be overthrown as Sodom and Gomorrah (Isa. 13:19): by fire and brimstone (Gen. 19:24).

The Doom Of Satan

And the devil that deceived them was cast into the lake of fire and brimstone, where the beast and the false prophet are, and shall be tormented day and night for ever and ever. Rev. 20:10

At this point, Satan is finished. His days of deceiving, plotting and tempting are over. The nations of the new Earth (chpt. 21) will not have any concerns about this deceiver, for he will be tormented day and night for ever and ever. The devil knows his plight and is trying today to take as many individuals with him as possible. It's not because he enjoys the company of others or even remotely likes people; he doesn't. He entices people to stay away from God so that God may lose some of His creation. His fight is against God and His plan. We are but pawns in Satan's game.

Note that the beast and the false prophet are still in Hell. It is where they "are." At this point, it will have been 1,000 years since they were cast into the lake of fire. This reveals the eternal aspect of Gehenna Hell, the lake of fire. They, like Satan, will be tormented day and night for ever and ever. What a terrible plight. Yet this is the same plight that follows everyone who rejects God. Hell was not prepared for mankind (Matt. 25:41). However, if anyone rejects God's plan through Christ, he or she chooses Satan's way (Eph. 5:6; Lu. 16:19-31; I Jn. 3:10). We must reach everyone we can with the message of Christ.

And I Saw A Great White Throne

And I saw a great white throne, and him that sat on it, from whose face the earth and the heaven fled away, and there was found no place for them. And I saw the dead, small and great, stand before God; and the books were opened: and another book was opened, which is the book of life: and the dead were judged out of those things which were written in the books, according to their works. And the sea gave up the dead which were in it; and death and hell delivered up the dead which were in them: and they were judged every man according to their works. And death and hell were cast into the lake of fire. This is the second death. And whosoever was not found written in the book of life was cast into the lake of fire. Rev. 20:11-15

This passage will be fulfilled after the Millennial Reign and before, or in conjunction with the Earth's purification by fire. It is the Great White Throne

Judgment. In chapter nineteen we reviewed the Judgment Seat of Christ, which is for believer's only and occurs immediately after, or in conjuction with, the Rapture of the Church. Those appearing at the Judgment Seat stand before Christ; this is a judgment of loving compassion, where all who are saved receive reward or loss of reward. Those appearing at the Great White Throne Judgment, however, stand before God. This is a judgment of condemnation, where all those judged are eternally damned.

Upon the Great White Throne is the one from whose face the Earth and the Heaven shall flee. There is no place for the Earth or the heaven for they, too, will come under a fiery judgment (II Peter 3:7).

We have seen that the believer's judgment is for those alive at the Rapture of the Church and those who are "dead IN Christ" (I Thess. 4:16). On the flip-side of the coin are those who die without God. They are the "dead." They are those who have died and who shall die without accepting the grace of our Lord. They are "dead without God." There are those who profess to know God, but have not accepted His sacrifice (I Jn. 5:12). They too shall appear at this Great White Throne Judgment.

> And to you who are troubled rest with us, when the Lord Jesus shall be revealed from heaven with his mighty angels, In flaming fire taking vengeance on them that know not God, and that obey not the gospel of our Lord Jesus Christ: Who shall be punished with everlasting destruction from the presence of the Lord, and from the glory of his power; II Thess. 1:7-9

At the Great White Throne Judgment the fallen angels will also be judged and cast into the eternal lake of fire. We, the Church, will judge them (I Cor. 6:3). All those who "have died" and "shall die" without God, those on Earth, those whom death and Hell shall deliver up, those in the sea, everyone who has ever rejected God, will be judged. This judgment is not for reward, or loss of reward, but for condemnation according to works. Good intentions will be of no avail. Good works of individuals or godless organizations will be void of meaning concerning eternal reward. Being without Christ is a serious matter.

The Two Types Of Books

Two types of books will be opened at the Great White Throne Judgment (Rev. 20:12-15), the "books," (collection of books into one book) revealing the facts of judgment concerning lost individuals, and "another book," which is the Book of Life. We discussed these in chapter three (under "Sardis Spiritual," "What is the Book of Life?"). However, here we must review these books.

The Books

The "books" is a collection of books known to us as the Bible. We know that God would not judge individuals without first offering a guideline to follow or a rule book to study, hence, we have the Bible, a book of books (II Tim. 3:16). Christ relates in John 12:48 that those who reject Him and His words will be judged in the last day. Paul also expresses the importance of this in Romans 2:16, where he states that there will be a day when God will judge the secrets of men by Jesus Christ, according to the gospel.

The Book Of Life?

The "books" reveal the facts of the life lived, while the Book of Life will validate the facts. The Book of Life will be present at the Great White Throne Judgment as proof of whether or not any given name is recorded. Whosoever is not found written in the Book of Life will be cast into the lake of fire (20:15).

Some thirty books are mentioned in the Bible, for example: book of curses (Num. 5:23), book of wars (Num. 21:14), book of cities (Josh. 18:9). The Book of Life is distinctly mentioned only eight times in the New Testament (Phil. 4:3; Rev. 3:5; 13:8; 17:8; 20:12,15; 21:27; 22:19) and is only alluded to in the Old (Ex. 32:32-33; Psa. 69:28; Mal. 3:16). From these mentions we gather meaning for the Book of Life.

In Philippians 4:3, we find that the Book of Life is for record of those men and women who have accepted Christ and share the gospel message. This reveals that the Book of Life is for those who have been born again into Christ's family (Jn. 3:3,7; I Peter 1:23). It is for Christians and Old Testament saints only (Gal. 3:21-26).

The Book of Life proves that those judged at the Great White Throne do not belong to Christ, for Christ is life. They do not inherit eternal life, for their names do not appear in the Book of Life. Thus, they have no part in that book. The blotted names will also reveal the rejection of life, which is Christ.

Blotted Names?

Another particular note of interest concerning the Book of Life is that names will be blotted out.

Moses prayed that God would blot him out rather than doom his fellow Israelites (Ex. 32:32). God replied to Moses saying that, "Whosoever hath sinned against me, him will I blot out of my book" (Ex. 32:33). The word "blot" is "*machah*" which means to "stroke or rub; abolish." This "abolishment" is not limited to Old Testament times. Those of Sardis are warned to overcome or have their names blotted out. We must remember that this letter was to the "Church" at Sardis, those who have their names written in the Book of Life. He goes on to say that the overcomers, those who watch, strengthen and hold fast, are safe from having their names blotted out. In contrast to having their names blotted out, their names will be confessed before the Father. We cannot take part of the Word and leave out the parts which may offend us or others.

Moreover, this blotting-out strictly applies to those who tamper with God's Word. To tamper with God's Word is to tamper with every soul of every Christian who follows after such mistakes. We are to be judged according to the words of God (Jn. 12:48; Rev. 22:19). To tamper with God's Word is to sabotage our guidebook and spiritual roadmap. How tragic this is and how horrendous the results to those who have added to and taken away from God's Word (see chpt. 7).

In connection with this thought, we must consider two categories ("sorts") of persons who do not appear at the Judgment Seat of Christ (discussed in chapter nineteen): the "sinner" and the "ungodly."

> And if the righteous scarcely be saved, where shall the ungodly and the sinner appear? I Peter 4:18

The word "sinner" comes from the Greek word "*harmartolos*," meaning "sinful." This refers to those who have never accepted Jesus Christ as Lord and Saviour, who by "nature" are the children of wrath (*"orge,"* "desire" Eph. 2:3). Such persons may or may not be of good moral character. Moral character will not be the issue. The issue will be that they have rejected Jesus Christ as Lord.

The word "ungodly" comes from the Greek *"asebes,"* which means "irreverent." To be irreverent is to be lacking in respect or dutifulness. This lack of respect or lack of dutifulness engulfs those who may know of God and/or rebel against everything godly (sinners), as well as those who know God and do not perform Christian duties, thus, becoming ungodly, irreverent. There will be such persons whose names have been blotted out of the Book of Life. Sad, but true. Such persons will not appear before the Judgment Seat of Christ, but will appear at the Great White Throne Judgment.

Purification By Fire

> But the heavens and the earth, which are now, by the same word are kept in store, reserved unto fire against the day of judgment and perdition of ungodly men.....But the day of the Lord will come as a thief in the night; in the which the heavens shall pass away with a great noise, and the elements shall melt with fervent heat, the earth also and the works that are therein shall be burned up. II Peter 3:7,10

Chapter twenty takes us to the end of the Earth as we now know it and to the doorway of a brand new Heaven and a brand new Earth (chpt. 21). The importance of this subject, at this point in our study, is due to the souls of those who live in their natural bodies during the Millennial Reign. What happens to their bodies when the world is set on fire?

We know that God has given us a promise and covenant that the Earth will never again be destroyed by flood (Gen 9:13; Rev. 4:3; 10:1), but it will be burned. To put it another way, it will be purified by fire. The apostle Peter tells us that the heavens and the Earth which are now, are to be kept intact until the judgment and perdition of ungodly men. That refers to the Great White Throne Judgment when the ungodly will be judged. We have just seen this in our study. Then, the heavens and the Earth will be purified by fire to prepare the heavens and the Earth for the new city, new Jerusalem. There are a few things however, that we need to know about the Earth in order to better understand its fiery judgment.

The Earth

The Earth was created to perpetuate itself. That is, it was created to continue to grow vegetation and spring forth in its appointed times. The psalmist David tells us that the Earth is "established for ever" (Psa. 78:69) and that its "foundations should not be removed for ever" (Psa. 104:5). Solomon recorded that "one generation passeth away and another generation cometh: but the earth "abideth for ever" (Eccl. 1:4). This tells us the Earth will not dissolve away into nothingness, but rather the opposite is true. The Earth that we now enjoy will always exist. It will be changed, but will never cease. Nuclear blasts will not wipe it out. No huge meteor will hit it and cause it to cease. The Earth is here to stay.

We must ask, then, what do the apostles Peter and John mean when they say that the heavens and the Earth will melt with fervent heat and be burned up (II Peter

3:10) and pass away (21:1)?

This is easily determined when we look at the Greek word from which the term "passed away" (21:1) comes. It is *"parerchomai."* This word does not mean "to annihilate" or "terminate an existence, "but "to come aside, to be nigh," and in some cases, "friends." It is as if to take a friend aside to change a behavior or action. Thus, "passed away" means "to cause to pass from one condition to another." Jesus also gives this idea concerning the heavens and the Earth and the Word (Matt. 24:35; Mrk.13:31; Lu. 21:33).

The heavens and the Earth will melt with fervent heat which will change them from one condition to another. They will be purified by fire. Thus, John sees a new Heaven and a new Earth, for the first Heaven and the first Earth were passed away, changed from an impure state to a pure state.

When the Earth is set on fire, the inhabitants, occupying natural bodies, will pass through the transformation in the same manner as Shadrach, Meshach, and Abednego were brought through the burning fiery furnace. The "fourth man" will be there. They will pass into the everlasting state of the Earth (that is, those of God). We know this, for there are nations that shall bring their honor and glory into the new city. They are those who will live outside the city on the new Earth (21:24-26). Those for whom the leaves of the Tree of Life will bring healing and restoration.

Ω

Whose
Builder And Maker
Is God
Chapter 21

And he that sat upon the throne said, Behold, I make all things
new. And he said unto me, Write: for these words are true and
faithful Rev. 21:5

Chapter 21 marks a new beginning. There will be a
new Heaven, a new Earth, a new city, a new temple and
new conditions. Everything will be brand new. It will be
heaven indeed. Oh, what wonderful things await!

A Pure Heaven, A Pure Earth

And I saw a new heaven and a new earth: for the first heaven and
the first earth were passed away; and there was no more sea. And
I John saw the holy city, new Jerusalem, coming down from God
out of heaven, prepared as a bride adorned for her husband. Rev.
21:1-2

Here we view the new status of God's ancient works
of art, the heaven and the Earth. The new heaven and the
new Earth are the results of the purification and renova-
tion of the old ones. We saw in the previous chapter that
the words "passed away," from *"parerchomai,"* means to
"change from one condition to another." This is exactly
what will happen to the Earth and its atmospheric heaven.

They will be changed and purified by fire (II Peter 3:10). These changes of the heaven and the Earth are also exemplified to verify the unchangeable Word of God (Matt. 24:35; Mark 13:31; Lu. 21:33).

John sees no sea on the new Earth, for the prophesied fiery judgment given it will lap up all waters. The absence of the seas does not mean that there will be no more waters at all, for waters will once again flow in abundance on the new Earth. This will be discussed in chapter 22.

A New City

In addition to the new heaven and new Earth, John sees the holy city, new Jerusalem, coming down from God out of Heaven. Note that it is the city not the Earth which descends. The new Earth shall be, and indeed already is, in place. However, it will be purified by fire. Thus, the new city descends to the new Earth. This city is adorned as a bride awaiting her husband. It is beautiful, radiant, and glowing.

This new city, new Jerusalem, is the place that Jesus has presently gone away to prepare (Jn. 14:1-7). It is the Father's "oikia," His residence, His abode, His house of many mansions. Lyrics to an old familiar hymn read, "Just build me a cabin in the corner of glory land." Those are humble words, but unscriptural. We've got mansions, many mansions, and they are in a brand new city. The materials used for this new city are not mere wood, brick or mortar, but they are the best of the best. It is a very real and literal place. We call it Heaven. God calls it new Jerusalem. It's the city that Abraham searched for, whose Builder and Maker is God (Heb. 11:8-10).

God Dwells With Man

And I heard a great voice out of heaven saying, Behold, the tabernacle of God is with men, and he will dwell with them, and they
shall be his people, and God himself shall be with them, and be
their God. And God shall wipe away all tears from their eyes; and
there shall be no more death, neither sorrow, nor crying, neither
shall there be any more pain: for the former things are passed
away. Rev. 21:3-4

Note that the people of Earth do not go to where God
dwells, that is, to the third Heaven into which Paul and
John were caught up. It is God who comes to dwell with
man, on a perfectly purified Earth, in a brand new city. It
is God's tabernacle that is to be with men. The word
"tabernacle" comes from the Greek word "*skene,*" which
means "a tent or cloth hut." This denotes a temporary
dwelling. However, "*skene*" also means "habitation."
God will not take up temporary residence, but will
"dwell" with men. The new city will be His habitation.
Imagine, that out of all the celestial bodies in the heavens,
God chooses to dwell upon this beautiful planet called
Earth. It will be purified by fire and flourish once again
for that habitation (II Peter 3:10; Psa. 78:69).

The tabernacle of old was a symbol of the protection
and communion of God with man. We will enjoy the protection and communion with God in the new city on the
newly purified Earth. We will reside with God and continually commune with Him. It is the time in which God,
Christ, and the Holy Spirit will be all in all (I Cor. 15:28)
and we will live with Him (I Thess. 4:17). There will be
no tears, no death, no sorrow, no crying, no pain.

Perfect Security

Not only will we have direct communion with God, but we will have the security of His omnipotence. He is all powerful. He is the Almighty. Nothing will threaten God's people. Such total and complete security is incomprehensible to man in his present state. We can only imagine what such security, peace and contentment will be like on the new Earth. However, in the presence of God Almighty, we will experience all the bliss of total security.

Only through faith are we able to accept the fact that such a world will exist and that the words of God are true and faithful concerning it (Heb.11:6). Our faith is a wonderful blessing, for through faith our spirit bears witness with God's Spirit that the Word of God is sure! (Rom. 8:16-17).

Another Immediate Message

And he that sat upon the throne said, Behold, I make all things new. And he said unto me, Write: for these words are true and faithful. And he said unto me, It is done. I am Alpha and Omega, the beginning and the end. I will give unto him that is athirst of the fountain of the water of life freely. He that overcometh shall inherit all things; and I will be his God, and he shall be my son. But the fearful, and unbelieving, and the abominable, and murderers, and whoremongers, and sorcerers, and idolaters, and all liars, shall have their part in the lake which burneth with fire and brimstone: which is the second death. Rev. 21: 5-8

"Behold I make all things new.... Write: for these words are true and faithful." Immediately after these statements, we see another "it is done." The things John heard are true and faithful. We can rest assured that wonderful things await. Christ himself is witness and we can fully trust the witness of Jesus Christ, for He "is" truth (Jn. 14:6). The "it is done" marks these things as a sure word of prophecy (19:10).

In the above verses we once again see the appellation of Alpha, Omega, the beginning and end, given to Jesus. As seen in chapter one, Alpha and Omega are the first and last letters of the Greek alphabet. This reveals the completeness and totality of Jesus Christ as the Word of God. Everything, even life itself, begins and ends in Him. He is the source of the "fountain" of eternal life (v.6). Partake of that fountain now! Thirst no more! Be an overcomer! Those who come to the fountain of the water of life and are overcomers will inherit all things, the new heaven, new Earth, everything!

The immediate message also warns that those who do not partake of the fountain of life will inherit the lake of fire. This lake of fire is Gehenna Hell, the second death. Those who will inherit that plight are the fearful (timid [not to be confused with humility]); unbelieving (without Christian faith); abominable (detestable, ungodly); murderers (those who commit homicide); whoremongers (male prostitutes); sorcerers (magicians and the such, also concerns witchcraft and illicit use of drugs); idolaters (such as those who worship idols); liars (untrue and deceitful persons). Thanks be to God that He will forgive such sin, but we must ask, repent of sin, then live by faith in His Word (1 Jn. 1:8-9).

The Second Death

What is the second death? We see in the passages above that the lake of fire and brimstone "is" the second death. We have discussed in chapter nine that those who die without accepting God's plan of escape will go immediately to Hades, the Old Testament *"Sheowl."* We have found that this place of torment is within the Earth. In chapter one, we discussed how Jesus descended into Hades before ascending into Heaven (Acts 2:24-27; Eph. 4:8-10; I Peter 3:18-20). Those not accepting God's plan of escape are held in Hades until the Great White Throne Judgment (20:12). At that time, they (the "dead" without Christ) will be resurrected. However, after that resurrection and after the Great White Throne Judgment (chpt. 20), they will be cast into the lake of fire, the everlasting Hell. It is the second death.

You may have heard the saying, "Born once, die twice. Born twice, die once." That is, if you have only had a natural birth, you will die twice: the physical death followed by the second death. However, if you have been naturally born, then at some point in your life accept Jesus Christ as Lord and Saviour, thus becoming "born-again" by the Spirit of God (born twice), you die only once, physically.

Come Hither

> And there came unto me one of the seven angels which had the seven vials full of the seven last plagues, and talked with me, saying, Come hither, I will shew thee the bride, the Lamb's wife. And he carried me away in the spirit to a great and high mountain, and shewed me that great city, the holy Jerusalem, descending out of heaven from God, Having the glory of God: and her light was like unto a stone most precious, even like a jasper stone, clear as crystal; Rev. 21:9-11

This marks the fourth major vision of Revelation. It is the fourth "Come hither" connected with John's being "carried away in the spirit."

Note that it is one of the seven angels who had one of the seven vials who came to talk with John. This also marks the vision as pertaining to the future. The angel tells John to "Come hither, I will shew thee the bride, the Lamb's wife." This also marks the fulfillment as being in our future. Here we gain additional assurance that it is the bride, the Church (II Cor. 11:2), that becomes the wife after the "catching away." Here, the term "wife" does not refer to the Jews, as some claim. Only those who have accepted Christ during the present age are to be part of the bride. This is true, whether Jew, Gentile, bond or free (Gal. 3:27-28).

The Glory Of The City

Instead of directly viewing the wife, John is shown the new city, new Jerusalem. This is significant. We know that a city is not made up merely of buildings, businesses and parks. It takes occupants, as well as buildings, to make a city. The occupants of the new city are those who make up the bride. Thus, John sees both the city and the occupants in the form of God's "glory." Why? Because the new city, new Jerusalem, is the place of God's residence, as well as that of the bride. We know this, for we are joint heirs with Christ. We will be with Him forever (I Thess. 4:17) and He will dwell in the new city (v.23). Thus, John views the glory of God, the glory of the wife, and the glory of the city. We see then, that the wife and the city are inseparable references. Thus, alongside the glory of God, the

Lamb, we, too, will lighten the city. The wife lightens the city? How?

Here is the significance. With the beginning of the New Testament, the glory of God has been shown mainly in Christ (Lu. 9:29-32; Jn. 2:11). As joint heirs, we, too, share that glory (Jn. 17:5-6, 22). Thus, we are to be transformed into the glorious image of God (II Cor. 3:18) and will be fully glorified when in God's presence (Rom. 5:2). Thus, John saw a combination of both the city and the wife having the glory of God. The brightness of God's glory is the primary reason John sees the city instead of a woman. The brightness of the glory of God, as witnessed by Paul, will outshine the midday sun (Acts 26:13).

Twelve Gates, Twelve Foundations

And had a wall great and high, and had twelve gates, and at the gates twelve angels, and names written thereon, which are the names of the twelve tribes of the children of Israel: On the east three gates; on the north three gates; on the south three gates; and on the west three gates. And the wall of the city had twelve foundations, and in them the names of the twelve apostles of the Lamb. Rev. 21:12-14

Here we begin to get a foreview of what the new city, new Jerusalem, will look like. There will be a great wall which sits foursquare (v.16) and has twelve gates, each one having the name of a tribe of Israel inscribed on it (7:4-8). There will be three gates to the east, three to the north, three to the south and three to the west. Each gate is made of one great pearl (v.21). Thus, there will be twelve great pearls.

Twelve, the number for "government by divine appointment," is used as the signature of Israel. In

Numbers 1:5-16, twelve princes are named over the twelve tribes of Israel. There are twelve stones in the high priest's breastplate which represent the nation of Israel (Ex. 28:17-21). Ishmael begat twelve princes (Gen. 17:20). Elijah built an altar of twelve stones, and fire came down from heaven and consumed the offering (I Kings 17:30-40). Jesus chose twelve disciples. If Jesus had requested, the Father would have sent twelve legions of angels. There will be twelve angels, one at each of the twelve gates of the new city.

It is not stated as to which of the twelve tribes are listed and which of the twelve apostles are listed. The twelve tribes are undoubtedly those mentioned in chapter seven: Juda, Reuben, Gad, Aser, Nepthalim, Manasses, Simeon, Levi, Issachar, Zabulon, Joseph, and Benjamin. However, there is somewhat of a dispute over which apostle will be the twelfth replacing Judas Iscariot, Paul or Matthias. Matthias, not Paul, was numbered with the twelve after prayer and the casting of lots (Acts 1:26). The name "Matthias" means "gift of God." Although Paul is considered as great among the apostles and a great influence through his epistles, he was not numbered among the twelve. It is thus more likely that it will be Matthias whose name appears on one of the foundation stones. (The name "Paul" from *"Paulos,"* means "little.")

The Size Of The City

And he that talked with me had a golden reed to measure the city, and the gates thereof, and the wall thereof. And the city lieth foursquare, and the length is as large as the breadth: and he measured the city with the reed, twelve thousand furlongs. The length and the breadth and the height of it are equal. And he measured the wall thereof, an hundred and forty and four cubits, according to the measure of a man, that is, of the angel. And the building of the wall of it was of jasper: and the city was pure gold, like unto clear glass. Rev. 21:15-18

The angel had a "golden reed" in which to measure the city, the gates and the wall. This reed is undoubtedly pure gold, denoting purity. The city measures 12,000 furlongs. Thus, the city is 1500 miles long and 1500 miles wide. Such a city would extend from Maine to Florida and from the East Coast to about 600 miles west of the Mississippi River. That's one large city!

Note that the city lies foursquare, that is "tetragonos," meaning four-cornered. The length is as large as the breadth. The singular form of the word "wall" is used because it will be a continual wall which surrounds the city, having no breaks or joints. It is unblemished, seamless.

It would seem reasonable that this great wall is shaped like a mountain peak rather than a cube. Note that it "lieth" or "sits" foursquare, "four-cornered," not upward in a cube shape. The main reason for this assumption is that the wall is only 216 feet thick (144 cubits). A relatively thin wall with a cubical shape would seem to be completely out of proportion. Remember that the wall extends 1500 miles in length and in width. Nothing is said of the top, whether it's canopied or open. A mountain peak shape would appear to have better supporting qualities. In addition, it would stand to reason that the throne would be positioned in the center and upward as the river of life originates and flows "out of the throne."

The structure of the wall is of jasper, a variety of

quartz or silicon dioxide. Silicon constitutes more than one-fourth of the Earth's crust and is used in steel-making. Although the wall is crystal clear, it will be as strong, or stronger than, steel. Thus, with these things considered, it would appear that the city has the shape as that of a mountain peak.

The wall, like the entire city, is crystal clear and is constructed without the use of human hands. It is the city whose builder and maker is God (Heb. 11:10). A song describes this wonderful place: "Oh, What a city." It is truly beyond description.

The Twelve Foundation Stones

> And the foundations of the wall of the city were garnished with all manner of precious stones. The first foundation was jasper; the second, sapphire; the third, a chalcedony; the fourth, an emerald; The fifth, sardonyx; the sixth, sardius; the seventh, chrysolyte; the eighth, beryl; the ninth, a topaz; the tenth, a chrysoprasus; the eleventh, a jacinth; the twelfth, an amethyst. Rev. 21:19-20

The wall of the city has twelve great foundation stones. These stones will be inscribed with the names of the twelve apostles (v.14). One would assume that each stone would bear the name of one of the apostles. However, great speculation and many extended applications would be necessary to make such a connection. The apostles' names are inscribed to give credence to the fact that the new city is the dwelling of those of the Church (born-again believers). The apostles helped build the foundational truths of the spiritual house called the Church. Jesus Christ is the foundation stone (I Cor. 3:10) and the chief cornerstone (I Peter 2:2-6).

Although assigning the apostles with a particular

foundation stone requires a far stretch into speculation, the colors and numbers of the stones are significant. In the natural realm, foundation stones provide the necessary connections between the Earth and the building. However, the foundation stones of the new city supply more than just physical connecting points. There are symbolic applications as well.

We have seen in our study the significance of numbers. The same method of interpretation applies to colors. Thus, when we compare the colors and numbers of the foundation stones, we see a pattern that helps us better understand the passage. (We must remember, of course, to stay within the context supplied by this chapter. The context consists of the new heaven, the new Earth and the new city.) The colors and numbers concern the redemption of the Earth and all things connected to the Earth.

1. Jasper: Jasper, the first foundation stone, is usually red because of the presence of iron, but it is sometimes brown, yellow, green or crystal clear. The wall of the new city is "of jasper" (21:18), thus, it is more likely that the first foundation stone contains a mixture of colors and is diverse from the wall itself which is clear. It is obvious that this first foundation stone is a mixture of colors polished to excellence. The Hebrew name for Jasper, "*yasyhepheh,*" from which the Greek comes, means "to polish." It was the third stone in the fourth row of Aaron's breastplate (Ex. 28:20; 39:13).

The number one is the number of unity. The mixture of colors of the jasper stone, representing diverse qualities, refers to the unified plan of God concerning the atmospheric heaven, the Earth, and the new city. Although the applications of unity may be applied to the Church, among other Biblical things, we will restrict our application of the foundation stones to the context of the new heaven, the new Earth and the new city. We must keep in mind that Christ not only returns to redeem mankind (although made from the dust of the Earth), but will return to redeem the Earth back to Himself. (Earth dominion was lost through Adam and must be redeemed - See chapters 5 & 10).

2. Sapphire: Sapphire, the second foundation stone in the new city, was the second jewel in the second row of Aaron's breastplate (Ex. 28:18; 39:11). It is the Greek "sappheiros" coming from the Hebrew "cappiyr." The sapphire of the ancients was not our sapphire, the transparent blue corundum, but usually the opaque stone known to us as lapis lazuli, varying from ultramarine to dark violet blue. The curtains of the tabernacle of old were blue. Blue was the color of the ephod, a vest interwoven with golden threads. Mordecai wore the royal color of blue. The blue sky denotes the eternity of Christ Jesus with the Father. Thus, the color blue denotes the royalty, righteousness, and eternity of Christ.

The number two is the number of unity, division and witnessing. Thus, "unity" denotes the Godhead, while "division" denotes the curtains and veil of the tabernacle, as well as Father and Son of the Godhead. The aspect of "witnessing" corresponds with the royal apparel of priests. Thus, we see represented in the sapphire, the righteous witness of the eternity of the one true God as Father and Son in the creation. This definition corresponds with the old and new heaven (Workings of the Holy Spirit identified later).

3. Chalcedony: The chalcedony, the third foundation stone in the new city (Rev. 21:19), is a translucent variety of quartz occurring in a variety of colors. Agate, bloodstone, carnelian, chrysoprase, flint, jasper, and onyx are all varieties of chalcedony.

The number three is the number of holy things and represents the resurrection, divine completeness and perfection of God. The seraphim of 4:8 cry "holy, holy, holy" to the lamb. Three comprise the Godhead: Father, Son, and Holy Spirit. The eternity of Jehovah is given in the three-fold expression of "who is, who was, and who is to come." Jesus arose after three days.

As quartz is one of the most common minerals, and is an important constituent of many kinds of rocks, chalcedony is a good representation of the Earth itself. Its diversity of colors also supports this thesis. Almighty God has established the Earth forever for the purpose of habitation. It is on the Earth that God will live with His people. Thus, Chalcedony, along with the number three, exemplifies diversity and administration of Almighty God concerning the Earth, its formation for habitation and its various stages that will bring it to perfection. All this is accomplished through the Godhead of Father, Son, and Holy Spirit.

4. Emerald. Emerald, the fourth foundation stone in the new city, is a deep green variety of beryl. It was the

third jewel in the first row of Aaron's breastplate (Ex. 28:17; 39:10), and was used to describe the rainbow around the throne (4:3).

The words for green normally describe vegetation. It is used of pastures (Psa. 23:2); herbage (II Kin. 19:26); trees in general (Deut. 12:2; Luke 23:31; Rev. 8:7); a hypocrite compared to a papyrus plant (Job 8:16); and grass (Mark 6:39). The color green thus represents the regenerative life of Earth vegetation. We saw earlier that the color of the emerald also concerns the covenant between God and the Earth in the rainbow (Gen. 9:17).

Four is the number of the world. There are four seasons, four elements and four major directions of the compass. Thus, the emerald foundation stone represents God's covenant with the Earth that it shall continue to perpetuate itself.

5. Sardonyx: Sardonyx, the fifth foundation stone of the new city, is a red and white variety of chalcedony. This is the only mention of the sardonyx in the Bible (21:20).

The color red is a picture of God's divine providence and abundant life given to mankind, especially at the crucifixion (Acts 20:28). Several attributes of God's provision are described by the color red. Among such we find Jacob's stew (Gen. 25:30), and the sacrificial heifer (Num. 19:2). However, Isaiah 1:18 reveals red (scarlet) as that applied to sin. Christ not only provided the perfect sacrifice for man, but He became sin for us (II Cor. 5:21). The reddish color thus represents God's care and provision toward man through His redemptive plan.

The significance of white is that it portrays purity, righteousness, and joy. The white horse is seen as a sign of victory.

Five is the number of grace and of God's goodness. There were five offerings upon the altar of sacrifice: the burnt offering, peace offering, sin offering, trespass offering, and meat offering. Five ministries reveal God's grace: apostles, prophets, evangelists, pastors, and teachers (Eph. 4:11). David gained victory over five giants. There were five wise and five foolish virgins. Grace is mentioned five times in succession (Romans 11:5-6). Sardonyx (red and white stone) thus represents God's grace through the shed blood of Christ, thus making way for purity, righteousness and victory given to the saints. By grace are we saved through faith (Eph. 2:8). Concerning the Earth, God's grace has provided us with the Earth and new city for an eternal home (after Earth's purification by fire).

6. Sardius: Sardius, the sixth foundation stone of the new city, is red and considered by many to be carnelian, a reddish brown variety of chalcedony. It was the first stone in the first row of Aaron's breastplate (Ex. 28:17; 39:10) and was included as the covering of the King of Tyre (Ezek. 28:12-13).

The color brown is mentioned only four times in Scripture. These references are applied only to sheep (Gen. 30:32,33,35,40). They were the sheep chosen by Jacob that were to be distinguished, that is, set apart, from those of his father-in-law, Laban. There are many Biblical comparisons between sheep and human beings. The

Church collectively is referred to as the sheepfold (John 10:1). Thus, the color brown represents those who have accepted God's provision. They are of the sheepfold, the born-again believers.

Six is the number of man, created on the sixth day. His days to labor are six. Six years the land was to be worked by man and left to rest on the seventh. The reddish-brown Sardius stone thus represents the blood that was shed for man's redemption. Note that man was made from the dust of the Earth. It is the blood of Christ shed on the cross of Calvary, that, upon believing and accepting, brings one into the sheepfold.

7. **Chrysolyte:** Chrysolyte, the seventh foundation stone in the new city, is a yellow stone that may have been the same as topaz or some other yellow gem such as beryl, zircon, or a yellow quartz. Its name comes from a Greek word that means "goldstone." The chrysolite known today is the peridot, an olive green silicate of magnesium and iron. This is not believed to be the same gem as that referred to in 21:20.

The word "yellow" appears only four times in the Bible. The Hebrew word *"yeraqraq"* is translated as yellow and indicates the greenish cast of gold (Psa. 68:13). Many objects of Old Testament times were made of gold: the high priest's vest (Ex. 28:5), crowns (Psa. 21:3), chains (Gen. 41:42), rods (Song 5:14); rings and coins (I Chr. 21:25; Acts 3:6). Hiram brought gold to Israel for Solomon's palace (I Kin. 10:16-21) and for furnishings for the temple (I Kin. 6:20; 10:2,10). Gold was also taken as plunder in war (II Kin. 24:13).

Although gold is a very precious commodity, the yellow color of the chrysolyte ("goldstone") denotes impurity. Gold in its purest form is crystal clear. Impurities in the gold cause the yellowish color. However, gold is used by the apostle Paul to reveal the most precious of man's works (I Cor. 3:12). We must know though, that works hold no significance concerning eternal life without first accepting Christ and the purification He brings. Good works are a very vital part of the Christian's life, but only after accepting Christ as Saviour.

The Hebrew word for yellow *"yeraqraq"* denotes the greenish cast of gold, as seen earlier, and also refers to the regenerative life of Earth vegetation. In addition, three out of the four mentions of the color yellow, *"tsahob,"* describes the light-colored hair in a leprous spot (Lev. 13:30,32,36). Leprosy is a form of impurity often associated with sin or uncleanness.

Seven is the number of completeness and perfection. The Word of God rests upon the number seven. It stands for the seventh day of the creative week concerning the completion of creation. The seven one-thousandth year of man's history is connected with the Millennial Reign, at the end of which, the Earth will be cleansed by fire. Such words as "complete" "finished" and "it is done" are connected with the number seven. There are also seven churches, seven spirits, seven stars, seven seals, seven trumpets, seven thunders, and seven vials which complete the last days. Noah took the clean beasts into the ark by sevens. After seven days, the flood came.

Thus, yellow, green, and gold (pure) along with the number seven, stand for the cleansing of the impurities of

Earth, including man (made from the Earth), and God's completion of all things concerning it.

8. Beryl: Beryl, the eighth foundation stone in the new city, ranges in color from bluish green to yellow, white, light crimson to a pale reddish purple, and deep green. It was the first stone in the fourth row of Aaron's breastplate (Ex. 28:20; 39:13). Many scholars render the word for beryl as chrysolite and topaz. The wheels in the prophet Ezekiel's visions were described as resembling beryl (Ezek. 1:16; 10:9).

The number eight stands for the "new order of things." The eighth day is the beginning of a new week. God commanded Abraham to circumcise every male child on the eighth day. Noah's family consisted of eight persons. Noah was the eighth person (II Peter 2:5).

We have seen that blue represents the righteousness and eternity of Christ, whereas green represents the regenerative life and continuance of Earth vegetation, and yellow, of the chrysolyte, represents impurities. The light crimson denotes the blood shed on Calvary. We saw earlier that the plan of redemption also applies to the redemption of the Earth, as well as the souls of men. The reddish-purple denotes the blood-bought royal atmosphere enjoyed upon the new Earth.

Thus, the colors of beryl, combined with the number eight, the "new order of things," refers to the establishment of the new Earth and the new atmospheric heaven which surrounds it. These will be enjoyed by all those living on the new Earth. It is for those dwelling inside and outside the city.

9. Topaz: Topaz, the ninth foundation stone of the new city, is a yellowish-green form of chrysolite. The topaz was the second gem in the first row of Aaron's breastplate (Ex. 28:17; 39:10).

We saw that the Biblical yellow denotes the greenish cast of gold. The color yellow represents the impurities found in gold. Thus, the color yellow refers to impurities. We have also seen that green represents the regenerative life of Earth vegetation. Thus, the yellowish-green foundation stone symbolizes the impurity of the Earth. However, when connected with the number nine, which represents the fruit of the Spirit and the divine act of completion from the Lord, we realize that the topaz stone represents the Earth's cleansing from impurity and its completion for the eternal state. Thus, the act of cleansing itself.

10. Chrysoprasus: Chrysoprasus, the tenth foundation stone in the new city, is a light green color variety of chalcedony.

The color green, as we have seen many times already, represents the regenerative life and continuance of Earth vegetation.

The number ten is the number of testimony, law and responsibility. There were ten plagues upon Egypt during the days of Moses (Ex. 7:12). There are ten commandments. There were ten virgins. These refer to responsibility as well as to the Law itself. Ten Psalms begin with "Hallelujah" (Psa. 106, 111, 112, 113, 135, 146, 147, 148, 149, 150), pointing to the testimony of God. Thus, the tenth foundation stone, chrysoprasus, represents the covenant between God and the Earth concerning the perpetuation of the Earth. In particular, the Earth's testimony concerning the covenant in that it responds by springing forth, once again after purification by fire, with abundant vegetation.

11. Jacinth: Jacinth, the eleventh foundation stone in the new city, is a yellow-orange variety of the mineral zircon. The jacinth was the first stone in the third row of Aaron's breastplate (Ex. 28:19; 39:12).

Again we see the color yellow representing impurity. However, the jacinth is a yellow-orange. Orange is a color blend found between yellow and red. Thus, there is a connection between the impurities represented in the color yellow and the red which denotes the provision and cleansing of the blood of Christ. The color red also gives a picture of God's divine providence and abundant life given to mankind through the blood shed on Calvary (Acts 20:28). Note, that the blood shed on Calvary was also necessary for the redemption of the Earth. Without that sacrifice, death, burial and resurrection, Earth redemption would not be possible.

The number eleven is the number of judgment and disorder. When connected with the colors yellow and orange, we see a representation of impurities coming head-on with the pure blood of Christ. Impurity meets purity. Christ is the only one capable of true judgment over disorder and is the only one who can make impurities pure. This is exactly what He will do with the Earth. It will be judged as impure, then purified by fire in order to make way for the new city. Thus, jacinth represents the fulfillment of the covenant that God made with the Earth that it should spring forth in its appointed times. It is God's part of the covenant fulfilled, in that He purifies the impure.

12. Amethyst: Amethyst, the twelfth foundation stone in the new city, varies from light to deep violet and was used for jewelry. It was known in Egypt, India and Ceylon. Amethyst was the third stone in the third row of Aaron's breastplate (Ex. 28:19; 39:12).

The deep violet color consists of a bluish-purple. Blue, as depicted in Proverbs 20:30, describes the color of a wound, but usually refers to the wound itself. Purple was also the color of royal robes (Judg. 8:26), as well as the garments of the wealthy (Prov. 31:22; Luke 16:19; Rev. 17:4). The robe placed upon Jesus was purple (Mark 15:17,20). In New Testament times, purple was an important item of trade (Acts 16:14; Rev. 18:12).

The number twelve, as seen earlier, represents God's government by divine appointment. Surely, Christ Jesus was wounded (blue) that the divine government may be set upon the new Earth. That divine government will be above all forms of government that have ever been (purple-royalty). Thus, considering the royal color of purple and the number twelve, the amethyst represents the establishment of a royal divine government upon the Earth. Accepting the sacrifice of Christ Jesus makes it possible for us to be a part of that divine government as joint heirs with Christ. That privilege was purchased on Calvary by the blood of Christ Jesus, who was wounded for our transgression (Isa. 53:5).

Color-Number Scheme

By connecting the colors and numbers of the foundation stones, we see a plan concerning the atmospheric heaven, the Earth, and the new city. Let's review:

1. The jasper stone represents the unified plan of God concerning the atmospheric heaven, the Earth, and the new city.

2. The sapphire represents the righteous witness of God as Creator. It exemplifies the three-fold nature and eternity of God as Father, Son, and Holy Spirit.

3. The chalcedony represents the physical make up of the Earth.

4. The emerald represents God's covenant with the Earth for a perpetual existence.

5. The sardonyx represents God's grace in providing the Earth and city for an eternal home.

6. The sardius stone represents the blood shed for man who was made from the dust of the Earth.

7. The chrysolyte represents the impurities of Earth and man (made from the Earth). It also stands for the bringing of the impurities of Earth and man to completion and purity.

8. The beryl stone stands for the establishment of the new Heaven, the new Earth and the new city.

9. The topaz stone represents the act of cleansing and completion of the new Heaven and new Earth, particularly the act itself.

10. The chrysoprasus represents the Earth's testimony concerning the covenant of perpetuation in that it responds by springing forth, once again, with abundant vegetation after its purification by fire.

11. The jacinth represents God's fulfillment of His part of the covenant with the Earth, in that it is He who purifies.

12. The amethyst represents the establishment of a royal divine government upon the new Earth.

Twelve Gates To The City

And the twelve gates were twelve pearls: every several gate was of one pearl: and the street of the city was pure gold, as it were transparent glass. Rev. 21:21

We saw earlier that the twelve gates are overseen by twelve angels (v.12). Obviously, gates are used for coming in and going out. The angels oversee the glory and honor brought into the city by the kings of the Earth (v.24). This refers to people who will live outside the new city upon the new Earth. These people will enter and exit through the gates. Imagine the sight: a gate made from one great pearl. Not only that, but there are twelve. Note that each of these twelve gates provide entrance into a city some 1500 miles long and 1500 miles wide. The gates to this gigantic city must be of tremendous size. Note also that the street of the city is pure gold and crystal clear. Imagine the quantity of pure gold necessary to supply such a city! Yet it shall be just as God has said in His Word. Again, "Oh, What a City!"

Temple In Heaven

And I saw no temple therein: for the Lord God Almighty and the Lamb are the temple of it. And the city had no need of the sun, neither of the moon, to shine in it: for the glory of God did lighten it, and the Lamb is the light thereof. And the nations of them which are saved shall walk in the light of it: and the kings of the earth do bring their glory and honour into it. And the gates of it shall not be shut at all by day: for there shall be no night there. And they shall bring the glory and honour of the nations into it. Rev. 21:22-26

We saw in chapter seven that a temple generally refers to a building in which a god or gods are worshipped. It is the place where particular gods or goddesses manifest their presence. Thus, temples are considered holy or sacred, even by pagans. There is no earthly temple in the new city, new Jerusalem, but there is a temple. The Lord God Almighty and the Lamb are the temple of it. (See chapter seven for temple discussion under "God's Temple")

Nations Of The Saved

We find here that nations of people upon the new Earth will walk in the tremendous light of the city. The light is so clear that it is likened to a crystal clear jasper stone (v.11). The nations of the saved will walk in the light of the new city. This speaks of those who will walk outside the new city. Kings of these nations will bring the honor and glory of the nations "into" the city.

Note: The nations will walk in the light of the city as its light is brilliant and the city is transparent. However, this does not nullify the existence of the sun and the moon (explained under the "Sunshine On The New Earth").

Who Are They?

It is also evident that there will be a hierarchy among the nations, for they have "kings." We must ask then, who are these kings and nations living outside the city? We know that these nations and kings are not comprised of the bride, the Lamb's wife, for they (we) will dwell inside the city. Isaiah says that "all flesh" will come to worship before the Lord. However, this too refers to the nations outside the new city. Note that it cannot refer to those who dwell inside the new city, for they (Raptured saints) have glorified bodies and are the "joint heirs" with Christ. The glory and honor brought to the Lord from the nations will be ours also.

Isaiah settles the matter by identifying those who will walk outside the city on the new Earth.

Thy people also shall be all righteous: they shall inherit the land for ever, the branch of my planting, the work of my hands, that I may be glorified. Isa. 60:21

It is evident that these nations are those who will claim the eternal plot of land promised them. Who are they? They are "thy people," the children of Israel. They are the nations of people who will come out of the kingdom age (millennial age). They will pass through the Earth's purification by fire in their natural bodies just like Shadrach, Meshach and Abednego came through the burning fiery furnace. They are not the "Church," but are those of the tribes of Israel of the earthly lineage of Christ.

The children of Israel, those saved during the Tribulation Period, will, in their physical bodies, live eternally due to the leaves of the tree of life. The leaves of the tree of life are for the "healing of the nations" (22:2). They will exist as Adam and Eve would have existed, if not for their sin of disobedience.

> For as the new heavens and the new earth, which I will make, shall remain before me, saith the LORD, so shall your seed and your name remain. And it shall come to pass, that from one new moon to another, and from one sabbath to another, shall all flesh come to worship before me, saith the LORD. And they shall go forth, and look upon the carcases of the men that have transgressed against me: for their worm shall not die, neither shall their fire be quenched; and they shall be an abhorring unto all flesh. Isa. 66:22-24

Isaiah tells us that the children of Israel will be upon the new Earth. Although the Lord will be their everlasting light (Isa. 60:19), they will observe new moons and sabbath days. Isaiah also observes that they will be able to peer into Gehenna Hell. This is realized due to the torment of those who will take the mark of the beast. The smoke of their torment will ascend forever (14:10-11). Some scholars believe that the site of Babylon will be one of the openings of Gehenna Hell on Earth, where men of Earth will be able to see the ungodly in everlasting fire (Isa. 14:9-17; 66:22-24; Rev. 19:3).

Sunshine On The New Earth

The prevailing thought among Christians is that there shall be no sun or moon to lighten the new Earth at all, that these creations of God will be completely annihilated. Note that this city has "no need of the sun, neither of the moon, to shine in it, for the glory of God did lighten it, and the Lamb is the light thereof" (v.23). This does not mean that there will be no sun or moon at all, but that it is impossible for their light to penetrate the overwhelming brightness of God's glory within the city. The prophet Isaiah also reflects this thought.

> The sun shall be no more thy light by day; neither for brightness shall the moon give light unto thee: but the LORD shall be unto thee an everlasting light, and thy God thy glory. Isa. 60:19

The nations of the saved, which dwell outside the new city, will be drawn to the everlasting light of the Lord. They will observe new moons and Sabbaths (Isa. 66:23), but their worship will center around Jesus, the light of the world (Jn. 8:13; 9:5). This is something the children of Israel have not yet fully observed. This application is realized due to the following verse.

> Thy sun shall no more go down; neither shall thy moon withdraw itself: for the LORD shall be thine everlasting light, and the days of thy mourning shall be ended. Isa. 60:20

At first, one would think that this verse reveals that the sun and moon will cease to exist. However, it reveals the perpetual blessedness of the sun and moon. The sun will never go down and the moon will not withdraw itself. It also reveals that Christ will be the desire of the hearts of the people. It must be noted again that it is the city which will "need no light of the sun, neither of the moon to shine in it: for the glory of God did lighten it, and the Lamb is the light thereof." There is also reference made that the gates of the city will not be shut at all by day, for there is no night "in the city." The gates are significant in that they also concern those "outside the city," upon the new Earth, who bring their honor and glory into the city. They will live in the sunshine of the day and the moonlight of night upon the Earth forever. If not, they could not observe the Sabbaths and the new moons (Isa. 66:22-23).

The eternity of the sun and moon in the aspects of day and night are also seen in reference to the eternal punishment of Gehenna Hell. Note, that the beast, the false prophet, and Satan are to be tormented day and night for ever and ever (20:10). Reference is also given of those who will worship the beast, who will be tormented day and night forever (14:10-11). Day and night have no relevance to eternity unless they are literal. Thus, the light of the sun and moon will exist to mark Hell's ongoing existence. Their light will be upon the new Earth to assure the Earth's covenant of perpetual production of vegetation. The brightness of the sun and moon will exist, but not "in the city." The brightness of God's glory will outshine the sun and moon in the new city and outside its wall for prescribed distances. God's glory is not restricted from shining outside the city, for the city is transparent.

We know also that the gates of the city are positioned toward the east, north, south and west (v.13). The sun fixes these positions of the hemisphere, represented by the "rising of the sun," the "setting of the sun" (Isa. 45:6; Psa. 50:1), the dark quarter (Gen. 13:14; Joel 2:20) and the "brilliant quarter" (Deut. 33:23; Job 37:13; Ez. 40:24), or by their position relative to a person facing the rising sun as "before, behind, on the left or on the right hand" (Job 23:8,9). In addition, we have seen that the Earth will abide forever (Psa. 78:69; 104:5; Eccl. 1:4). Thus, according to the size of the city, versus the perpetuality and circumference of the Earth, nature tells us that there would be darkness upon half of the Earth continually. That is, unless the light of the sun and moon are allowed by God to continue to exist. Note also, that if God allows His glory to shine bright enough to encompass the entire Earth from the new city (without doubt He can do all things), His brightness would make void the purification and usage of the new heaven and all it contains. Considering the perpetual nature of the Earth and comparing it with the direct words of God from Genesis, the whole matter is quickly put to rest:

> While the earth remaineth, seedtime and harvest, and cold and heat, and summer and winter, and day and night shall not cease. Gen. 8:22 (See chart, pg. 485)

An Immediate Warning

> And there shall in no wise enter into it any thing that defileth, neither whatsoever worketh abomination, or maketh a lie: but they which are written in the Lamb's book of life. Rev. 21:27

This verse does not imply that there will be sin or wickedness on the new Earth that might bring harm or hurt to the new city. It simply reveals that neither the new Earth nor the new city will ever be contaminated by any kind of sin. Sin will have been delivered to its place in Gehenna Hell. We are assured of this because death and Hell (Hades) will be cast into the lake of fire (20:14). Death is the wage of sin (Rom. 6:23). There will be no sin for there is no death. The above verse is a warning to those of John's day and our day that sin will not inherit the kingdom of God (I Cor. 6:9; Gal. 5:21). We are to separate from sin.

Those who will inherit the eternal kingdom of God are those whose names are written in the Lamb's Book of Life. We saw in chapter twenty that the Lamb's book stands as the record book for those who have accepted God's plan for eternal life. Thus, the verse above consists of more than just a warning. It is an invitation for every individual to have his or her name written in the Lamb's Book of Life.

You cannot write your name or register for life on your own. Christ Jesus does the recording. If your name is not written down in the Lamb's Book of Life, don't put it off! Accept Christ Jesus as Saviour and Lord right now! Have your name entered in the Lamb's Book of Life!
Ω

I Jesus,
Have Sent
Mine Angel
Chapter 22

I remember as a child how my parents, my brother, my sister, and I moved from place to place quite often. During that time, we lived in several old farm houses, many of which were drafty and cold. However, many fond memories still visit me occasionally of those times, wide open spaces, fresh country air, and the freedom to roam.

My fondest memories revolve around the ponds, lakes and creeks scattered across the countryside. I would romp and play all day along many a creek bank. The water seemed so clear and the flowing waters so soothing. I would catch frogs, snakes, fish and whatever else that moved. I remember one fish in particular that I took home in an Ole' Judge coffee can about one-third full of water. I set it by my bed, which was close to the fireplace. No, he didn't cook; quite the opposite. Sometime that night after the fire went out, he froze solid in that coffee can. It was so cold. I would have so many quilts piled on me that I could hardly move. At any rate, those were the good ole days.

However, the new Heaven and new Earth will far exceed anything this world has to offer. The waters will be pure and crystal clear. The nights won't freeze the fish in the coffee cans and quilts will be a thing of the past. Everything will be perfect, for God himself will be there and our home will be permanent. I truly look forward to the things that await. Don't miss it! I know you'll love it, too.

We must keep in mind as we ponder the new Earth and new city that John was allowed to give us only small portions of information about the city. Thus we have very few particulars with which to work. We can only imagine the grandeur of the city through our spiritually dimmed eyes. However, the information we do have helps us to readily see that the new city and the new Earth will be a tremendous and glorious place.

A Pure River

> And he showed me a pure river of water of life, clear as crystal, proceeding out of the throne of God and of the Lamb. Rev. 22:1

The waters of our present Earth are muddy, polluted with toxic sewage and a myriad of other contaminates. Water purification plants are a necessity in just about every city. There will be no need for such cleansing methods in the new city. There we will have a pure river, as clear as crystal and life-giving. This pure river is the "water of life" flowing from the throne of God.

The mountain peak city will undoubtedly afford for the throne to be located in the center of the city, near its highest peak. The waters will stream from terrace to terrace to supply the new city and the new Earth with the purest of waters. Although beginning as one pure river, it will divide into at least twelve pure rivers at some point.

The river of life will flow out each of the twelve gates. Each gate will be large enough to provide the space needed for open fields, vegetation, trees, a river, and much more. Each gate will provide safe passage to those who will bring their honor and glory into the city. This is a reasonable assumption due to the size of the city and the direction of each gate. We must remember that John gives very few details of the city and there are many, many things not recorded about this wonderful place.

The Tree Of Life

> In the midst of the street of it, and on either side of the river, was there the tree of life, which bare twelve manner of fruits, and yielded her fruit every month: and the leaves of the tree were for the healing of the nations. Rev. 22:2

Here John gives a single view of a street, a river and a tree. However, the Greek word for "street" is translated in the plural six other times in the New Testament. It is "plateia" (Matt. 6:5; 12:19; Lu. 10:10; 13:26; 14:21; Acts 5:15). The Greek for "river" is "potamos." Potamos is used in the plural six times (floods - Matt. 7:25,27; rivers - Jn. 7:38; Rev. 8:10; 16:4; waters - II Cor. 11:26). The Greek for "tree" is "xulon." Xulon is used as plural six times in the New Testament (staves - Matt. 26:47; 26:55; Mark 14:43; 14:48; Luke 22:52; stocks - Acts 16:24). Thus, we can surmise that there are streets (plural), rivers (plural) and trees (plural). The question is, would it be reasonable, considering the enormous size of the city, for there to be but one river, one street and one tree of life? Most scholars agree that the one river will divide into several rivers and that there are streets of gold interconnected, not just one street. The same applies to the tree of life. The tree of life is actually a number of trees bearing a specific variety of fruit for each month (Ez. 47:12).

And by the river upon the bank thereof, on this side and on that side, shall grow all trees for meat, whose leaf shall not fade, neither shall the fruit thereof be consumed: it shall bring forth new fruit according to his months, because their waters they issued out of the sanctuary: and the fruit thereof shall be for meat, and the leaf thereof for medicine. Ezekiel 47:12

The leaves of this "tree of life" also hold healing qualities. It is revealed that the "leaves" are for the "healing of the nations." These nations, as seen in chapter twenty one, are the nations of the children of Israel. They are those who have been promised the land of Palestine as a perpetual inheritance for ever. They are those surviving the Millennial Reign and passing through Earth's fiery judgment as Shadrach, Meshach and Abednego passed through the burning fiery furnace. The fourth man will be there. (See chapter twenty-one, "The Nations Of The Saved.")

No More Curse

And there shall be no more curse: but the throne of God and of the Lamb shall be in it; and his servants shall serve him: And they shall see his face; and his name shall be in their foreheads. Rev. 22:3-4

Note that there will be no curse in the new city. This also applies to the new Earth. There will be no more aging, decaying, deterioration, death, corruption, evil or disasters. The list could go on and on. The Earth and man are presently under the curse of sin (Gen. 3:17). Sin, its curse, and the effects of sin will all be abolished.

Servants Of God

We saw in chapter seven under "Servants In The Temple" that the servants mentioned above are those martyred for the cause of Christ during the Tribulation Period. They will not only be with Christ during the Millennial Reign, as will the Church, but they will also inhabit the new city, new Jerusalem. They will serve in God's temple (See chapter seven, "God's Temple"). They are those who escaped the mark of the beast and will bear the mark of God's protection and security in their foreheads (See chapter seven, "Not The Mark Of The Beast").

Blessed Is He

And there shall be no night there; and they need no candle, neither light of the sun; for the Lord God giveth them light: and they shall reign for ever and ever. And he said unto me, These sayings are faithful and true: and the Lord God of the holy prophets sent his angel to shew unto his servants the things which must shortly be done. Behold, I come quickly: blessed is he that keepeth the sayings of the prophecy of this book. Rev. 22:5-7

(Note: For no night, no candle, and no sun, see discussion in chapter twenty-one, "Sunshine On The New Earth.")

The deity of Christ once again shines through. He is the Almighty. He is God. He is the Lord God of the holy prophets who has sent His angel to reveal the events for the end of the age. It is Jesus. He has sent the angel (v.16). Note also the divinity of Jesus revealed in verse three. "But the throne of God and of the Lamb shall be in it: and his servants shall serve him..." Did you catch it? Of God, of the Lamb, and HIS servants shall serve HIM! A greater realization of the deity of Jesus is just another of the many blessings received from the study of Revelation.

Worship God

> And I John saw these things, and heard them. And when I had heard and seen, I fell down to worship before the feet of the angel which shewed me these things. Then saith he unto me, See thou do it not: for I am thy fellowservant, and of thy brethren the prophets, and of them which keep the sayings of this book: worship God. And he saith unto me, Seal not the sayings of the prophecy of this book: for the time is at hand. He that is unjust, let him be unjust still: and he which is filthy, let him be filthy still: and he that is righteous, let him be righteous still: and he that is holy, let him be holy still. Rev. 22:8-11

Upon seeing the glories of Heaven, John falls down to worship, as he did when viewing the Marriage Supper (19:10). Many times man falls prey to the emotion of the moment or to the awe of a given spectacle. He quickly places his allegiance and worship in the wrong place. John falls down and worships at the feet of the angel. As with the instance before (19:9-10), the angel quickly rebukes John and tells him to worship God. Angels are but servants of God, as we are, and are not to be prayed to, worshipped, or placed upon pedestals of high esteem. They are fellow-servants with all of humanity. There is only one we are to worship: God. Jesus accepted worship because He is God (Matt. 9:18; 20:20; Mrk. 5:6; Lu. 24:52).

Instruction is given from the angel (v.10). The book of Revelation is not to be sealed up or concealed. It is to remain opened. The time of the unveiling and opening up is now. Revelation is the opening up of what Daniel was told to shut up (Dan. 12:4).

The Just And The Unjust

Verse eleven is an immediate call and statement concerning the eternity of the soul. While the ages of the new Heaven, the new Earth and the new city roll on, Hell will also continue to exist. Those who do not make preparations to enjoy the heavenly glories will continue to exist in the eternity of Hell forever. Those who die without accepting God's plan of escape, the unjust, will remain unjust eternally. There is no "praying out" to be done by earthly priests or anyone else. The fate of the soul will be sealed. The time is coming when it will be too late to repent. It will be impossible to come to God. If you haven't already, please prepare for glory now. Those who have accepted God's plan for life, the righteous, will remain righteous eternally and enjoy the glories that await.

Another Immediate Message

And, behold, I come quickly; and my reward is with me, to give every man according as his work shall be. I am Alpha and Omega, the beginning and the end, the first and the last. Blessed are they that do his commandments, that they may have right to the tree of life, and may enter in through the gates into the city. For without are dogs, and sorcerers, and whoremongers, and murderers, and idolaters, and whosoever loveth and maketh a lie. Rev. 22:12-15

The immediate message begins to flow from verse eleven into these next four verses. Everyone should be made aware that Jesus Christ is coming soon to bring judgment.

These verses do not imply that there will be sin upon the new Earth. They are verses which are directed at the readers and hearers of Revelation. They offer clear distinction between those who will live eternally and those who will die eternally. Those who adhere to the commandments of God will live. Those who are "without," that is, those not adhering to God's will, will die the second death (See chapter twenty-one, "The Second Death.") What are His commandments?

> Jesus said unto him, Thou shalt love the Lord thy God with all thy heart, and with all thy soul, and with all thy mind. This is the first and great commandment. And the second is like unto it, Thou shalt love thy neighbour as thyself. On these two commandments hang all the law and the prophets. Matt. 22:37-40

The Testimony Of Jesus

> I Jesus have sent mine angel to testify unto you these things in the churches. I am the root and the offspring of David, and the bright and morning star. And the Spirit and the bride say, Come. And let him that heareth say, Come. And let him that is athirst come. And whosoever will, let him take the water of life freely. For I testify unto every man that heareth the words of the prophecy of this book, If any man shall add unto these things, God shall add unto him the plagues that are written in this book: And if any man shall take away from the words of the book of this prophecy, God shall take away his part out of the book of life, and out of the holy city, and from the things which are written in this book. Rev. 22:16-19

Here we find the signature of Jesus Christ himself upon the book of Revelation. It is the testimony authenticating the book of Revelation to the churches. How sad it is that some Christians think that the book of Revelation should be avoided and set aside. It is a wonderful book, the only book in the Bible to which Christ Jesus has openly ascribed His name.

We have seen the mention of the deity of Jesus throughout this book. The above verses reveal the deity, earthly lineage, and authority of Jesus. As the "root" of David, Jesus is Creator God by whom all men were created. As the "offspring" of David, Jesus reveals His earthly lineage as being of the house of David (Matt. 1:6). Thus, David sprang through Christ and Christ through David. Jesus is also the bright and morning star. Note that the so-called "star of David," or "Mogen David," is not the six-pointed star, as many claim. Jesus is the star of David. The six-pointed star, today's symbol of Judaism, descended from the practice of idolatry. It was adopted when King Solomon, David's son, brought idolatry into Israel by marrying pagan wives. Solomon then built temples in honor of their gods and goddesses. Among the symbols used by these pagans was the six-pointed star. It derived from the Egyptians long before Solomon's or David's time and was the chief article of the pagan worship of Ashtoreth (Astarte - star). The hexagram (six-pointed star) of Ashtoreth worship represents the masculine and feminine aspects in the yin and yang of divination. It is the hexagram by which people are said to be "hexed." In western magic and mysticism the upward triangle represents the masculine and the downward triangle the feminine, a clear reference to phallic worship.

Jesus is the bright and morning star. This aspect reveals His authority above all of creation, even above angels. The word "star" in the Bible is used as a figure of speech for angels. In the Old Testament, Job 38:7 speaks of "the morning stars" singing together and all "the sons of God" shouting for joy. "Morning stars" is a poetic way of speaking of angels.

The Invitation

There is an invitation sent to those who have not yet accepted God's plan of salvation (v.17). It is an immediate reference to the work of the Spirit and the bride (through the Spirit). "Come and take of the water of life freely."

Note that the invitation may be tainted by men who corrupt the Word of God (vs. 18-19). It is a serious matter to change the content of the written Word. Note that interpretation and translation is a permissible and necessary part of spreading the Word, but we are not to change the content of the Word. To do so changes the meaning and intent of Scripture, bringing the most severe of penalties. Tampering with the written Word corrupts the nature of Christ's invitation directly concerning His ability, power and divinity.

John's Plea

> He which testifieth these things saith, Surely I come quickly. Amen. Even so, come, Lord Jesus. The grace of our Lord Jesus Christ be with you all. Amen. Rev. 22:20-21

It has been some two thousand years since Christ's first coming. This time span has been necessary for the building of the Church collectively and for the fulfillment of Scripture. This extended period of time does not alter the fact that Jesus is coming again. We are assured that He is coming because He said He is, and His words are faithful and true (v.6). This is but one aspect of the amazing facts of this chapter.

Amazing Facts Of The Revelation Message

At least eleven amazing facts about the message of

Revelation are revealed in verses 6-21 of chapter 22.

1. The message of Revelation is faithful and true (v.6).

2. The message of the book of Revelation will open many mysteries of the Word and bring them into focus. Such revelation provides blessing after blessing for those who study and obey the message of Revelation (v.7).

3. The message of Revelation will stir worship (vs.8-9). Worship God.

4. The message of Revelation is not to be hidden away and ignored. It is to be studied by everyone (v.10).

5. The message of Revelation brings into focus the Second Coming of Jesus Christ and His judgment (v.12).

6. The message of Revelation reveals those who will be accepted and those who will be rejected by the Lord (vs.14-15).

7. Jesus Christ himself proclaims the message of Revelation through his angel (v.16).

8. The message of Revelation displays one of the greatest invitations ever given to man: And the Spirit and the bride say, "Come" (v.17).

9. Those who tamper with the message of Revelation, indeed with the Word itself, will have his part taken out

of the book of life, and out of the holy city, and out of the blessings that await (vs.18-19).

10. The message of Revelation gives the greatest of assurances concerning the plan of Jesus Christ: "Surely I come quickly" (v. 20).

11. God's grace is with us. The grace of our Lord Jesus Christ be with you all (v. 21).

Ω

**I am but dust that God cares for.
Oh how gracious, how merciful,
how caring, how compassionate
and how wonderful
is our God, our Saviour, our Lord.**

Keith Harris

Revelation Outline

Index

CHARTS

New Heaven & New Earth Rev. 21:1

Earth cleansed by Fire II Peter 3:10   Great White Throne Rev. 20:11-15

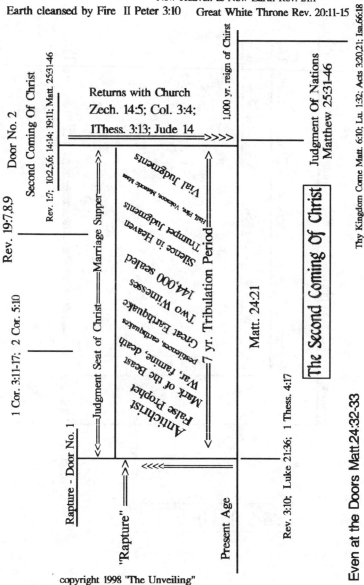

Returns with Church
Zech. 14:5; Col. 3:4;
1Thess. 3:13; Jude 14

Second Coming Of Christ

Door No. 2

Rev. 1:7; 10:2,5,6; 14:14; 19:11; Matt. 25:31-46

Rev. 19:7,8,9

1 Cor. 3:11-17; 2 Cor. 5:10

Rapture - Door No. 1

"Rapture"

Present Age

Rev. 3:10; Luke 21:36; 1 Thess. 4:17

Judgment Seat of Christ——Marriage Supper

1,000 yr. reign of Christ

Judgment Of Nations
Matthew 25:31-46

Vial Judgments

Hail, Fire, Volcanoes, Meteoric blast

Trumpet Judgments

Silence in Heaven

144,000 sealed

Two Witnesses

Great Earthquake

pestilences, earthquakes

War, Famine, death

Mark of the Beast

False Prophet

Antichrist

7 yr. Tribulation Period

Matt. 24:21

The Second Coming Of Christ

Thy Kingdom Come Matt. 6:10; Lu. 1:32; Acts 3:20,21; Isa.66:18

Even at the Doors Matt.24:32-33

copyright 1998 "The Unveiling"

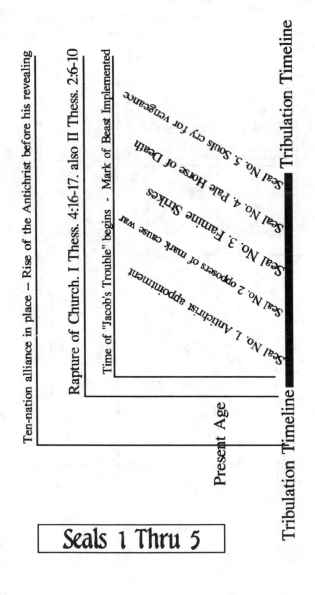

Ten-nation alliance in place – Rise of the Antichrist before his revealing

Rapture of Church. I Thess. 4:16-17. also II Thess. 2:6-10

Mark of Beast Implemented

Time of "Jacob's Trouble" begins –

Seal No. 1. Antichrist appointment.

Seal No. 2 opposers of mark cause war

Seal No. 3. Famine Strikes

Seal No. 4. Pale Horse of Death

Seal No. 5. Souls cry for vengeance

Tribulation Timeline

Present Age

Tribulation Timeline

Seals 1 Thru 5

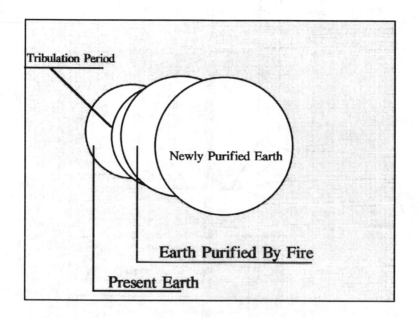

Tribulation Period

Newly Purified Earth

Earth Purified By Fire

Present Earth

Earth Stages

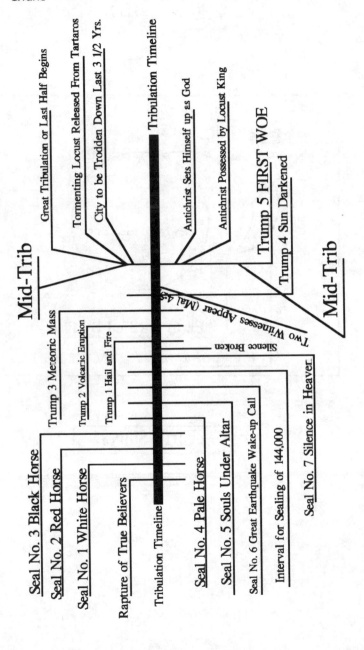

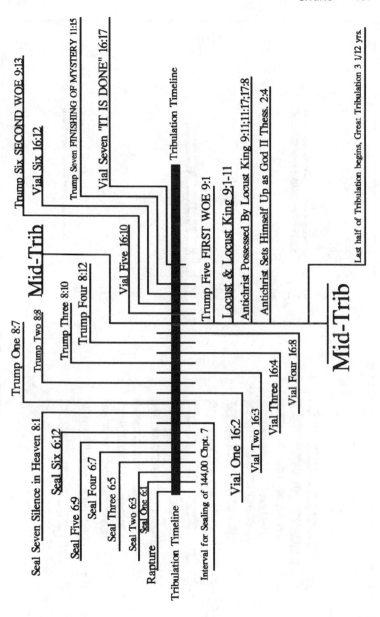

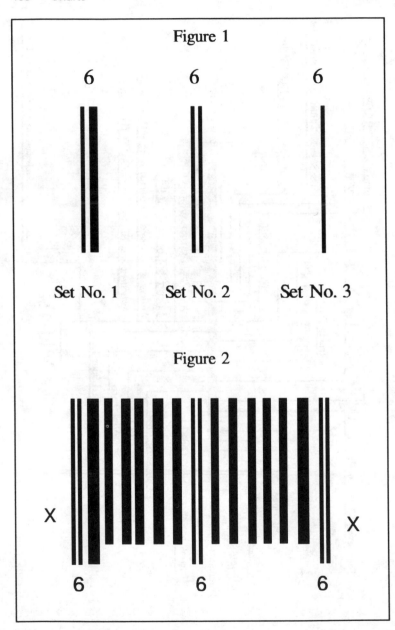

For dinosaurs, see author's book, "Jurassic Mark"

"In the beginning God Created the heaven and the Earth."

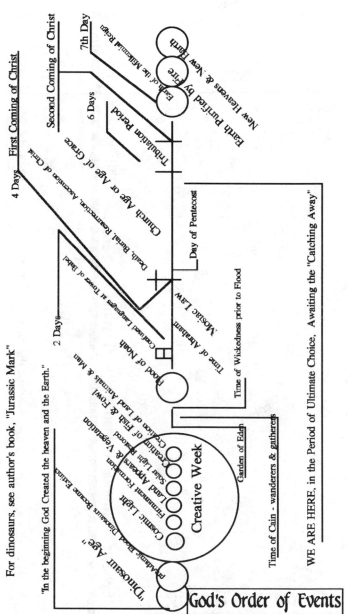

For days marked 2,4,6,7, see author's book "Jurassic Mark"

God's Order of Events

Creative Week

Cosmic Light
Firmament Formation
Land Appears & Vegetation
Creation of Fish & Fowl
Creation of Land Animals & Man
Solar Light Restored

"Dinosaur Age"
Pre-Adamic Flood, Dinosaurs Became Extinct

First Coming of Christ
Second Coming of Christ

4 Days
6 Days
7th Day
2 Days

Death, Burial, Resurrection, Ascension of Christ
Church Age or Age of Grace
Day of Pentecost
Flood of Noah
Confused Languages at Tower of Babel
Mosaic Law
Time of Abraham
Time of Wickedness prior to Flood
Garden of Eden
Time of Cain - wanderers & gatherers

Tribulation Period
Reign of the Millennial Reign
Earth Purified by Fire
New Heavens & New Earth

WE ARE HERE, in the Period of Ultimate Choice, Awaiting the "Catching Away"

Church Age Timeline

	Ephesus	Smyrna	Pergamos	Thyatira	Sardis	Philadelphia	Laodicea
	Losing First Love	Falling Into Persecution	Accepting Nicolaitane and Balaam Doctrine	Outwardly Saturated with Paganism	Escaping the Over-lording Papal Religious System	Opening Missionary Doors	Binding Religions Together
	AD 70 - AD 170	AD 170 - AD 312	AD 312 - AD 606	AD 606 - AD 1520	AD 1520 - AD 1750	AD 1750 - AD 1948	AD 1948 - AD ??????
				Dark Ages			See Page 99

Note that each church age overlaps the other   Dates are approximate. See page 39, note 1.